QUEST WEST

QUEST WEST

American Intellectual and Cultural Transformations

RICHARD LEHAN

LOUISIANA STATE UNIVERSITY PRESS
BATON ROUGE

Published by Louisiana State University Press
Copyright © 2014 by Louisiana State University Press
All rights reserved
Manufactured in the United States of America
First printing

Designer: Laura Roubique Gleason
Typefaces: Ingeborg, text; SunDisplay, display
Printer and binder: Maple Press

Portions of chapter 11 are taken from the author's essay "Literary Naturalism and Its Transformations: The Western, American Neo-realism, Noir, and Postmodern Reformation," *Studies in American Naturalism* 7.2 (Winter 2012): 228–42, published by Nebraska University Press.

LIBRARY OF CONGRESS CATALOGING-IN-PUBLICATION DATA

Lehan, Richard Daniel, 1930–
 Quest West : American intellectual and cultural transformations / Richard Lehan.
  pages cm
 Includes bibliographical references and index.
 ISBN 978-0-8071-5391-8 (cloth : alk. paper) — ISBN 978-0-8071-5392-5 (pdf) — ISBN 978-0-8071-5393-2 (epub) — ISBN 978-0-8071-5394-9 (mobi)
 1. American literature—History and criticism. 2. West (U.S.)—In literature. 3. West (U.S.)—In mass media. 4. West (U.S.)—In art. 5. Popular culture—United States. 6. Popular culture—West (U.S.) I. Title.
 PS169.W4L44 2014
 700'.45878—dc23

2013023699

The paper in this book meets the guidelines for permanence and durability of the Committee on Production Guidelines for Book Longevity of the Council on Library Resources. ∞

To the memory of Blake Nevius and John Espey—
colleagues and friends in the best sense of those words,
and to the scholarly legacy of their generation.

> The existence of an area of free land, its continuous recession, and the advance of American settlement westward explain American development.
>
> —Frederick Jackson Turner, "The Significance of the Frontier in American History" (1893)

> So we beat on, boats against the current, borne back ceaselessly into the past.
>
> —F. Scott Fitzgerald, *The Great Gatsby* (1925)

> I see that this has been a story of the West after all.
>
> —Nick Carraway, in F. Scott Fitzgerald's *The Great Gatsby* (1925)

> Each age writes the history of the past anew with reference to the conditions uppermost in its own time.
>
> —Frederick Jackson Turner, "The Significance of History" (1891)

CONTENTS

Preface / xi

1. The Wilderness Frontier / 1
2. The Mythic West / 14
3. The West as a State of Mind / 35
4. The Realms of Identity Powered by an Illusion / 45
5. Historicism: Romantic Destiny Transformed / 57
6. The Urban Reach / 67
7. Populism: The Man behind the Curtain / 74
8. Progressivism: The Urban Crucible / 84
9. Visions and Revision: Frontier Variants / 97
10. The Dark Side of the Way West / 113
11. Literary Transformations / 143
12. Realms of Interpretation / 160

Coda / 178

Chronology / 183
Notes / 187
Works Cited or Consulted / 189
Index / 197

PREFACE

Quest West examines the frontier experience, its transformations, and its realms of interpretations: it pursues the evolving meaning of the frontier thesis and its ideologies that were turned into aspects of the American identity. *Quest West* is an intellectual and cultural history grounded on theories of meaning that resulted in variations of American historical ideas and literary movements as the country moved west. Of special concern are the way a sense of destiny was transformed by dictates of historicism and how each generation established its own critical agenda, especially the way racial, ethnic, and gender concerns have dominated recent criticism.

Central to the discussion are the idea of the wilderness frontier as formulated by Frederick Jackson Turner and the Jeffersonian myth of an agrarian America that helped produce it. As is well known, Turner first voiced his thesis at a meeting of the American Historical Association in 1893, a meeting held during the World's Columbia Exposition in Chicago that coincidentally connected Turner's discussion of the frontier with the celebration of Columbus's journey west four hundred years earlier. Between Columbus and Turner were historical dots that waited to be connected, especially in light of Turner's belief that the wilderness frontier ended in 1890, to be overtaken by the rise of an industrialized America. When the wilderness frontier was replaced by the urban frontier, its transformations came to stand for a lost American vision.

From Whitman and Twain, London and Norris, Cather and

Fitzgerald, Faulkner and Steinbeck, Hammett and Chandler, we can detect aspects of the two-frontier thesis at work as we move from Turner's state of national innocence to the pursuits of an industrial nation controlled by commercial markets and investment capital. We move, that is, from the fruits of the land to a realm where money makes money and material markets determine values. This has become the "ur" American narrative, the core story. At its center is the quest west and the workings of the primitive transformed by new forms of civilization.

The two frontiers became the basis for the divided America that then came into being and is still with us today in demonstrable ways: the wilderness frontier supplied the ideology for a conservative political platform; the urban realm questioned the rise of industrial-commercial priorities and called for changes that became the basis for a more liberal deployment. More than physical regions, these realms became mandates, political agendas creating reciprocity between the idea of the frontier and the idea of America, the source of ideological values that were transformed in the movement from a frontier to an imperial nation and the transnational and global realms beyond. One's choice of frontier pointed to the idea of what one wanted America to be.

Preference for a frontier vision found equivalence in fictional narratives: subgenres such as the literary Western depicted elements of the wilderness frontier, while the urban frontier was seen in literary naturalism and neorealism and later noir; both were subject to the realms of doubt that came with postmodern critical change. As depictions of political values, the two frontiers were states of mind as well as historical realities, accommodating various theories of force, from the beneficent force of Emersonian transcendentalism to the more hostile forces of literary naturalism and noir.

The idea of the West was a major factor in the evolution of America from a set of colonies to a global power. We reach for worlds beyond the one we know. The West was the space where frontier ideology collided with European values. Early thinking concentrated on the history of an indigenous population making claim to the land, while later variations of historical assumption emphasized American Indians contesting that claim. The West was also the space where nascent and past cultures collided, where the primitive confronted the civilized.

Behind the idea of the West was a "myth of the land," involving the power of the "Volk," which had its origins in a philosophy of chthonic (underworld) gods, especially the life-from-death workings of Dionysus that accompanied the agrarian pursuits of romantic nationalism. The German element perpetuated here was influenced by the back-to-nature ideas of Johann Herder (1744–1803) and Johann Fichte (1762–1814); their sentiments were transformed in America by Jeffersonian agrarian values and trust in yeoman farming—ideals embodied by the American wilderness frontier, the ideology of which was kept alive by professional historians such as Frederick Jackson Turner.

This agrarian process combined history and myth (here defined as both an idealized and a fictitious explanation of history) and brought about catalytic change as it evolved. The compounded experience brought European ideas to America, where they were changed by religious and philosophical influences that eventually gave way to Enlightenment values, which were in turn transformed by romantic assumptions, creating an evolved moment infused with both historical and mythic meaning.

In this context, the historical meaning of America is inseparable from the march of seminal ideas westward. We see the West from the idealized prospects of European pilgrims; the West from a Puritan perspective; the West as a deviation from Enlightenment values; the West's response to Calvinism, Congregationalism, Unitarianism, and transcendental assumptions; the West as the end product of homesteading; the West and imperial ambition; the West as seen from the revisionist claims of Mark Twain and Walt Whitman. We most extensively see the West as frontier from the perspective of Frederick Jackson Turner's wilderness thesis, qualified by the realizations that the frontier was more extended in time than he claimed and that the West was more a product of urbanism and regional interplay than earlier thought.

The view is persistently a mixed one: we engage the dark side of the West once it becomes a material system of thought and action giving way to imperial mandates; unregulated behavior led to an era of reform, the object of Populist and later Progressive demands. We further see the West in sectional perspective, involving what the West had in common with the South and its Agrarian movement. We see the West as the end product of romantic destiny, subject to modern and postmodern transformations.

The call to romantic destiny opened history to the mythic

transformations of national ideas. These views were overtaken by the assumptions of the old historicism, as movement from agrarian to urban pursuits transformed the ideology of national destiny. Historicism contended that historical ideas could be understood only when placed in a larger context, most often ideological or cultural in nature, such as the rise of, say, German nationalism or the meaning of a historical occasion like the Italian Renaissance. In America the idea of the frontier was inseparable from the political pursuit of nationalism and, in cultural terms, the rise of literary modes such as the Western. Historicism also gave us the belief that each era or culture or region had an inspiring principle of unity, often the product of geographical determinism (such as fertile land, a water supply, river transportation, forest resources for log cabins, beneficial weather, and access to a market to buy or sell the products of the land). The realms of history and nature shared process: the assumption was that the laws of history were as functional as the laws of nature.

Such concerns brought testimony from a host of witnesses to the folding and unfolding of both political and cultural history. These ideas were inseparable from the movement west, as well as inseparable from mythic assumptions that were in turn the product of literary influence. Special attention was brought to bear on a major historical problem: why so many of the modern writers (Pound, Faulkner, Fitzgerald, Dos Passos, and the southern Agrarians, to name just a few) advocated a Jeffersonian tradition and a belief in agrarian pursuits long after the Jeffersonian yeoman's life was obsolete, its values mostly irrelevant to the new commercial-industrial order.

As the American political agenda changed, so did the idea of the frontier, giving rise to variant frontiers, becoming the basis for domestic expansion (manifest destiny) as well as foreign expansion (imperialism). These pursuits were justified by a theory of American "exceptionalism": the belief that the United States had a special destiny based on its being different from other countries—a destiny that mandated it to spread the idea of democracy that sprang from the revolutionary nature of American origins, engendering today's pride in global influence, including nation-building. Manifest destiny was merely one of many value systems the idea of the West brought to a developing nation: this study contends that each generation formulated its own sense of frontier reality—from the West and the transformation of European values, to the West as a crucible for an American individualism that anticipated an American egalitarianism, to the West as a source of eastern investment that involved military and legal conquests, to the West as the spearhead of expansionism, to the West as transformed by modern and postmodern historical movements. Since change was the one constant, we are always looking at the old through the new as we vainly seek to keep alive ideals that once determined the past.

There have been numerous books on the subject of the West—some amplifying the Turner thesis, others contesting it, still others revising the historical assumptions that sustain it. We will look at these works from a perspective of intellectual history and with strategies of interpretation in mind. A change in a theory of history or a variation in the definition of the frontier can alter historical meaning: historical conclusions stem from starting-point assumptions; context is as important as content. The West can be seen as a political and cultural phenomenon from the many historical and literary perspectives suggested above (from the Puritan idea of the West to the revisionist claims of Mark Twain and Walt Whitman, from the West as the end product of homesteading to the West as an imperial mandate).

For two generations, Turner's idea of the wilderness frontier dominated interpretations of the origins of American ideology, even challenging the dominant influence of the Constitution. But a generation ago, the Turner thesis was radically revised: more attention was given to the role of American Indians, especially to the history of their lost land; more concern was expressed about racial matters, especially the role race played in the history of new immigrants; and more study focused on the role of women and gender matters in general. These interpretive changes brought ideological change, transforming assumptions and altering the meaning of the Turner thesis. We thus have two images of Turner: we have the brilliant historian, capable of original thinking, whose understanding of the origins of American ideology dominated historical interpretation for the better part of forty years; and we have the lesser figure, who was indifferent to the way the West was won at human cost.

To better understand Turner's achievement, despite revisionary claims, we must pursue peripheral matters, some previously acknowledged and others relating to new concerns: to the origins of American ideological values; to distinctions between the wilderness frontier and the idea of the West; to the depiction of the frontier as a composite of history, myth, and a philosophical and religious state of mind; to the historical change involved in viewing the idea of the West as the end product of an illusion; to the transformation of romantic destiny by forms of historicism; to the response of Populism and Progressivism to the emergence of an urban nation; to the evolution of forms of frontier experience as the product of manifest destiny and imperial pursuits; to the reconciliation of history and literature by means of narrative modes and their transformations; to the even more radical change that came with an emerging postmodernism.

I became interested in the "Quest West" project because I could not understand how a Jeffersonian-agrarian vision—along with Turner's frontier thesis—could survive, indeed prosper, in an urban-industrial culture. I have discovered that it lives on because it carries a lot of baggage, much of it pure nostalgia. Nostalgia can fool us into desiring products of the wilderness frontier that we have embellished beyond their worth. But it can also remind us of what we have lost in an era of change. It is a mixed affair, carrying both a positive and a negative agenda—from a worthy celebration of a kind of rugged individualism that sustained Emersonian self-reliance, to a more ambivalent response to the Volk movement in Germany with its heightened call to the soil and its ersatz claim to Aryan supremacy, to an obsession for guns and gun culture that defines our sense of identity.

From Cooper to Twain, from Emerson to Whitman, from Cather to Fitzgerald, we can find major American authors who have sought the Jeffersonian-agrarian vision even though it is no longer manifestly relevant to what have become lost pursuits. They chase an illusion often grounded on evangelical principles, rife with antigovernment, anti-intellectual, vigilante, gunslinger assumptions; they create a culture that is the product of values that thrived west of the one-hundredth meridian. At the end of *The Great Gatsby,* Fitzgerald told us that it was an American tendency to locate ideals in an exhausted past—to seek the future in a lost past. That is the story that *Quest West* seeks to tell.

In that context, this study examines mandates built into realms of time, especially, as anticipated above, the American obsession with nostalgia, the longing for the return of an idealized moment. Despite the revisionist process, there are still those who long for the steadfast values that sustained the Turner wilderness idea. Dissatisfied with the present, they see the past with a romantic aura and desire to relive a more idealized existence, ignoring the fact that such a past may have been historically transformed. The persistence of this desire demands rethinking the meaning of the original frontier, both as a historical phenomenon and as a state of mind, questioning the embodiment of an ideal of what we once were or hoped to be.

Paradoxically, the one constant is the inevitability of change, even as that change leaves a residue of past meaning. Both the Jeffersonian vision and the Turner frontier thesis live on, if only as states of mind. We look to the past for what the future may hold. In the realms of the past we preserve our lost ideals. While its transformations linger on, we struggle to keep alive a residual myth of the West as a product of romantic destiny and a by-product of historicism, even as we know that such an ideology resides in a realm that will never come again.

Albert Bierstadt's *Oregon Trail* (1869) is reproduced with the consent of the Butler Institute of American Art, Youngstown, Ohio.

I am grateful to the staff of the English Department at the University of California, Los Angeles, especially Jeanette Gilkison and Rick Fagin; and to the staff of the circulation desk at the UCLA Research Library, especially Valerie Rom-Hawkins.

At LSU Press, I am in the debt of Margaret Lovecraft and Catherine Kadair for continued assistance. Thanks also to Lois Crum, copyeditor, and Betsy Dean, indexer.

And for help and encouragement during these many years, I thank my wife, Ann.

QUEST WEST

1

The Wilderness Frontier

I

From 1803 on, the story of America has been a story of the West. It was generally accepted that because of an open frontier the historical "center" of America moved west. Since the sun sets in the west, the jump from a metaphorical to a literal application of the setting sun was perhaps inevitable. But built into the idea of pilgrims' progress was this sense of movement, from Europe to America, and then in America across the continent, spearheaded by a frontier, to an emerging Pacific realm.

The migration experience was best embodied by Daniel Boone, a pathfinder who in 1775 led the way through the wilderness to the Cumberland Gap, settling the village of Boonesborough, Kentucky, one of the first settlements west of the Appalachians. Supposedly Boone supplied the model for James Fenimore Cooper's depiction of Natty Bumppo, the hero of Cooper's *Leatherstocking Tales*. It has been estimated that by the end of the eighteenth century, more than two hundred thousand Europeans had migrated along the same trail that Boone opened to the West.

The interior realm of the continent was initially in French control, and the French left behind place names like Fond du Lac and St. Louis. The British had relinquished much of their claim to the interior as they concentrated on authority over the seven seas. The motives that fueled the way west stemmed partly from the myth involving the Passage to India—the belief that the New World was a bridge between Europe and Asia, an idea promoted by Thomas Hart Benton and William Gilpin (for a detailed discussion of Benton and Gilpin, see Smith 20–46). Thomas Jefferson foresaw a highway across the continent—a pathway that eventually became the Oregon Trail. The outward extension of this highway took the pioneer to India and the Orient—a belief sustained by Emerson, then Whitman, then Hart Crane. The inward extension of the highway led to three realms of imperial advancement: the first by sea; the second into the interior, involving the work of the hunter and trapper; and the third into arable land for farming. The Turner thesis deals primarily with the third option, the implementation of which became the basis for the frontier thesis.

The frontier thesis is as well known as it was influential. In Europe, men were many and land was scarce; on the American frontier, men were scarce and land was plentiful. As a result, the old laws governing the working of land no longer applied. Mobility (the continual move to better land) and profligate living (creating an abundant waste in its wake) naturally followed. One's right to the land encouraged hard work; class distinctions were ameliorated by the abundance of free land; ownership encouraged an individualism that in turn accommodated the idea of democracy (Billington 1996, 16). The American character conformed to the interpretations of historicism—the belief that every era and a given region were products of their historical determinants and the process of change.

Historical determinism went along with historical change. There are essentially two sources of historical determinism: a physical or environmental factor and a social or cultural factor. Studies have shown that each has an effect on the subject, with the social or cultural factor asserting the greater influence. This has relevance to frontier life, where the social factors were more relaxed and less constraining than in a more established social environment and where, as a result, there was a greater sense of individual freedom on the frontier than in the more settled areas to the east. As Ray Billington has put it, "Change, not tradition, was the order of life." Anomie (social disruption, the result of the erosion of social codes, and not social cohesion) helped determine the frontier state of mind and led to the lawlessness characteristic of the wilderness frontier experience (Billington 1966, 53–54).

The idea of the wilderness frontier as solely the province of rugged individualism and egalitarian principles needs to be slightly qualified. In their most idealized sense, these characteristics were as much an illusion as a reality. As the frontier expanded, class and ethnic distinctions began to emerge. A professional class, composed of doctors, lawyers, and bankers, assumed superiority by dint of its education and social functions. A middle class emerged in which the participants—yeoman farmers, herdsmen, innkeepers, wagoners, river men, laborers, and miners—shared more or less the same status. A lower class was made up of recent Irish and German immigrants in the Mississippi Valley and the Chinese in the Far West (Billington 1966, 98–99).

Regardless of class, the trek west was long and arduous, an extended journey rife with transformations. Initially the settlers pushed into the interior up the eastern rivers: the Connecticut, the Hudson, the Delaware, the Susquehanna, the Potomac, the James, and the Savannah. Once regions like the forest of New York were settled, a second wave went beyond the Appalachians and the Alleghenies to the Ohio River valley and later the valley of the Mississippi.

A third wave of settlers emerged from the prairies of Illinois and the plains of Kansas and Nebraska and began the upward climb to the Rockies. West of the Rockies are three intermountain plateaus: the Colorado Plateau; the Great Basin Plateau, extending to the Sierra Nevadas (an arid, essentially desert, region settled by the Mormons, whose political authority stemmed from controlling the sources of water); and to the north the Columbia Plateau (an immense lava bed of two hundred thousand square miles). Ignoring the plains, the third wave of settlers went beyond the Rockies to the desert, encountering more mountains and more desert, at which point they could choose the southwestern route to California or the northwestern route to Oregon, either way completing the progression westward from coast to coast. It has been estimated that migrants moving to California and Oregon along this trail annually numbered in the early 1850s between fifty thousand and sixty thousand (Merk 1978, 383).

The Oregon Trail began in Independence, Missouri, at the bend of the Missouri River. The journey to the Pacific, about two thousand miles, took approximately six months (averaging about twelve miles a day). It began with the onset of grazing in the late spring. May and June were spent crossing the Great Plains, following the Platte River to Fort Laramie, and then crossing the Rockies at South Pass to Fort Hall, which settlers reached in early August. The closer they got to the Pacific, the more difficult the journey became, because they needed to transcend the ledges of the Snake River and get beyond the almost inaccessible Blue Mountains. Once this part of the journey was completed, settlers reached the Columbia River in early October and traveled the final hundred miles on the Willamette River to its mouth, which was their destination. What Cumberland Gap was to the East, South Pass was to the far West. It was the central opening in the Rockies, the highway to the West—the Missouri, the Platte, the Arkansas, the Rio Grande, the Colorado, and the Snake all had their headwaters near it.

A fourth wave eventually settled the plains of Kansas and Nebraska, which initially were described as uninhabitable. The first frontier looked back to Europe; the second to coastal settlements; and the third, in the Mississippi Valley, looked west with a newfound sense of independence.

The journey beyond the plains was facilitated by the completion of the transcontinental railroad in 1869. The railroad had to decide on a transcontinental route. Northern and southern routes ultimately lost out to a central route, roughly along the lines of the Oregon and California trails, the route taken later by the Union Pacific and the Central Pacific railroads, with their eastern terminus in Omaha and connecting branches in Chicago and St. Louis.

II

The "idea" of the West was as old as the country itself, hardly limited to historical concerns; but it was a key concern of many modern historians, and it established a theme that connected literary thought with other currents of American history. The modernist in America took from European thought the belief that the land was the source of spiritual meaning, endowed with the intrinsic blessing of a nation-state waiting to realize its destiny. While one can find this idea in its modernist form in post–World War I historians such as Oswald Spengler, it had a sustained historical background, evolving out of the old historicism and myths of the noble savage: the idea that in a state of nature humans are essentially good, an assumption credited to the Earl of Shaftesbury. He believed humans had an innate moral sense stemming from a natural innocence, as opposed to Thomas Hobbes, who believed that humans were involved in a perpetual state of war. In America, Shaftesbury's more beneficent assumption took on institutional (i.e., establishment) meaning—we find it in Jefferson, and in many ways it is at the heart of modernism (the foundation built upon by Pound, Faulkner, Fitzgerald, and Dos Passos).

More to the point, this idea influenced the myth of the West—the West as the locus of an ideal. In his "Farewell" address, George Washington pointed to a country that would look to the western frontier and not to Europe—an idea later promoted by Emerson, later still by Frederick Jackson Turner, and then by Thorstein Veblen. The belief in national identity led to academic disciplines such as American studies, with its search for origins, an imbued intellectual embryo, which made America America. The quest was west, and the West took on special meaning in the works of Cooper, Whitman, Twain, Cather, Fitzgerald, West, and others.

Frederick Jackson Turner dominated the field of academic history at the turn of the twentieth century. His portrait here, in keeping with our emphasis on modes of interpretation, is a mixed one: a brilliant historian with an original cast of mind, whose theory of the wilderness frontier generated a call for revision. After having dominated conceptual concern for two generations, it was faulted for not giving proper attention to ethnic, race, and gender matters. His assumptions were that history was a determined process, that physical and social environment accounted for the historical condition. He was skeptical of the "germ theory" of history taught at Johns Hopkins, where he did his graduate work—the assumption that European ideology simply took hold in America, independent of geographical or political cause. That assumption led him to investigate the idea of the frontier as a determinant of American identity and later to engage American history as having sectional—that is, regional—meaning.

His most important claim had to do with the wilderness frontier. Turner rejected the idea that America was a cultural appendage of Europe. He resisted the notion that America was the transplanted incarnation of European "germs," substituting a belief in the indigenous nature of the American frontier, both as a place and as a process. The American wilderness thus became the reconciliation point for a savagery and a civilization that transformed Old World values: here European feudalism gave way to American pragmatism. But in 1893, largely on the basis of the census of 1890, Turner argued that the American frontier, which was the source of national identity, had ended.

This was a major historical event, because the American frontier was unique in history, different in kind from the European frontier. The European frontier was the place where two nations came together—for example, France and Germany or Germany and Poland. The American frontier brought with it an edge of free land. This free land, or wilderness, transformed those who entered it before they transformed it in turn. In Europe a feudal system controlled by an aristocracy prevailed; in America the gift of free land established a host of yeoman farmers who could think in democratic terms. These terms were often more idealized than real, but they suggested what was historically unique and drew the line between European and American values.

And yet, while there was nothing in the European frontier that matched the American frontier, there was in European history what might be called "affinity" relations to the American frontier: the German theory of the Volk, for example, brought the same worship of the land, celebrated the same sense of national (romantic) destiny, privileged the same racial types, and admired the same benefits of rugged individualism that defined those who populated the wilderness frontier. America was the realm of transformation, transforming European ideas and values into a separate reality. But there were residual concerns that, before they were transformed, America and Europe shared in common.

III

Turner's task included seeing America as an agency of historical transformation. He was concerned with cultural identity, what was involved in being an American. His concern was the opposite of that held by such expatriates as Henry James, Henry Adams, Ezra Pound, and T. S. Eliot, who defined themselves by the culture of the Old World, although both Adams and Pound looked to Jefferson for an ideal embodiment of the New World. Turner's basic argument about the workings of the American frontier was simple and direct: life on the frontier was by nature a lonely condition, perpetuating by necessity the need for inhabitants who were individualistic and self-reliant. Besides cultivating rugged individualism, the American frontier, Turner maintained, encouraged a pragmatic disposition, practical and materialistic values, and a restless mind. These qualities were needed in living day by day, engaging the moment to the exclusion of utopian concerns. What followed was the myth of the West: the belief that the abundance of land, a sense of the plentiful, freedom from restraint, and a shared feeling of equality encouraged the spirit of democracy.

But the rise of the democratic impulse turned primarily on the possession of free land: the perpetuation of democracy was thus built into the American frontier experience, and Turner insisted that it was free land that "differentiated the American democracy from the democracies which have preceded it" (Turner 259–60; Pierson). Elaborating on this statement, Turner concluded: "American democracy was born of no theorist's dream; it was not carried in the Sarah Constant to Virginia, nor in the Mayflower to Plymouth. It came out of the American forest, and it gained new strength each time it touched a new frontier. Not the constitution, but free land and an abundance of natural resources open to a fit people, made the democratic type of society in America for three centuries [before] it occupied [the pursuit of] empire" (Turner 293; Pierson 31).

IV

The original colonies were separated from the frontier by the Appalachian Mountains before the pioneers crossed the Alleghenies and settled Kentucky and Tennessee as well as the upper waters of the Ohio. Between 1816 and 1821, six states were created: Maine, Indiana, and Illinois (free states), and Mississippi, Alabama, and Missouri (slave states). The boundary between settled land and frontier, or the "fall line" as it was called, kept changing as the frontier moved west. The frontier encountered the arid lands at approximately the ninety-ninth meridian; terrain reached subsequently brought more mountains and more deserts before the frontiersmen reached the Pacific coast.

Each stage of the successive frontiers involved combat with the displaced Indians. Indian tribes responded to white migration in different ways: some adapted; others retreated to the reservations. Those on the Plains and in the Southwest fought back. Sioux tribes, supported by Cheyenne and Arapaho bands, were the most militant, as the 1865 Fetterman Massacre proved, when eighty troops from Fort Kearney in the Dakota Territory were wiped out, anticipating a decade later the annihilation of Custer and his men at Little Bighorn. The Cheyenne and the

Arapaho also attacked white settlements in Kansas, as did the Apaches on the Mexican border. But by 1887 American Indian opposition to the westward expansion had ended, in great part because of the provisions of the Dawes Act, which curtailed tribal life (Deverell and Hyde 25–26).

Dee Brown in *Bury My Heart at Wounded Knee* (1970) describes the fate of the different Indian tribes from 1860 to 1890, concentrating on the plight of the Sioux and Cheyenne bands on the northern American plains, the last of the American Indians to be moved to Indian reservations. Wounded Knee is a village on a reservation in South Dakota, where the last major confrontation between the U.S. Army and the American Indians occurred. There more than 130 Sioux Indians, most of them unarmed, were killed.

Conflict with the Indians slowed but did not stop advancement, and the frontier unfolded along the lines of various pursuits: first came the pathfinder, then the tracker, then the hunter, then the trader, and finally the rancher and farmer; people of each group brought their different values to the land and created an archetypal polarity. Following the farm came the village and then the town with its commercial and merchant help that addressed the expanding demands of the agrarian agenda. A major city (e.g., Chicago, St. Louis, Omaha, and Kansas City) was part of the lifeline of the West.

Turner believed the frontier accommodated its inhabitants as it evolved; the pioneer came when his expertise was needed; this was the basis for what Turner referred to as historical "process." Ray Allen Billington, basing his idea on an essay published in 1874 by Francis A. Walker, suggested that the outer edge of the frontier was first taken up by fur trapping and ranching, but as the population increased, the ways of life became more diverse and settlement became a bit more haphazard than Turner suggests; settlers of all trades came in a more random way (Billington 1966, 17–18).

As the country moved west, there was a natural tendency to see life as a struggle between the human will and the environment. The task at hand was to dominate the wilderness, within which evil (forms of the devil) was at work. The Puritan obsession with evil—before Emerson could dispel it—gave the movement a missionary as well as secular calling. Turner saw the march west as "an irresistible attraction": the various stages of the frontier "passed in successive waves across the continent." He suggested that one could "[s]tand at Cumberland Gap and watch the procession of civilization marching single file.... Stand at South Pass in the Rockies a century later and see the same procession with wider intervals between" (6). The trading posts reached by these trails were on the sites of what had been Indian villages, situated to control the water system of the region. Each village later became the central city of its region, as was the case with Albany, Pittsburgh, Detroit, Chicago, St. Louis, Council Bluffs, and Kansas City.

As the frontier moved west, it left a civilized trail behind with a populace that had been transformed by the experience. Turner believed "[i]t was this nationalizing tendency of the West that transformed the democracy of Jefferson into the national republicanism of Monroe and the democracy of Andrew Jackson" (14). He concluded: "This, at least, is clear: American democracy is fundamentally the outcome of the experiences of the American people in dealing with the West. Western democracy through the whole of its earlier period tended to the production of a society in which the most distinctive fact was the freedom of the individual to rise under the condition of social mobility, and whose ambition was the liberty and well-being of the masses. This conception has vitalized all American democracy, and has brought it in sharp contrasts with the democracies of history, and with those modern efforts of Europe to create an artificial democratic order by legislation. The problem of the United States is not to create democracy, but to conserve democratic institutions and ideals" (32).

V

Turner's critics have been quick to point out weaknesses in his thesis. One response faults him for combining contradictory claims. He conflates nationalism and sectionalism, individualism and community, savagery and civilization, equalitarianism and upward social mobility, materialism and idealism, and innovation and conformity (Billington 1966, 16). The claim here has some merit: Turner often promoted seemingly contradictory ideals. But he seldom weighted those ideals equally, and his preferences (sectionalism, individualism, idealism, innovation, equalitarianism, and frontier values) outweighed their opposites and became the basis for his frontier thesis. Moreover, some of what the hostile critics took as contradictions were not unwarranted contradictions. Turner had created an idealized frontiersman who in reality was not always ideologically consistent with the ideal. The frontiersman at times needed the help of the community (to respond to Indian hostility, for example) but at other times felt superior to his neighbor. But these lapses (if they are lapses) may qualify, but do not negate, the claim of rugged individualism or of a working egalitarianism. Despite the heroic claims, Turner's frontiersman, beneath his trappings, was more human than often portrayed, a far more contradictory person than the product of the illusions that were needed to sustain his mythic role.

Recent historical assessments have also insisted that Turner put too much emphasis on the West alone for the implementation of the frontier. But he had never seen the West as a static entity. Anticipating T. S. Eliot's belief that each literary work added to the literary "tradition" changed the nature of the whole, Turner believed that each segment of the westward procession added to the sequence of movement changed the idea of the frontier: the movement into the Ohio and Mississippi Valleys was different from movement on the prairie, the movement beyond the Rockies was different from that of the plains, and the movement along the Oregon and California trails was a different kind from what preceded it. This unfolding, as we have seen, became a matter of what Turner termed "process," changing the nature of the historical whole. There was thus no single "West," but a series of "Wests"—and each was the product of interior change, transformed by landscape and by state of mind in the transition from eastern colony to pioneer settlement. Each segment was part of an evolutionary process that was self-defining and a product of dynamic (as opposed to static) history.

Turner argued for the connected nature of social, political, economic, and cultural matters as they relate to each other and to historical development. Before Turner, the West was considered simply as an annexation of territory with no impulse of its own or ability to transform history. Because the dynamics of the West were constantly changing, Turner believed that the frontier was not synonymous with the West and that the West was not a static frontier. But in retrospect, as brilliant and as influential as Turner's frontier thesis was, reconsideration was in order. Perhaps a statement most obviously in need of correction was Turner's insistence that the frontier ended in 1890. The fact is that more public land was taken and put into production between 1890 and 1920 than during the decades following passage of the Homestead Act, 1862 to 1890.

Another overstatement involved the singularity of the West. One can now argue that the settling of the West was in part a collaborative effort between East and West, implemented by Jeffersonian Republican support and encouragement. It is true that the federal government limited the financial support given to the western movement, but some funds were available that supplied the means to sponsor homestead laws, to implement canal and steamboat technology, to provide an alternative way west by helping to finance the transcontinental railroad, and to supply the military components (cavalry and forts) necessary for settlers to work the land taken from (understandably) hostile natives, among other efforts that encouraged the western movement.

It is also misplaced to attribute all of the tendencies toward democracy to the workings of the frontier. Such a claim ignores the European influences (e.g., the workings of parliaments) and eastern influences (e.g., the workings of colonial legislatures and New England town meetings). Turner also ignored the influence that Protestant theology played in general: the self-government, for example, of Congregational churches and the anti-establishment impulse that promoted a mandate toward limited authority within the major Protestant sects. As for the move west resulting in the rise of individualists and a self-reliant population, one could equally argue that the move itself would be most attractive to those who were individualistic by nature *before* they went west.

The same scrutiny casts doubt regarding the difference between migration and settlement. Americans are by nature a migratory people: by age fifty, 40 percent of native-born Americans live outside the state of their birth (Lee 67). But there is a substantial difference between the restless desire to move beyond established communities and the conclusion that such desire created a political ideology that perpetuated the spirit of democracy. Career moves are not always the product of restlessness; there were exodus movements motivated by economic necessity: the need, for example, of the New England farmer to move from rocky soil to the more fertile land of western New York and the Ohio Valley, and the need in Oklahoma to leave what had become a dust bowl for the lush groves of California and the Northwest. But the most substantial migrations were not from farm to farm but from farm to the city: the cities can be added to what Turner referred to as the "safety valve." An eastern laborer could not simply pack up and start a farm in the West. But the laborer could find new employment and the means to support himself and his family (if just barely) in the new industrial city.

The skeptic could also question Turner's idealizing the wilderness movement beyond its workings: the personal attributes that Turner celebrated often come freighted with limitations. Turner's frontier is composed mostly of a white, male, Protestant population. It is primarily self-contained and rarely encounters urban or modern concerns. It depends almost totally on free land and is thus a product of Homestead Act largesse as it moved west. The ideal product of the wilderness experience is the rugged individualist who is often indifferent, when not hostile, to aesthetic matters and is by nature anti-intellectual. The desire for liberty led to unregulated behavior, including monetary abuses (mostly the tendency to promote inflated paper currency and wildcat banking). Most telling, the rugged individualism that Turner so admired encouraged a militant tendency that promoted the warlike disposition that became a major factor in the wilderness legacy. That legacy also included the tendency to question and go beyond the law when one was dissatisfied with its workings and to rely on violence (gunfighter behavior) when peaceful means seemed ineffective, a point convincingly documented by Richard Slotkin.

One of the more informative and groundbreaking attacks on Turner's frontier thesis comes from Alan Trachtenberg, who faults Turner in *The Incorporation of America* for lack of what he calls "cultural multiplicity"—that is, for Turner's failure to recognize that the southwestern frontier, for example, involved the role of Spanish Americans, Roman Catholics, Mormons, and Indians. Trachtenberg goes on to discuss the frontier as a post–Civil War phenomenon that the federal government held in colonial (that is, dependent) status and insists that this fact necessitates a revisionary look at Turner's belief in the function of free land: the frontier was part of the incorporation of America—the idea of free land gave way to myth and myth to exploitation. "Turner's frontier, then, is as much an invention of cultural belief as a genuine historical fact" (Trachtenberg 2007, 16).

Like so many other revisionary attacks on Turner, Trachtenberg's attack is the product of a misplaced context: he conflates the wilderness and urban frontiers, compressing agrarian and industrial modes of thought, rather than seeing them as independent views of two realms of different time. The agrarian view, while aware of urban workings, is primarily a preindustrial view. The industrial frontier was a product of the gilded age and worked from a different agenda. While the agrarian frontier had to cope with hostile Indians, the industrial frontier had to cope with the working conditions of new immigrants and women—that is, with racial, ethnic, and gender matters. Trachtenberg faults Turner for not treating these concerns, unfairly expecting him to address matters more relevant to the industrial than to an agrarian frontier thesis; he attacks the wilderness thesis for being incomplete because it lacks relevance to industrial components. As an interpretive strategy, it is a little like condemning the apple for not being an orange. Trachtenberg has written an influential work, but his tendency to read the wilderness frontier in the light of urban mandates is as flawed as anything he can point to in Turner.

The idea of the frontier has become a bit of a Rorschach test, fertile ground for speculation on interpretive theory, especially the use of starting points that guarantee prescribed conclusions. For the most part, one can find what one looks for in the idea of the wilderness frontier. Emerson could look to the western wilderness and see an idealized nature at work. Henry Adams could look to the western wilderness and see hostile forces at work. They began with different interpretive assumptions and ended up defining reality through different perspectives; they observed the same world, one optimistically, the other pessimistically. A critic of myth like Northrop Frye could find both a comic and a tragic unfolding in the way west. One view anticipated the Western novel, the other literary naturalism. While the world observed has changed drastically, the divergent perspectives are still alive, if only as states of mind. As we shall see, like the wilderness frontier, the urban frontier created its own history, with a mythic-reality by-product, complete with its own set of contradictions.

2
The Mythic West

I

Henry Adams told us that there is no order in nature—just the illusion of order. But the illusion can energize society and determine its historical future. *Quest West* is an intellectual study of a construct, a historical realm and a changing state of mind that became an illusion. Both the historical reality and the illusion had to do with the fate of agrarian myth in the face of industrial change. That there was a mythic frontier does not negate the fact that there was also a historical frontier. The mythic frontier supplied an ideal that encouraged militant pursuit. The major point here is that the historical frontier gave rise to several stereotypes (a belief in rugged individualism, a sense of self-reliance, and a pragmatic disposition that accommodated domestic adaptability); these qualities eventually became idealized, and then historical reality took on new, mythic dimensions—such as American "exceptionalism," the belief that America was uniquely endowed and its history was a product of destiny. When recast in literary naturalism, these qualities took on an idealized nature to be sought, but seldom realized, in the face of hostile, antagonistic forces.

As we have seen, Frederick Jackson Turner gave us the myth of the wilderness frontier and the transformations that evolved from it. In retrospect, we can see that Turner's frontier thesis was seriously flawed. His definition of the frontier went beyond historical justification and became a call to romantic destiny, a mandate for rugged individualism, a testimony to resilience and adaptability. Turner abstracted national virtues out of his frontier thesis, creating a political fantasy that became an ideal, a way of thinking for a land-centered, expansionist nation that was moving onward—that is, westward. The wilderness frontier gave way to myth, became a romantic state of mind, an illusion. Both the myth and its historical reality became inseparable from the quest west and its providential way of thinking about America.

For close to two generations, Turner's frontier thesis prevailed, generating ideas that helped to define America. Turner's thesis had appeal to both politicians and academicians. His idea of the frontier was conducive to a belief in democracy and to a rudimentary capitalism that was in turn sanctioned by American Protestantism; it left a legacy that encouraged the political program of an expansionist nation intent on global status. The idea of a frontier was also rich in intellectual possibility, because it redefined the idea of America and marked the place where nascent and civilized matters came together. The frontier supplied the boundary of what Mark Twain's Huck Finn referred to at the end of the novel as "the territory ahead," realms of space and time waiting to be settled and defined, a wilderness waiting to be worked and tamed. The idea of the West was as much—or perhaps more—a state of mind, both as an idea formulated by Turner and, in literary expression, as the Western.

As national harbinger, Turner's thesis was aggressively challenged when America changed and in the process lost its agrarian base: a new America demanded a new definition of a national self. The change brought Old World immigrants to work in the new industrial city along with freed slaves from the South. After the Civil War, there were more than 4 million freed slaves in the South, many of them ready to move on. Some went west, equating the West with the biblical Promised Land (Deverell and Hyde 4–5). Others went to cities in the North, engendering places like Harlem in New York and transforming Chicago. As a result, the idea of the wilderness frontier gave way to its opposite and to another construct—the myth of an urban counterforce. Both the wilderness and the urban realms had their dark sides, but each offered an ideal—one to the yeoman farmer and the homesteader, the other to the industrial baron and the factory worker. Both in different ways encouraged the enterprising seeker. The wilderness illusion and the industrial transformation created two political realities: one was based on the priority of the individual, the other on the priority of the community, and the two created a system of diverse values that is still with us today. The discussion of the relationship between individualism and community—really the discussion about the social values of the two frontiers—constituted a substantial part of the debate in the emerging discipline of sociology and mirrored the changes relating to the breakdown of individualism and the loss of community in the transformation from a wilderness to urban society The prevailing opinion maintained that with the rise of the machine, the self was fragmented and an organic realm was transformed into the mechanist. Modernism saw the rise of a normless individualism that presumed a disharmony between the individual and the community.

Relevant to this discussion was Ferdinand Tönnies (1855–1936) and his theory of Gemeinschaft versus Gesellschaft. Gemeinschaft emphasized community and motives beyond self-interest based on common beliefs, family, division of labor, and trust in the organic. Opposed was Gesellschaft with its prevailing belief in the breakdown of community based on individual self-interest, motivated by money, and marked by class or social conflict rather than cooperation.

Another participant in the discussion was Emile Durkheim (1858–1917), who distinguished between traditional society and modern society. Traditional society assumed that common purpose and collective consciousness subsumed individual consciousness, created social norms, and regulated social behavior. Opposed to traditional society was modern society with its division of labor that created different social roles, sponsoring individual consciousness distinct from collective consciousness. The transformation from traditional to modern society accounted for a feeling of anomie, alienation stemming from the loss of social and moral codes.

A third participant in the debate was Max Weber, who argued that capitalism took its being from forms of Protestant religion (especially Calvinism) that promoted an individualism that accommodated the breakdown of community by encouraging a capitalism that put emphasis upon the individual to engage in personal enterprises through trade and investment wealth.

The two realms (each in its own way a frontier) mark more than just regional difference: they establish a crossroads that involves our national origins, supplying the interpretive bases for how a nation should function. Both the conservative and the liberal agendas that we know today had their origins on the frontier. The wilderness frontier accommodated a Jeffersonian idea of an agrarian nation intent on limited government, prizing individualism and self-reliance. The urban frontier, rooted in commercial enterprises and industry, eventually and by necessity encouraged a New Deal vision.

An industrial nation rarely employs the full resources of its labor force; there is a minimum of at least 5 percent of its citizenry that remains unemployed and in need of local, state, or national welfare. Moreover, there are many services that are best, sometimes only, provided by forms of government, from waging war and supplying disaster relief, to building dams and interstate highways, maintaining national parks, postal delivery, and regulations of various kinds. We can see the legacies of the two frontiers in today's geopolitical realms of the red (conservative) and blue (liberal) states, with the red states mostly located in the interior rural realms and the blue states mainly situated along the coasts in metropolitan areas.

Those who criticized New Deal activity were often living by agrarian ideals that no longer had relevance; they had created an idealized past that lacked historical application, were unappreciative—sometimes even unaware—of federal benefits, and failed to value the physical differences and needs between the two frontiers. Even today, according to Suzanne Mettler, 40 percent of people on Medicare, 44 percent of Social Security recipients, and 43 percent of those receiving unemployment benefits deny that they have participated in a government program.

The two frontiers competed with each other: which frontier a person privileged carried over to what the person wanted America to be; it became an agenda. As a territory, the frontier was the focal point of an expanding nation. Once America became an imperial nation, the idea of the frontier was transformed again, until after World War II the idea of the frontier went beyond national to transnational scope, beyond domestic to global significance. The idea of the frontier remained, but its nature, its purpose, and its cast of characters was unalterably changed.

II

Frontier experience gave us the origins of modern America, and those origins were subject to processes of interpretation. As the political agenda changed, so did the idea of America; and as the idea of America changed, so, conversely, did the idea of the frontier. Processes of interpretation—a new definition of the frontier or a different concept of history that was brought to the equation—accommodated such changes. There is thus reciprocity between the idea of the frontier and the idea of America. The frontier became a prism through which to interpret and assess the transformations that have defined the idea of America.

The closing of Turner's frontier brought us into a realm of the past where the illusion of the frontier lived on, reinforcing the idea of a mythic West. We now locate frontier goals in a mythic past. As previously noted, it was Scott Fitzgerald who told us that it was axiomatic that Americans seek their destiny in an exhausted past, search the past for an idealized realm no longer present, and long for ideals long gone that would give romantic substance to what the present lacks: "[S]o we beat on, boats against the current, borne back ceaselessly into the past" (1957, 182).

The theme of pursuing a lost past is well treated in American literature by Fitzgerald himself and by earlier writers or contemporaries such as James Fenimore Cooper, Walt Whitman, Mark Twain, Willa Cather, William Faulkner, Nathanael West, and John Steinbeck—writers whose concerns treat a large swath of American history. Fitzgerald's belief that we keep alive illusionary ideals in a world that no longer accommodates them finds examples in multiple sources, from a strict construction (an "originist" interpretation) of the Constitution to preserving the heroics of the Western novel; both the Constitution and the Western contain ideas relevant to the wilderness thesis. A wilderness frontier—both its opening and its closing—reinforced the agrarian pursuit of ideals displaced by the second industrial revolution. The history of this conflicted ideal was kept alive in the literary imagination of the times and in various literary genres, including the Western novel, literary naturalism, and neorealism as embodied in noir fiction and film, and by a radical revision of the idea of the pioneer West in modern and postmodern literature and history.

Intellectual concern is a composite matter taking in social, political, economic, philosophical, and cultural issues, best summarized by the realization that history and literature are intertwined pursuits. A change in one discipline necessitates change in another. The literary imagination takes its being from history, and history is enlarged—deepened and sustained—by the literary imagination. Both are narrative systems; if not interchangeable, they often reinforce each other. The study of the American frontier—both its wilderness and its urban components—is a product of historical pursuit deepened by literary representation. The wilderness frontier finds its literary embodiment in the subgenre of the Western; the urban frontier finds its literary embodiment in literary naturalism. Transformations in one system have demanded transformations in the other: the Western accommodated aspects of literary naturalism (cf. Norris's *The Octopus* and Steinbeck's *The Grapes of Wrath*), and literary naturalism anticipated noir fiction (dealing with fated characters and the dark side of marginal life that was part of the urban experience, as in James M. Cain's *The Postman Always Rings Twice*).

There have been historical studies of the westward movement, and there have been works that have touched upon its literary aspects. What needs reconsideration involves the transforming effect history demands of those literary factors—most aptly illustrated by the connection between a closed frontier and the need for the harsher realism that literary naturalism brought to the Western. A factor in this process is also the way the frontier movement became a state of mind separate from its historical reality. Another factor is the meaning of what resulted when and where the primitive and the civilized merged. Coupled to these concerns is the assumption that historical interpretation follows institutional authority: the idea of an urban frontier, for example, came into being with the rise and influence of metropolitan America.

The dichotomy between a rural and an urban mentality has been treated in various ways. One involved the distinction David Riesman formulated in his monumental *The Lonely Crowd* (1950). According to Riesman, there are two distinct cultural types: inner-directed and other-directed personalities. The inner-directed person works out of strong sense of internal conviction, consistent with the character of rugged individualism grounded in evangelical belief. The other-directed person is more flexible, more the product of a tolerance needed to survive in a more complex urban environment. The formulation of these terms accommodates the assumptions of the old historicism with its belief in historical determinism, its emphasis on environmental meaning, and its belief that historical meaning can be reduced to general explanation.

Whatever the historical assumptions that we bring to the dichotomy between rural and urban reality, we move to the way history is transformed into forms of cultural myths, including modes of literary expression. In its extended application, the frontier became a composite of history, myth, and a philosophical and religious state of mind. Extended once again, it influenced our domestic and foreign policies; in literary terms it transformed major narrative modes; and as a process it kept alive belief in the original frontiers, if only as a postulate of what we once were. As both a state of mind and a physical presence, the frontier accommodated various theories of force, from the beneficent force of Emersonian transcendentalism to the more hostile forces of literary naturalism and noir. As the American political agenda changed, so did the idea of the frontier, becoming the basis for domestic expansion (manifest destiny) as well as foreign expansion (imperialism), anticipating a policy of "exceptionalism" that led ultimately to today's nation-building.

Each generation saw the frontier anew—from the West as the transformation of European culture, to the West as the basis of an American individualism that anticipated an American egalitarianism, to the West as an eastern dependency, to the West as a series of military and legal conquests, to the West as the radical transformation of modern and postmodern reality. Each generation brought its own demand for change and left as a state of mind an idealized reservoir of meaning now located in an irrelevant past.

III

There is both an internal and an external meaning connected with each frontier: the idea of each realm, as previously stated, can be transformed by changing the terms within which it is defined or by changes in the concept of history that grounds that interpretation. As we shall see, our fundamental beliefs evolve from interpretive strategies, and interpretive strategies often arise from ideologies of one sort or another, mostly political and economic.

The "idea" of America has been in keeping with a changing historical process. As a result, a sense of American identity has been radically transformed since Turner gave us his frontier thesis, although variations on that thesis can be found elsewhere—for example, in the American South. Both visions have come under scrutiny from various perspectives, but most notably from New York intellectuals, such as Richard Hofstadter, examining the wilderness frontier from an urban perspective, working from essentially historicist assumptions similar to those of Charles Beard. Another version of the frontier stemmed from an expansionist policy with variations of imperial politics that carry us from the Spanish-American War to the many and varied skirmishes that followed World War II, to the nation-building that prevailed in places like Iraq.

The idea of a frontier has given us a historical record at the same time as it has supplied a sense of national purpose. From the call to rugged individualism, to the awe of industrial power, to the imperial reach as a product of manifest destiny, the purposes embodied in the idea of the frontier have reflected the agendas of an evolving America. The history of such transformations—from an agrarian frontier of the American West to an imperial realm with national purpose—is a story of putative destiny, national quest, lost innocence, and transformed ideals. All of these factors are elements in the story this book seeks to tell.[1]

IV

Central to all of these historical elements was the transformation from an agrarian to an industrial culture. The persistence of agrarian values was also a mandate of the idea of the West, especially the romantic idea of the West as a mythic realm with a transformative power that shaped American history. Most of the mythic belief was inspired by Frederick Jackson Turner's idea of a wilderness frontier. The West for Turner was an unbounded landed realm, a law unto itself, a frontier haven waiting to be settled when not a safety valve relieving the dissatisfaction of the discontent, allowing new opportunities to those resolute enough to take advantage of the occasion, encouraging an idealized rugged individualism (at least in theory) that approached narcissism. The West became a crucible, transforming founding ideas and European values into something distinctly different, indigenous and ultimately American.

Both Turner and Charles Beard believed 1890 was a transformational date in American history: by then an agrarian world had given way to an industrial world. Turner emphasized the agrarian aspect of this process, while Beard emphasized the capitalism-industrial aspect of the transformation. Turner's agrarian America had its roots in the Republican dictates of Jefferson, Jackson, and Lincoln. Beard, however, according to David Noble, maintained "that history was evolving from the medieval stage through the stage of capitalism and would culminate in the stage of industrial democracy" (Noble 1970, 24). Henry Nash Smith's *Virgin Land* (1950) supported Turner's view; Walter Prescott Webb's *The Great Frontier* (1952) leaned toward Beard's, as did William Appelman Williams's *The Tragedy of American Diplomacy* (1959). It was Beard's conclusion upon which Patricia Nelson Limerick later built her own transformational work. Turner's frontier anticipated an egalitarian America; Beard's frontier claimed that "[p]ower, not liberty, was the essential Euro-American experience" (Noble 1970, 31). Both Turner and Beard believed in the centrality of the frontier, but each brought his theory to a different conclusion.

The difference between a feudalistic Europe and a democratic America turned on claims to the land. European feudalism put the ownership in the hands of a lord, the land itself worked by tenant farmers. American democracy put the land in the hands of yeoman farmers—subsistence beings, independent in the pursuit of livelihood, living off the land as both owners and workers. One view looked back to medieval economics; the other looked ahead to the prospects of modern democracy. Turner's distinction between the two was the difference between two political worlds, Europe and America, and the rise of America as a new political option. The idea of a new America brought with it a belief in romantic destiny.

The theme of romantic destiny reinforced the claim that the idea of the West involved a historical reality separate but subject to a mythic counterpart. From the very beginning, even before there was a mandate from the land, there was a sense of history as destiny. The Puritans hoped to achieve "a new heaven and a new earth"; this was another way of saying that being an American involved "exceptionalism," a special mission to a higher way of life, the call from a beaconed hill, an idea expressed on the Great Seal of the United States by the words "Novus Ordo Seclorum" (Parkes 81–82). Even on the level of cliché, the idea of destiny is with us. Belief in "the American dream" implies that there is something in the American experience that beckons to success (variously defined), which in turn suggests a rudimentary way of thinking about America as a product (divine recipient) of destiny. And the belief in material "progress" that accompanies the fulfillment of the dream carries with it the anticipation that there is an ideal waiting to be realized in the American future, which takes us to still another expression of belief in an American destiny. The influence of the Enlightenment comes into play, and with it a transformation of authority based on a belief in the rights of the individual—rights that when extrapolated carried the belief that power resides with the people and not with the king or the feudal lord.

But the Enlightenment was the product of its own limits. Romantic destiny emphasized the organic nature of being and was intrinsic to romantic history, in part a reaction to Enlightenment history. The idea of science was challenged by the idea of myth; the belief in physical (mechanistic) matter gave way to the belief that matter was infused with mind, which encouraged a belief in a vitalistic nature and a romantic sense of history as inborn and ordained.

V

The play between Enlightenment and romantic values is best seen in one of our major themes in this study: the role of "savagery" ("primitivism" in its largest sense) in relation to the institutions of civilization. In the eighteenth century, the prevalent thought was that nature was man's enemy unless tamed by man's intelligence. In this context, depicting the Indian was a mixed affair. There were "good" and "bad" Indians, and their moral merits were often arbitrarily imposed. In Karl May's stories, all Apaches were good and all Comanches bad. The good Indian was the product of civilized forces: "[A]ll that was 'good' about the red man would be traceable to civilization, all that was 'bad' to Nature" (Billington 1981, 101).

Under the influence of romanticism, this claim was reversed: nature was glorified; the savage was made noble; the wilderness when tamed became the transformed garden (Billington 1981, 13–14, 18–20). But there was a fictional need for both good and bad Indians. The bad Indian tested the prowess of the Western hero, while the good Indian— in a tradition that stretched from Uncas and Natty Bumppo to Tonto and the Lone Ranger—served as a faithful companion (107). While there were individuals who justified the idea of the good Indian, their tribe never reached that status: the image the tribe projected was that of a "decayed race, steeped in violence and indolence, unable and unwilling to adjust to the modern world, and hence doomed to rapid and justifiable extinction" (Billington 1981, 124).

As the white settler advanced in the face of the wilderness, the tribal Indian declined in the face of civilization. As American culture became more industrial, the idea of nature became nostalgically more benevolent. In Puritan America the wilderness embodied the unknown, a belief that was later expressed as a mystical aspect to nature, when the land was tamed by agrarian pursuits and there was an idealized longing for the lost wilderness, expressed in demands for national parks and urban gardens. Yellowstone National Park, established in 1872, was the first of such national parks ("national" because Wyoming and Montana at that time were territories, not states, and the federal government assumed responsibility for its claim to the land).

In the city, New York had its Bronx, but it also had its Central Park, which opened in 1857 on 843 acres of city-owned land. (In 1858 Frederick Law Olmsted won a contract to expand and improve the land; construction began that year but was not completed until 1873, fifteen years later, a year after the opening of Yellowstone.) The zoo (including the zoo in Central Park with its 130 species) came into being as a reminder of the wilderness that was now relegated to the remote past.

These escapes from urban reality helped keep alive, at least as a state of mind, a sense of the wilderness that was being transformed by the new urban-commercial-industrial society. In the dialectic between primitivism and civilization, the moral terms randomly changed. On the whole, the forces of civilization worked for the good, even as such forces brought degeneration to the tribal Indians and distrust to Natty Bumppo and Huck Finn, who questioned the legal and religious institutions (including the decorum) that civilization advanced.

In his belief that the determining aspect of land was transformed wilderness, Frederick Jackson Turner was deeply indebted to a belief in romantic destiny: his ideas were essentially the product of material being, the belief that the history of America had its basis in fundamental law similar to natural law like that of entropy or gravity. There is a sense of the inevitable in his thinking that often goes unnoticed. In his essay "The Significance of the Frontier in American History" (1893), he tells us that initially history was concerned with political happenings, but history as politics had given way to history as economics—and the laws of economics were now the foundation of historical meaning.

Turner believed that the historian should go to primary sources. As we have seen, he had doubts regarding the "germ theory" of history, the belief that political ideas have their origin in Europe and are carried full blown, like viruses, to America. The germ theory rejected the belief that political ideology was determined by geographical or social influences. He qualified this theory, claiming that European ideas had infiltrated America but that their influence was exaggerated; he insisted that they took on a different cast once they crossed the Atlantic: became more egalitarian and democratic once they shed their feudal origins, became more subject to American individualism when transformed by the geography of the West.

There was reciprocity between the individual and the environment (what later came to be known as "bioregionism"): one reinforced and infused the other. Like the proponents of the old historicism, Turner believed that regional factors (what today would be called "ecosystems," including watersheds) created foreordained historical conditions. But most important, he believed that a nation's fate was determined by the abundance or scarcity of (free) land and open recourse to the wilderness. All of these factors had a determinate aspect, but Turner believed that they did not diminish the dictates of individualism and the play of free will, even if such individualized power was only an illusion.

To this end he maintained that the wilderness frontier created an American type. He claimed: "[T]he true point of view in the history of this nation is not the Atlantic coast, it is the Great West." What the Mediterranean Sea was to the Greeks, the West was to America. He substituted the continuous recession of free land and "the advance of American settlement westward" for Plymouth Rock and the settling of the eastern seaboard (Turner, "Significance of the Frontier," 11–13, 37–38). He was primarily concerned with frontier intersection and the effect of civilized intrusion into the wilderness. He saw the movement west as a circular process, both given and willed. The human will found its expression in the historical given: it began with a desire for new land and the ability to perpetuate that desire, creating a westward movement composed of optimists who were the potential rugged individualists and proto-democrats who infused the movement with historical purpose, completing the circle and encouraging the belief (in retrospect, the imagined conclusion) that expansion was divinely sanctioned.

Turner believed that the resulting American frontier transformed its population and contributed to what was unique in the American character, promoting a forward-looking adventurous disposition, independent in character, resilient, self-involved and closed-minded, tolerant of values if complementary to its own, wary of the foreign and strange, inventive and pragmatic, more a product of action than of words, guilty of anti-intellectualism, willing to resort to gunplay when words failed, prone to vigilantism, restless by nature, perpetually dissatisfied, continually looking west.

An America destiny, or so it was claimed, stemmed from drawing upon the traits that went with the character of rugged individualism: it created a state of mind and made possible or encouraged other institutions—drawing selectively from a legacy of ideas residual in Protestantism, capitalism, and democracy, including a trust in God's grace, the promotion of investment and land speculation, and the belief in the people as the source of political power—diverse motives that prevailed so long as they never challenged the priority of the individual.

VI

The idea of a frontier has long been embedded in the American mind, as a quick look at the American presidency reveals. Jefferson created an extended western frontier with the Louisiana Purchase of 1803. As a young man, Andrew Jackson moved to western Tennessee: he thought of himself as a product of the frontier; as president (1829–37), he moved the Indians farther west (into what is now Oklahoma), keeping the West open to the emerging pioneers. Lincoln was a product of the western movement, which took him from Kentucky (1809–16) to Indiana (1816–30) to Illinois (1830–61) in his journey to the presidency (1861–65). Others added to the idea of a "fated West" with mythic dimension: Theodore Roosevelt reinforced the idea of the move west as the working of destiny in his *The Winning of the West* (1889–96). Harry Truman grew up and lived in Independence, Missouri, the starting point of the Oregon Trail. And John F. Kennedy, in his inaugural address as president (1961), spoke of facing west in the symbolic terms that suggested a new frontier.

As a historian, Turner emphasized reading history as literal record, but he was also capable of turning secular history into sacred legend; he saw that the move west had a mythical component and supplied analogues that connected western history with religious Jewish-Christian legend, including the exodus myth: Jefferson was its John the Baptist; Jackson its Moses; and Lincoln its Christ, redeeming man from the sin of slavery (Noble 1989, 21).

With the ending of the frontier wilderness, the values embodied by the idea of the West were transformed by a new national agenda: rugged individualism, the trait most suited to the wilderness frontier, now encouraged imperial reach. Moreover, the transformation of both urban and frontier America was fueled by the influx of immigrants, primarily from Europe. In the nineteenth century and up to World War I, 50–60 million persons left their native land for the New World, and another 5–10 million were brought to America by force from Africa. Henry Bamford Parkes believes this was the largest movement of people in history (3).

What motivated those who came by choice? Some were escaping the upheaval of the Napoleonic Wars. Others came because they believed the hype of the shipping lines and their agents, or the romantic tales about America they heard in school, or the tall tales of guidebook authors, or the favorable accounts of life in the New World in letters from relatives or friends in America. Whatever the immediate cause, almost all who came from Europe were in search of a new and better life. And with them came the transformation of America itself.

The transformation from an agrarian to an industrial country brought new national mandates into being. The rise of the new corporation, the exploitation of mineral wealth, the creation of the factory system, the implementation of the transnational railroad, the rise of a consumer culture that brought with it a market economy involving commercial and industrial mandates—all of these factors led to an economy that turned on money, institutionalized in the new stock exchange that extended the power of capitalism. People became constrained by the new industrial function that gave priority to profit; the idea of democracy was narrowed; and the individual became less resilient as agrarian opportunity became more limited.

Theodore Roosevelt bridged the dictates that accompanied the transformation of rugged individualism to a more conformist state of mind. He was a man of and for the times, able to celebrate the wilderness frontier and still consent to an expansionist foreign policy, reconciling contrary frontier and imperial values, an ardent capitalist and yet a trust-buster. Built into both worlds were metamorphic elements. The decline of the agrarian life and industrial abuses led to protest movements, especially the Populist and later the Progressive movement, which brought with it racial and religious biases (especially an anti-Semitism). Imperialism brought limits: the move toward becoming an imperial nation challenged an earlier isolationism and stretched the militant reach for new land and natural resources, all at a national cost.

The rise of an industrial America transformed the wilderness frontier. The new frontier gave us an America material in nature, dependent on the workings of capitalism, and cognizant of economic and military power that at the end of the nineteenth century competed for imperial place with other advanced world nations, especially those in Europe. The loss of a national innocence accompanied the rise of a new capitalism responding to imperial pursuits. The pursuit of wealth became an end in itself, often pursued as an abstraction in the form of stocks and bonds, or in the form of land no longer farmed but owned as investment property. Walt Whitman was sensitive to what these changes involved. Mark Twain disapproved of the obsessive call to wealth in his contribution to *The Gilded Age,* as did Frank Norris in *The Octopus* and Willa Cather in *A Lost Lady.* The West became the historical symbol of a new and different America that took its meanings from both the internal and the external fulfillment of imperial design.

The idea of the West as an open and then a closed frontier had many witnesses. In the realm of politics, George Washington and later Thomas Jefferson encouraged the move west. Washington said, "We have opened the fertile plains of Ohio. . . . [A]nyone . . . who wants land to cultivate may repair thither and abound in the Land of Promise" (cited in Smith 236). Jefferson, who was unsympathetic to the rise of urban industry, saw the agrarian West as a way out of what he considered demeaning work: such workers could "quit their jobs and go to laboring the earth" (cited in Smith 237).

In the realm of literature, James Fenimore Cooper, Ralph Waldo Emerson, Walt Whitman, Mark Twain, Henry Adams, Willa Cather, and Scott Fitzgerald all looked to the West with renewed expectation, often followed by a sense of disappointment at failed achievement. A historical determinism was at work. Emerson spoke of a new city in the West, an idea later advocated by Whitman. The idea of the frontier was kept alive, as we have seen, by historians like Frederick Jackson Turner, who believed in regional forces—or sectional forces, as he later called them—as a determinant of history; the idea was kept alive as well by other historians who contested Turner's fundamental ideas.

VII

Turner's view of history can be clarified in two important ways. First, it is consistent with the old historicism—the belief that every era or nation has a principle of unity within it, an informing principle, usually economic-political in function, which operates like the laws of nature, helping to explain a historical movement such as the Italian Renaissance (fueled by the national rise of humanist pursuits) or a national culture such as Germany's. An agrarian-urban frontier supplied insights that held other historical assumptions in place. And second, despite Turner's insistence on a wilderness frontier, it can be argued that we need not choose between two frontier theses: a closer look at this ideological impasse suggests that both a wilderness frontier and an urban frontier existed at different times and occasionally at the same time in different places.

Revisionary thinking places the urban frontier at the head, the spear point, of historical progress. Earl Pomeroy (1955) and Patricia Nelson Limerick (1987) have argued that the West was an eastern dependency, or at least that its development was more of a collaborative effort. There is much to justify this contention: eastern support of homesteading has long been documented; eastern investment money facilitated the building of a transcontinental railroad; and eastern speculation in land, cattle, timber, oil, and water contributed to an emerging West. The main concern of Patricia Nelson Limerick, in her book *The Legacy of Conquest,* is the belief that speculative investment, militant pursuit, and conquest (rather than rugged individualism and egalitarian thinking) prevailed in the frontier movement, as she deals primarily with economic matters in a study rich in anecdotal reference. She substitutes sustained legal conflict and an "unbroken past" for the "creation myth"—the belief that each generation of pioneers mastered nature, bringing civilization to the wilderness in serial fashion as they moved westward to the Pacific.

VIII

Despite being contested, Turner's thesis supplied a way of looking at America that substituted an all-defining regional development for national achievement. His definition of a wilderness frontier had historical relevance, but its exaggerated claims went beyond reality and became illusionary in their call to romantic destiny and in their belief in rugged individualism—values that the urban crucible transformed in the workings of an industrial community and the theory of historicism and its belief in the cohesiveness of historical eras.

The claim for a special nature of the frontier is documented in literary terms by the Western and by the transformation of the Western into literary naturalism and later into literary noir. Owen Wister's cowboy anticipates the workings of literary naturalism when he confronts life forces, especially the forces of nature. When the cowboy reaches the city, he becomes Raymond Chandler's private detective, Philip Marlowe, whose solitude, resilience, and steadfast dedication to a personal code gives us the transformed equivalence to frontier character; and Marlowe's tough-guy manner is just one step away from both literary and film versions of noir.

The idea of the West supplied many literary masks. We have, for example, Jack Kerouac and Alan Ginsberg's short-lived, drug-infused pilgrimages in search of the idealized West that exists only in the addled mind. Transformed once more, the idea of the West takes us to Thomas Pynchon's Oedipa Maas's confused journey to Narcissus (Los Angeles?) in search of the American legacy. The sense of promise realized and promise lost, as well as the transition from one view to the other, allows a depiction of both the bright and the dark sides of this unique American experience.

The frontier experience leads us to the realms of two different cultures, and the transformation from one realm to the other is rife with consequences. The first culture features a yeoman perspective in which the farmer is self-sufficient and lives mostly off the land; this yeoman structure eventually gives way to a commercial agrarianism in which the farmer produces a cash crop and then buys what he needs to live.

The second culture takes us to the urban-commercial-industrial realm. The intellectual historian Oswald Spengler has long argued that the movement from an agrarian to an urban world is marked by cultural decline, when institutions that dehumanize usurp the function of the individual.

An agrarian nation looks inward, concentrating on domestic concerns; an industrial nation looks outward, concentrating on global matters. The theme of a national frontier anticipates the idea of an imperial nation. The common denominator is the taking of land—domestic land in the case of the wilderness frontier, foreign land in the case of empire. The move west seemed to encourage a move beyond. Both intrusions upon the land were justified in the name of manifest destiny: the God-given right to expand into and possess the whole of the North American continent was extended to Puerto Rico and Cuba in the Caribbean and Guam and the Philippines in the Pacific realm (see Jones 2012). When the call to expansion was justified in the name of history itself, when it took on privileged status, it became romantic history as well as manifest destiny.

Manifest destiny justified the right of America to expand westward. That authority supposedly stemmed from the desire for more land to the justification of slavery. The claim to the continent, the right to expand in the northern hemisphere, eventually gave way to imperialism, the right to global possession. But as Albert K. Weinberg argued in his *Manifest Destiny* (1935), the appeal was not to "objective need" but to "instinct and impulse in the glorious prospect of World Empire" (cited in Malone 1989, 84). In other words, manifest destiny stemmed from an empowered state of mind: desire combined with power justified the basis for imperial pursuit.

The expansionist mandate brought with it serious consequences, primary among them the inevitability of national decline, which stemmed from the expense involved in facilitating and sustaining the imperial reach. This principle has proved true whether it was imperial Rome or the other imperial nations—the "falling towers" (Jerusalem, Athens, Alexandria, Vienna, London)—that T. S. Eliot catalogs in *The Waste Land*. As the imperial nation extends its base, it becomes responsible for nation-building. It takes on the burden of colonial infrastructure, the need of an army to secure international rights and a police force to keep domestic harmony, the cost of welfare demands—especially medical and educational care—of colonized people, and the other costs that come with nation-building, all of which weaken the imperial nation at home, overloading its center as domestic needs compete with foreign and military spending, creating domestic discontent.

The story that is here to be told is as old as history and as recent as the urban riots that have shaken modern American cities from Harlem to Los Angeles. Every great empire has eventually experienced decline, as if the process were built into nature, analogous to the human process of decline that comes with aging, or to the rhythm of a day (sunrise to sunset), or to seasonal change (spring to winter). Such a view arises from a fundamental romantic sense of time as a given—a natural, even cosmic—process. This symbolic unraveling takes us to a romantic view of nature, to what Perry Miller calls "nature's nation," to the "visionary company" that in America found its most eloquent expression in the commentary of Emerson and Whitman.

The Jeffersonian vision was sympathetic to the belief that political rights had their mandates in nature. This belief did nothing to prevent—indeed, it may have perpetuated—the belief that expansionism was part of those national rights. Moreover, working the land itself had a therapeutic effect. The Jeffersonian vision—with its principal mandates rooted in the land, its sympathy with the rural yeoman farmer (who owned and cultivated his own land), its belief that the government that governs least is the government that governs best—lived on long after its components were no longer viable.

The ability of the Jeffersonian mandates to survive in the new industrial age stemmed from a number of sources: first, the agrarian call brought with it the political authority of the founding fathers, a sense of sacred testimony, and the appeal to cultural roots and tradition as a God-given mission; second, there was a need for a more simplistic vision of reality as the commercial-industrial society became more complex and overly powerful; and, third, in keeping with the previous reasons, there was a nostalgia for the lost ideal, a remorse that the yeoman tradition of agrarianism was being eclipsed by the new system and the desire to preserve the old system as long as possible. Such nostalgia played into the modernist belief—well expressed, as we have seen, by Scott Fitzgerald—that we perpetuate past ideals long after they have become exhausted and that we cannot, as Nick Carraway tells Gatsby, repeat (buy back) the past.

The concern for a lost idealized past is a continuing American theme. We have a dozen or more works—among them Twain's *Life on the Mississippi* (1883), James's *The American Scene* (1907), Dreiser's *Hoosier Holiday* (1916), Pound's "Patria Mia" (1911), Eliot's *After Strange Gods* (1934), Fitzgerald's "My Lost City" (1932), and Henry Miller's *Remember to Remember* (1947)—in which a writer returns to an American scene, usually after an absence of twenty years, to find that world sadly transformed and the values he considered so deeply American transformed with it. Such an experience is of course subjective, since one person's diminished world becomes the basis for another's ideal. Yet in each case the author pays homage to a lost innocence, an exhausted past, and conveys a vivid sense that we have used up a moment of possibility that will never come again. So it was with two idealized visions of America: Jefferson's agrarian vision and Turner's vision of the wilderness frontier.

Fitzgerald's *The Great Gatsby* is a fictional account that parallels the transformation from an agrarian to an industrial frontier. Gatsby rejects his agrarian rearing in the name of a more romantic (individualistic) self, only to be confronted by the new kingdom of force embodied by Tom Buchanan—a transformation that parallels the American metamorphosis from agrarian society to industrial power. The realm of Henry Adams's Dynamo curtailed romantic possibility: "Chaos was the law of nature; order was the dream of man," Adams wrote (1946, 389). The machine was going to bring about a new order of nature: technological man had gone beyond nature, had forced his mechanical will on the land and turned that control into the wealth that Twain depicts in *The Gilded Age*, which is the concern of the Progressive movement and constitutes one of the major themes of American literature. This transformation, the spirit of which Fitzgerald captures in *The Great Gatsby*, is also the story of America and the story of the two frontiers that are the subject of this book.

The Jeffersonian agrarian vision and the Turner frontier view were both compelling and enduring, encouraging a transformation of the ideals and values that defined America and supplied both a sense of national identity and of destiny before they were transformed by the forces of industrial and urban power. As part of the agrarian vision that won the commitment of the Populist movement and supported the reform that the Progressive movement mounted against corrupt elements in the new industrial order, the myth of the West helped infuse and transform historical reality. National identity was more the product of mythical than of historical influence. The Jeffersonian vision lived on in mythic function long after it became irrelevant in historical application—no longer a mandate in an industrialized America. Both as an earlier historical reality and as a current state of mind, it played a major role in shaping the identity of the new nation.

3

The West as a State of Mind

I

The idea of the West in its many facets has long been with us: it has existed as a physical region, as a cultural idea, as a religious mandate, as a political state of mind, and as a mythic realm. We have looked west for our ideals: in the West were the submerged island of Atlantis, Avalon, and the workings of Celtic mythology. As Walter Allen has told us, "the very notion of the west, or of westward, of what lay beyond the sunset, seems always to have had mythical, even mystical connotations" (13). And Allen moves us from mythology to history when he points out that "the great historic migrations that have peopled Europe, those of the Greeks, the Celts, the Slavs, the Goths, the Anglo-Saxons, the Norsemen have always been from east to west" (14).

The movement west involved the formation of European religious and political ideas that were transformed when put into practice in America. While there was reluctance to combine politics and religion, there was in fact a religious influence that had its residual political effect. The Puritans brought a rigid Calvinism to America that carried with it a sense of abiding evil. The Puritans located two sources of evil: they saw the wilderness as the main obstacle to be confronted and the primary source of danger, especially when populated by hostile natives; and they acknowledged their own sinful nature, locating evil within themselves. Thus they positioned evil both inside and outside their being.

Calvinism was best located in the Congregationalist faith. Congregationalists believed in the authority of the local congregation: each congregation asserted its own autonomy. This put them outside the authority of elders (Presbyterians) and bishops (Episcopalians). Following Calvin, they argued that Christ was the head of the church, not the king or the pope. Within the Congregationalist Church were fundamental evangelical believers as well as disciples of more liberal religion and society. The more liberal advocates led the way to Unitarianism and Deism.

In Massachusetts the Congregationalists embraced the Unitarians, and the Unitarians moved toward transcendentalism. Perry Miller's *Errand into the Wilderness* (1956, 1984) claimed that transcendentalism was not an alternative to Calvinism but evolved from it. The transitional figure was Jonathan Edwards, who found "images of divine things" in the physical world, situating the source of religious concerns in nature. George Santayana tells us that the Calvinist asserted "three things: that sin exists, that sin is punished, and that it is beautiful that sin should be punished." A Calvinist feels "pleasure in the existence of misery, especially one's own." The Calvinist painted "in sharp and violent chiaroscuro" a state of mind transformed by transcendentalism and the belief that nature "was all beauty, a source of aesthetic inspiration" (Santayana 16–17).

The most important practitioner of transcendentalism was Ralph Waldo Emerson. Emerson believed nature was alive with spiritual energy. This energy, which he termed "soul," could be found in the individual. When all men shared this energy, they became the product of the "oversoul," which revealed its truth through "intuition," a direct way of understanding, more conducive to knowing than that allowed by empirical or dialectical means (125–43).

Emerson's philosophy engendered an American paradox by engaging the contradictions between the idea of individualism and self-reliance and the ideal of democracy and political community. On an aesthetic level, organic form involved the belief that a literary work found its unity in the course of being written. Applied to politics, the Emersonian trust in a beneficent nature assumed that the individual had the indwelling means to manufacture truth—had an informing principle within the self that served the same purpose as that of outside social authority.

Emersonianism was transformed Calvinism: a religious mandate in which evil is eradicated by the belief in natural goodness. Emerson desired to reduce the influence of European reliance on political authority and social hierarchy and to put the emphasis on the connection between the individual and the beneficence of nature. He insisted that God was everywhere and that evil was an illusion. Emerson's concept of nature was fundamental to his belief that European ideas could be transformed in America. The presence of an American wilderness had much to do with Emerson's idea of nature. Turning away from the British idea of God as a deity separate from the nature of his creation, he held that nature is not outside but working in or through us. He believed that we know God through the spiritual energy of nature, which is the source of our well-being. Beauty had its origins in nature—language also. Since we best understand the world around us by identifying with nature, we are all "transparent eyeballs," conduits of nature's energy. He insisted that because of "the currents of Universal Being [that] circulate through me, I am part or particle of God" (6; see also 126–27).

Despite his desire to give his ideas an American cast, Emerson was influenced in his thinking by Frederic Hedge's essay on Coleridge, published in the *Christian Examiner* (March 1833). Along with Coleridge, Carlyle was also a major influence. Coleridge believed in the transforming aspect of a living nature, Carlyle in the masks nature supplied. But transcendentalism owed its basic assumptions to Immanuel Kant, especially his *Critique of Pure Reason* (1781, translated in 1830). Kant believed that there was an inseparable connection between mind and nature: reality was built into the mind in the form of modes (space, time, condition, relation, etc.); the mind worked through forms of reality that came into being instinctively. These forms were not beyond human experience but were the means by which experience was made accessible.

Transcendentalism marked a major movement toward radical individualism and liberal politics. Looking back to Congregationalist and Unitarian assumptions, the participant felt that no single code fit every situation and that each individual must judge for himself or herself what his or her moral duty might be. The appeal was to an inner reality, and it moved the core thought one step closer to the connection between mind and nature and to the intuition that unlocked forms of truth. As a radical individualism, transcendentalism worked against more community-based agendas: such transcendental experiments as

Brook Farm and Fruitland failed because this kind of philosophical individualism conflicted with the idea of community.

As a way of knowing, transcendentalism accommodated the rugged individualism that came with the movement west. We see it at work in the abstract in Emerson's theory of self-reliance, the basis for many of his essays and lectures. We see it in the interconnectedness of all things and the solidarity of the people, beliefs that give foundation to Walt Whitman's poetry. We see it in a naturalistic novel like Frank Norris's *Octopus* when Vanamee, the character who is most in tune with the spirit of nature, tells Presley that evil has no permanent meaning and that the forces of nature work together "for good" (1958, 448). We see it at the end of Hemingway's *For Whom the Bell Tolls* (1940), when Robert Jordan tells Maria that a spiritual presence binds them forever, even as they part. And we see it at on a Mississippi River raft when an inner voice tells Huck Finn that Jim is a human being and not property, even if acting on such knowledge sends him to hell. Huck's intuitive decision to free Jim at the expense of hell's fire takes us to that existential point where individualism and self-reliance go beyond social and religious teachings, where spiritual well-being means staying one step ahead of civilization.

The ability to intuit the spiritual meaning of nature often required the privileged workings of the "primitive" over the limits of the "civilized." A historicist like Herbert Spencer saw civilization as a progressive form of communal behavior, the culmination of social truths. A humanist like Mark Twain reversed the process, viewing civilized forms of behavior as arbitrary, if not misleading and wrong, to be corrected by primitive instincts that resided closer to the truths that come from nature rather than the delimiting institutions that falsely organize society. That is why it is important for Huck to seek the territory ahead, to stay—like James Fenimore Cooper's Natty Bumppo—in harmony with nature.

In defining themselves against the wilderness, the American pioneers instinctively gave consent to the insights of primitivism, locating in the transformation of the wilderness a state of mind that imbued nature with the foundation of human truth. The combined effect of determining human value as defined by a process of the wilderness, rather than defining such value against the landed estate, was to transform the European emphasis on aristocracy into the American desire for democracy. Locke's idea that the wilderness becomes property once worked by human hands was qualified by the need for national parks and wilderness regions and the need to keep a residual part of the city pristine, the basis for the long tradition of putting aside large tracts of unspoiled land for urban parks and gardens, best illustrated by Frederick Law Olmsted's Central Park in New York. There has always been the need for a wilderness region, allowing escapes from urbanism, as Hemingway escaped the Chicago suburbs in the wilder reaches of the Michigan woods. These values the frontier people carried west, creating an American type, combining the dictates of rugged individualism with an environment consistent with the spirit of democracy. Turner maintained that these frontier transformations created a new kind of person, a distinctly American self, the product of new-values ideology.

II

The belief that some idealized life coincided with the virgin land in the West that made up the American frontier found a compelling, albeit fanciful, narrative in James Fenimore Cooper's *Leatherstocking Tales*. Cooper creates two realities, one mythic and the other historical. The mythic sets man outside of time, at one with nature, in harmony with the land. The historical deals with man in time, confronted by the events that make up the pioneer movement. Cooper depicts Natty Bumppo's desire to be the American Adam, the mythic man independent of time, at one with the wilderness, a product of the land. But his *Leatherstocking Tales* ultimately demonstrates the impossibility of fulfilling this desire, as Natty's expectations are questioned by Judge Temple's idea of civilization and the need of law to control mankind's fallen nature.

In *The Deerslayer*, we first see Natty Bumppo as an American Adam. He initially embodies the European romantic idea concerning the spiritual meaning of the land. This idea was Americanized by 1830, especially after 1828 and the election of Andrew Jackson, who looked to the frontier to complete a process of national destiny that had its origins in the American Revolution and was confirmed by Jefferson's Louisiana Purchase in 1803. Once the land was reclaimed from the French and the Indians, Deerslayer becomes Hawkeye, the warrior soldier—the man of nature transformed by the military needs of history.

The next novel, *The Last of the Mohicans,* continues the transformation of the myth in the face of history. When Chingachgook joins Hawkeye, his mythic function is taken over by his son, Uncas, the last of the Mohicans, who dies when the French are defeated at the hands of Magua, who embodies the Indian resistance to the western movement. With the defeat of the French, the Ohio and Mississippi Valleys are open to conquest from those who have remained east of the Appalachian Mountains, and Deerslayer-Hawkeye now becomes Pathfinder.

Cooper tells us at the end of *The Pioneers* (1823): "[Natty] had gone towards the setting sun—the foremost in that band of pioneers who are opening the way for the march of our nation across the continent." But Cooper, like many of his contemporaries, had mixed feelings: he, and they, were proud of the movement west but wary of its cost in human and environmental terms. The people Natty leads into the West have all the limits of human nature, which are at odds with an Adamic natural innocence. Cooper asks in *The Prairie* (1827) to what extent the movement west was at society's expense.

This theme is addressed at length in *The Pioneers,* where, on the assumption that human nature must be subject to law if there is to be civilization, Cooper questions whether the natural rights of Leatherstocking are beyond the laws of Judge Temple. Judge Temple's position prevails when the people—turned into a mob—drive Natty Bumppo from the community. Leatherstocking has been eclipsed by historical time, and the last novel in the sequence, *The Prairie,* depicts his death, now as a withered old man (although a concluding scene suggests his mythic past when he appears as a colossus, distantly outlined against a symbolic western sun). Natty dies and is buried on the prairie, where Cooper believes the myth of the West also died, once the Louisiana Purchase lost its sense of innovation and no longer redefined the mystical nature of the land.

Cooper coalesces several frontier factors. He attracted the attention of Theodore Roosevelt, who saw the relevance of Cooper's Hawkeye and the connection between him and Francis Parkman, who gave us a historical version of Cooper's fiction—a cast of characters (Daniel Boone, Davy Crockett, and Kit Carson) whose personal virtues anticipated acts of national heroism.

Cooper's novels may be more thematically than realistically convincing. (One remembers how Mark Twain ridiculed the improbabilities of Cooper's romance.) But Cooper coalesced the events that made the pioneer impulse into an important mythic-historical event. Out of his narrative, four themes emerged in modernist literature: Cather treated the urgency that first motivated the drive west; Steinbeck treated the way its reality was turned into a mirage; F. Scott Fitzgerald treated how the pursued ideal was already lost in an exhausted past; and Nathanael West depicted how the quest west, when frustrated, turned violent: how a community of people desiring a new beginning—connected as it was to the promise of destiny—was turned into a destructive mob when expectation failed to materialize.

Along with the myth of the West, the modernists had two sources of literary reality to draw upon. One was the transcendental tradition that came from Emerson and Whitman. The other was a pragmatic tradition that came from William James. One led to a literary romantic symbolism, the other to literary realism.

Walt Whitman's vision involves the One in the Many, although he uses the Many to get to the One—that is, he takes us to the One through religion (the crucifixion), through the power of poetry ("O I could sing such grandeurs and glories about you"), and through the power of being one with the land ("I bequeath myself to the dirt to grow from the grass I love / If you want me again look for me under your boot-soles") (1964, 75). The path through the Many leads to the One (everything is connected).

The question that needs consequent attention involves the nature of the One. How do we get from the realm of the Many (the pragmatic and the commonplace) to the One (mythic unity)? Henry Adams believed the Middle Ages did it through the symbolic power of the Virgin—a symbolism so strong that it created its own reality, a unifying force opposed to the fracturing action of the Dynamo. From Emerson to Whitman, this quest for a principle of unity—the transforming power that takes us from the commonplace to the heroic and sublime—involved the Soul, or the Oversoul, as Emerson would have it.

Whitman's poetry stems from two sources: his work as a journalist in Brooklyn and New York and the Emersonian vision. The first source drew upon the historical reality and physical observations of life in the city, especially Whitman's concern for the "mechanic," who today we would refer to as the blue-collar worker. The second took us to a new hope for America, based upon Emersonian principles of self-reliance and a utopian vision of a new city. Out of this bifurcation of ideas came two main traditions of modern American poetry: the primarily European, urban visions of Pound and Eliot, as opposed to the mainly indigenous, idealized visions of Hart Crane and William Carlos Williams.

From Emerson's perspective, Europe offered the city of Cain; America gave us the New Jerusalem. Like the Israelites, the American people had been tested in the wilderness. The journey was from the city of man to the City of God. But like Whitman after him, Emerson secularized the city of God, locating it as an ideal in the West.

Emerson's vision was primarily preindustrial, but he anticipated both Whitman and the modern poet in his desire for a symbiotic connection between city and the hinterland. The desire for a "spiritual" connection between the city and the land found a "material" equivalent in the completion of the Erie Canal, which connected the commercial activity of New York with the vitality of midwestern land. In both instances, there was a desire to bring the material in touch with the spiritual.

Whitman's metaphor for the city was the crowd—but the crowd individualized: out of it stepped Poe, Lincoln, Daniel Webster, and Henry Clay. It combined all of humanity as well as the great men who were the instruments of history. Drawing upon the tradition that led to Emerson, Whitman depicted the particular realized in the universal, the One in the Many. Borrowing from Emerson's "Self-Reliance" (the great man in the crowd keeps "the independence of solitude") (Emerson 170), Whitman depicted himself, the artist, alone in the crowd. The American burden was to reconcile the masses and the individual. The poet extrapolated from the crowd to the nation. The crowd was inseparable from America's destiny as the nation moved toward urbanism (between 1810 and 1860 the population of the United States grew six times faster than the world average, reaching 30 million by the Civil War, and the proportion of Americans living in cities grew from 6 percent to 20 percent of that total). Whitman never separated himself from this urban transformation: his poetry takes its power from Emerson's vision transformed into street speech.

Leaves of Grass went through the radical revision of nine editions from 1855 to 1890 as Whitman sought to keep up with a changing America. He transformed with romantic assumptions the Enlightenment ideal, believing the destiny of America was to realize an ideal democracy rather than to pursue material progress. He held on to that ideal until after the Civil War, when his vision of hope, as we shall see in "Democratic Vistas," turned to doubt. There is in the American imagination a bifurcation that holds a sense of promise for an ideal America in contrast to the belief that the promise has been betrayed. Whitman's drift from hope to doubt in "Democratic Vistas" was anticipated by the major American writers who preceded or were contemporary with him: Hawthorne in *The Blithedale Romance,* Melville in *Pierre* and *The Confidence Man,* Thoreau in "Civil Disobedience," and almost everything Twain wrote from *A Connecticut Yankee* to "What Is Man?"

The various versions of *Leaves of Grass* reveal Whitman's ambiguity regarding the promise of America. But where does *Leaves of Grass* begin and end? Whitman saw the contents of the poem as elusive and kept rewriting it. Where do we locate the "sense" that for Pater turns "fact" into "art"—in the 1855 edition or in the 1881 edition? In the 1855 edition, "Song of Myself" was surrounded by eleven other poems, all of which were supposedly talking to each other. What happens to the integrity of *Leaves of Grass* when these poems are revised, or transposed, or omitted altogether? Whitman's poetry breaks with the idea of organic form (the assumption that a work finds its principle of unity in the process of its creation). To come to terms with *Leaves of Grass* is to read the various editions of the poem as they evolved, not in terms of some principle of unity, part defined by the whole, but in terms of its historical unfolding, the poem reflecting a changing America as seen through Whitman's troubled eyes. It is to this aspect of Whitman's poetry that we shall return in chapter 10.

The mode of fiction that takes the West as its subject is literary naturalism, one of the main themes of which involved the conflict between a protagonist and the fate of the land. A work that best illustrates this narrative situation is Frank Norris's unfinished "epic trilogy" (*The Octopus, The Pit,* and *The Wolf*) dealing with wheat—its growth in California, its distribution based on market speculation in Chicago, and its consumption in Europe. Like Zola, he wanted to describe the forces, biological and economic, that were transforming agrarian life. The wheat remains the primary force: even abstract matters like market speculation ultimately come back to nature—back to the land and the forces out of which life germinates.

A discussion of Norris ultimately brings to the surface the key question of where the West begins. On one level, it begins west of the colonies—the land beyond the Appalachian Mountains. But the city that plays a more central role in the history of the West is Chicago. Located near the center of the country, between the coastal cities of New York and San Francisco, Chicago became the center of agrarian and industrial activity—leading the way in the commodity markets, becoming the center of wheat distribution and the meat industry. Moreover, Chicago was the center of activity in many if not most of the naturalistic narratives, the literary mode closest (after the Western) to depicting life on the frontier (along with Norris are Dreiser, Sinclair, Wright, and Farrell).

Another force that Norris wanted to work out had to do with his idea of the West: his belief that modern civilization was moving westward, from Europe to America, to the Pacific, where America expressed its military might with Dewey's exploits in Manila and the engagement of U.S. marines in China during the Boxer Rebellion. These events were part of a global movement, and in their historical sweep, they paralleled the production, consumption, and distribution of wheat as an interconnected global force.

Norris's epic of the battle between the railroad and the wheat farmers and Steinbeck's saga of the Oakies displaced from their land by the bank are two of many novels that deal with the confrontation between nature and hostile institutional forces. The literary and political records eventually came together. As for the literary record, the subgenre that treated a variation of this topic was the Western. Turner's ideas, as we shall see, were relevant to both literary naturalism and the Western. As for the political record, both Washington and Jefferson anticipated Emerson in locating an ideal city or the future of the nation in the West.

4

The Realms of Identity Powered by an Illusion

I

Max Planck has told us, "A new scientific truth does not triumph by convincing opponents and making them see the light, but rather because opponents eventually die, and a new generation grows up that is familiar with [a new way of thinking]" (33–34, qtd. in Kuhn). There is a "reality" independent of mind, but we approach that reality through the mind—that is, through what Thomas Kuhn has termed "paradigm shifts." We progress from paradigm to paradigm, from one assumption of truth to another assumption of truth—from Newton's gravitational theory and laws of motion, to Planck's quantum theory, to Einstein's theory of relativity. Niels Bohr's work on the discontinuous nature of energy in subatomic particles advanced Planck's theory and was advanced in turn by Werner Heisenberg and Kurt Godel's work on the uncertainty principle and probability theory. Probability and uncertainty have replaced determinate knowledge: the complexity of the information we gain depends on the complexity of the questions asked, the paradigms produced.

Turner's theory was to history what Heisenberg and Godel's theories were to physics: it supplied a new way of thinking about a fundamental problem. As a way of defining America, it prevailed from the early 1890s to the early 1930s. Thereafter it still endured, to be sure in a weakened state, if not as a paradigm, at least as an illusion (a residual state of mind), thanks to its advocates in academia and to their belief that it still had relevance in regions of America, such as the plains states and the rural South.

Perry Miller in *Nature's Nation* has argued, "We may have come to the land by an act of will, but despite ourselves, we have become parts of the landscape" (11). Individual will and historical destiny combined to produce the yeoman farmer—the fused product of nature and human desire, commitment and the mandate to work the land. Turner's frontier provided a heightened realm of being that created an ideal that in turn became a transformative illusion: the claim always went beyond reality to the realm of romantic destiny. When the wilderness frontier closed, the emphasis shifted from the land to the city.

Each change of landscape involved a different America and a new sense of identity. Like a species subject to Darwinian natural selection, we had to adapt to new environments in order to survive as a nation. Miller believes that the defining element in America stems from the choices that were made in those transforming contexts. How different would we be if we had chosen colonial over revolutionary America, states rights over federalism with entitlement to secede from the union, socialism over capitalism, isolationism over imperialism, the priority of peace over the propensity for war, commitment to domestic matters over nation-building? Despite the antipathy to a federal mandate from many political factions, the need to protect the idea of federal union prevailed once it was threatened; and so too has the Jeffersonian vision prevailed as a lost ideal—as an illusion, albeit redundant and immaterial to an industrial America.

II

We are concerned with the significance of an evolving American identity, the persistent product of historical change. The combatants here involve the city and the wilderness frontier, civilization and the wilderness. In order to better understand the eventual melding of these antithetical systems, I have supplied a larger context, which includes the state of mind that perpetuated the myth of the land, the illusion that sustained the myth with its assumptions of romantic destiny, and the rise of an industrial force that eventually transformed the myth and the way we think about it. The myth of the West supplied indigenous elements that reduced the political influence of Europe and infused intellectual being into what was to become a transformed American polity.

Political change brought other kinds of change, including literary transformation. An agrarian movement and a wilderness frontier confronted an urbanism heavily populated by the new immigrant; the frontier movement gave rise to the genre of the Western, the urban phenomenon to literary naturalism. The move from an agrarian to an industrial base saw the idealized vision of Ralph Waldo Emerson supplanted by the material philosophy of mechanistic thinkers like Henry Adams. Beneficent forces competed with an antagonistic opposite. The recognition that both natural and national forces could be hostile replaced the belief that a spiritual energy was working in nature for good.

As Frederick Jackson Turner maintained, the idea of the West (as embodied in the frontier) was a major factor in the evolution of America from a set of colonies to a world power. The frontier brought with it a source of wealth for a specialized few working the fur trade, cattle ranching, and mineral mining. But the main frontier activity was farming, the provision of food and other goods by the working of the land. The myth of the land remained a Jeffersonian ideal, perpetuated by historians like Turner, even as it was reduced in importance by the transforming power of industry. It is thus appropriate that behind the idea of the West was a romantic illusion that took in the myth of the land and the legacy of the Volk.

The idea of the Volk (folk or people) inspired the "volkisch" movement, which had its origins in the romantic nationalism of early German romantics, especially Johann Gottlieb Fichte (1762–1814). Fichte was an idealist steeped in the thought of Immanuel Kant, an epistemological bridge between the idealism of Kant and Hegel. In his "Addresses to the German Nation," he advocated a romantic return to nature and anti-urban sentiments similar to those perpetuated in England by William Morris and in America by Thomas Jefferson. In his belief that self-consciousness was a social phenomenon, Fichte anticipated one of the first principles of modernism, was the father of German nationalism, and encouraged the idea of the Volk.

Another philosophical contribution to the idea of the Volk came from Johann Gottfried von Herder (1744–1803), a student of Kant's and an important spokesman for romantic nationalism, who based a claim to the land on the ethnicity of a homogeneous population. Herder based national rights on cultural factors, populist in intent, with a romantic focus on language, ancestry, and a celebration of German lore—all parts of an organic claim to national identity. The idea of the "organic" rested on the belief that life's principles find a unity within the self as a living thing, subject to the processes (growth, development, and fulfillment) inherent in natural life.

The volkisch movement assumed that human beings were "preformed" by inherited traits (racial blood); the movement was based on the idea of a "fatherland," the priority of nation with the need to root personal and national identity in the soil. Mandated was a back-to-the-land movement—with anti-urban, populist sentiments—stemming from a love of and ability to work the land. The aim was to produce a self-sufficient (yeoman) life grounded on a mystical relationship to the land; it was a reaction to the industrial revolution and to progressive liberalism that came with the rise of urbanism, and it rested on a belief in the superiority of race and national origins. In ideology the movement had popular appeal, but it was not immune to anti-Semitic, anticommunist, and anti-immigration sentiments.

In Germany, the volkisch movement had a special ideological meaning to Anton Drexler (1884–1942), a Munich locksmith. Drexler was a member of the Fatherland Party, which founded the German Worker's Party in March 1918, later known as the National Socialist German Workers (or Nazi) Party that came to power in 1933 under Hitler. As we shall see in a later chapter, the volkisch movement reinforced the assumptions of the Fatherland Party, especially the mandate to ground national identity in the land and to claim the priority of the German people based on the supremacy of the Nordic race and the assumption that it was a part of the Aryan or master race (*Herrenvolk*).

In America one was not immune from the prejudice that accompanied the sense of the superiority of working the land and the disdain for those who did not live close to the soil. A philosophy of the land and the dictates of the Fatherland Party shared some political assumptions. An idealized claim to the land encouraged a romantic sense of destiny, a belief in a mystical future. It was common to move from an affinity with slave-holding practices to racist ideology. One might also move from Turner's conviction that the American wilderness had produced a heightened individualism to belief in the superiority of a national type, like that found in the Fatherland Party. A sense of the heroic based on Nordic lineage ran through American classics like *The Virginian*. And Frederick Remington painted an idealized world by excluding immigrants, especially those from southeastern Europe, whom he called "scum."

The wilderness frontier encouraged neoconservative thinking—a matter of good or bad depending on one's politics. But racism is racism regardless of its origins in Germany or its perpetuation in America. Such matters must be weighed and recognized when less extreme. In America the ultimate application of these ideas was transformed and less ideologically noxious; they were ameliorated by Jeffersonian assumptions, a different agrarian purpose, and a mystical component based on evangelical assumptions: the belief in the authority of the Bible, salvation through Christ, and the need to be born again. The obsession with forms of religion distracted the evangelical American away from the more strictly racist assumptions at work in Germany.

Both those who agreed and those who disagreed with Turner failed to give much credence to the parallel assumptions that existed between Turner's wilderness frontier and German Volkism. The fact remains that one cannot ignore the claim to national identity that the frontier experience shared with the Fatherland Party. But in America the ideological consequences of such an identity were further blunted by an aestheticism that softened the role of the political. In the 1930s, the southern Agrarian movement gave rise to its own belief in agrarianism and to a more humane American version of romantic nationalism with its affinity to Turner's frontier thesis.

The New Criticism and the Agrarian movement can be best thought of as two independent movements. But a theory of the organic does connect the two—a belief that the literary text works as, say, a plant works in nature. This argument finds common "ground" in the connection between the agrarian belief that went with a philosophy of the land and new critical textual matters (e.g., the idea of the autotelic text, the concern with unity based on a theory of parts, and the belief in literature as the inspired product of the secondary imagination, working akin to the primary imagination of the Creator).

Seldom discussed is the fact that the frontier wilderness movement and the New Criticism shared neoconservative concerns. The Agrarian movement took pride in a sense of spiritual well-being. The New Criticism was not without its own ideology, including religious preference: it grounded itself in metaphysical poetry, especially the religious poetry of John Donne; it touted T. S. Eliot over all other poets, explicating his high-church ideology; and it favored paradox and irony over other rhetorical devices, rendering the literary text ambiguous, its ideological complexity, like "a well-wrought urn," a source of aesthetic pleasure. When all was said and done, religious and aesthetic matters moved these movements to the right, but they also overrode racist concerns and saved America from the full pursuit of the Volk.

III

The illusionary nature of self as abstracted from Turner's frontier thesis was reinforced by other cultural events—such as the popularity of novels like James K. Paulding's *Westward Ho!* (published in 1832 but still popular generations later), with its promise "[T]he tale we are about to relate connects itself with the early history of this vast and growing empire of the west," and William Gilmore Simms's *The Wigwam and the Cabin* (1845), a depiction of the southern frontier, advocating slavery in its response to *Uncle Tom's Cabin,* but a frontier novel that had relevance to the call of the West in its celebration of "the bold and hardy pioneer, the vigorous yeomen." The import of these works was intensified by the popularity of the dime novel and other commercial pursuits such as William Cody's (Buffalo Bill's) Wild West Show, which opened in St. Louis in 1883 and traveled throughout America; it also received an enthusiastic reception (including a performance before the queen) in England in 1887. The show was composed of 240 performers and a herd of buffalo and long-horn steers, and it displayed episodes of bronco busting, sharpshooting (featuring Annie Oakley) and replicas of western history, highlighting the Pony Express and mock battles with the Indians, including Custer's last stand. After England, the show moved to France, Spain, Germany, and Belgium, perpetuating in Europe a stylized and inauthentic portrait of the American West. When Prentiss Ingraham used the dime novel for purposes of transforming the basic identity of the hunter-tracker, as embodied by Natty Bumppo, into the more prosaic cowboy, less rugged and independent but as brave and sometimes as brutal as he needed to be, Ingraham changed the identity of an American prototype. The Wild West Show and the dime novel presented in Europe a sense of a new American type and an image of the West as complete as fantasy could make it (see Billington 1981).

The image of a pioneer America had a natural appeal as a corrective in Europe: with Europe more industrially developed than America, the Europeans harbored a nostalgic desire for an agrarian past. The European image of the American West was sustained by writers from every nation, but none was more popular than Germany's Karl May, who wrote more than seventy books—half of them depicting the American frontier he never saw—that determined the European view of the West as both a source of hostility and, when tamed, a realm of opportunity, including for the pursuit of democracy (for a discussion of May, see Billington 1981, 53–56).

IV

The West was an illusive phenomenon: as in May's case, it was a product more of imagination than historical presence. Some believe it began with the eastern slopes of the Rockies. Wallace Stegner suggests that it begins with the one-hundredth meridian and ends with the Sierra Nevadas and the Cascades. Stegner claims that one must drive east from Oregon or California to get to the West. For others, the boundaries of the geographic West are arbitrarily set at the forty-ninth parallel to the north, the Mexican border to the south, the Mississippi River to the east, and the Pacific Ocean to the west. These boundaries have been resisted as being both too inclusive and too restrictive (see Brian W. Dippe, in Limerick, Milner, and Rankin 115). It is difficult to define the western frontier specifically, because the movement involved varying frontiers as the journey unfolded, many jumping-off places in the journey west, multiple Wests and not just a West.

There are essentially four regions that make up the geography of America: the Northeast, the South, the Midwest, and the far West. When thought of as a whole, the far West begins with the ninety-eighth meridian and extends to the Pacific coast: it begins at the eastern borders of the Dakotas, Nebraska, and Kansas and the central region of Oklahoma and Texas and ends with the Pacific Ocean. As a locus of regional concern, such a division is too extended to supply a coherent or shared geographical meaning: the terrain here changes from plains to mountains to deserts to coastal areas. Each environment creates its own meaning: access to water alone varies in the extreme from region to region. The far West as a place makes more sense when it is divided into four geological regions: the plains, the Rockies, the Southwest with its desert, and the coastal region of the Pacific including the inner valleys.

Turner believed that each region created its own culture, which then worked in a determining way to form its own political and social reality, much of its meaning created by the character of the land involved. The local region distinguished itself from other regions and from the nation as a whole, which supposedly was a composite of sectional interests. Yet Turner's West is so fluid in its use of space and time that seemingly all of America becomes part of the West. Turner's failure to locate the West in a physical place only reinforced the idea that it was a state of mind. The best we can do in grounding the idea of the West is to see it as part of a historical condition rather than as a physical place: what distinguished the West and gave the western frontier special meaning was that it marked where civilization met and transformed the wilderness.

Between civilization and savagery stood the wilderness. Cotton Mather realized in 1693 that the wilderness was the stage "thro' which we are passing to the Promised Land" (Mather, "The Wonders of the Invisible World," qtd. in Nash 1982; see 24–27, esp. 26). The wilderness was the pioneer's task: the frontier left political and social meaning in its wake. But because even this aspect involved the frontier as a moving phenomenon, changing geographically as it moved west, it cannot be defined in any singular way.

The journey west coalesced into an era that combined myth and history before an industrial process brought a state of mind responsible for catalytic change in America. The participants thought a deity had spiritually blessed their movement, that manifest destiny anticipated romantic destiny—a state of being eventually subject to intrusion by a new order of technology and a new commercialism, both the bases for industrialization. The compounded experience worked toward more indigenous beliefs, thinning the influence of European ideas. From the beginning, religious and philosophical assumptions weighted these ideas before they eventually gave way to Enlightenment values that were in turn transformed by romantic and then by mechanistic assumptions.

The change in national identity from an agrarian to an industrial country was just one of several historical transformations, beginning with the Pilgrim hope in America as a community under God and followed by the Enlightenment trust in reason that usurped—or at least weakened—the role of God; reason was then softened into a universal (transcendental) energy, a spiritualized albeit natural force, culminating in the belief in romantic destiny. This sense of destiny supplied a mythic element, perpetuated an idealized vision of nature, and gave us the western frontier as a shaping (actually determining) force before it was transformed in turn by an industrial process. A mechanized nation, now newly militarized, heralded a mandate to empire and the call for a new national purpose. Such a purpose was infused with a residue of the historical past and sometimes defined by sectional difference: this was especially true in its application to the South. Such an agenda enlisted a host of witnesses to the folding and unfolding of both political and cultural reality.

While this study deals with the familiar topic of the American frontier and its conflicted encounter with the industrial city, it presumes that these ideas share a larger context: the role of the mythic West, the influence of historicism in the face of destiny, the idea of the West as an illusion, and the literary transformations that followed the transformations of history. The idea of the West takes on meaning when seen from the Puritan perspective; takes on still another meaning in its uses of and then deviation from Enlightenment values. Religion and philosophy come into play with the response of Calvinism, Congregationalism, Unitarianism, and transcendental assumptions. The industrial transformation involved the West as a participant in land reform and as subject to other reforms that accompanied such movements as Populism and Progressivism as well as those that came into being with the drift toward imperialism.

The view of the West cannot be separated from the idea of the extended frontier—the West as a product of urban, sectional, and national interplay. The view is persistently a mixed one: we see the dark side of the West once it becomes a material system of thought; we see the West comparatively in sectional perspective with its similarities to and differences from the agrarian South. In its historical unfolding, we see the ghost of the West (or, more accurately, the lost frontier) as the end product of romantic destiny; the agrarian presence was gone in reality (except perhaps in the South) but nostalgically alive in spirit.

A primary concern here is with the economic role that the land played in the historical development of the nation, especially the response of an agrarian nation to the commercial-industrial development that threatened its supremacy. Romantic destiny is a counterweight, if not a corrective, to mechanistic (material) force. Along with the mythical and ideological elements it engendered, it helps justify the belief in the foreordained rise of America as an international power and the use and sometimes abuse of that power.

V

One of the prime components of any study of the agrarian-industrial development in America involves concern with the frontier's symbolic meaning—along with its historical meaning—and the interpretive power of that meaning. The wilderness frontier went beyond material cause to the realm of romantic destiny, where it works as illusion, infusing the imagination with ideals, engendering a state of mind that is both inspiring and empowering. The idea here owes its historical form to Henry Adams (to his belief in the mythic power of the Virgin as a symbol to unify the Middle Ages) and its aesthetic form to Wallace Stevens (and his theory of Supreme Fiction).

Another form of critical difference here involves the literary dimension that is added to historical content: the West becomes a different historical reality when seen from the varied perspectives of Emerson, Cooper, and Whitman; or as seen from the disgruntled perspective of Mark Twain or the disillusioned view of Walt Whitman. The West takes on new meaning when examined as a major theme in the works of Cather, Fitzgerald, Nathanael West, and Steinbeck, just as the West takes on new dimensions when seen as the locus of varied literary movements or genres (for example, the Western was transformed by other narrative modes).

All of these concerns take us to the radical social change involved in the transition from an agrarian (romantic) to an industrial (mechanistic) America and the cultural transformations that accompanied that change. Henry Nash Smith pointed out in 1950 that Turner's frontier thesis sprang from the components of agrarian myth. In *The Age of Reform,* Richard Hofstadter argued that that interpretation exaggerated the realm of innocence and did not do justice to the dark side of the way west: the wanton land speculation, the vigilantism, the waste—both of nature and humanity—that accompanied expansionism. Hofstadter resisted limiting the frontier to agrarian, rural, and Protestant attributes, claiming that such a definition ignored ethnic, migrant, multireligious, and urban matters. In many ways, Hofstadter's critique was prescient, anticipating the changes that accompanied the political agenda of the 1960s that gave more attention to ethnic and racial matters, expressing sympathy for the victims, and challenging the idea of melting-pot homogeneity. Environment and feminist concerns added yet another dimension to a revised history of the West. Furthermore, the new historian does not accept the belief that the West ended in 1890 but argues that it continued to grow in homesteading, in investment speculation, in multiethnic population, and in urban culture. Among the important new histories (discussed in more detail in later chapters) are Gerald Nash's *The American West Transformed* (1985), Patricia Nelson Limerick's *The Legacy of Conquest* (1987), Richard White's *"It's Your Misfortune and None of My Own"* (1991), Richard Etulain's *The American West* (2007), and Dee Brown's *Bury My Heart at Wounded Knee* (1970), a view of the way west from an Indian perspective.

Another book that questions Turner's thesis is William Cronon's excellent study of Chicago, *Nature's Metropolis* (1991). Turner believed that the frontier was primarily a rural matter independent of other cultural influences. Cronon argues that the frontier and the city developed together—that the frontier was "the expanding edge of the . . . urban empire." He questions Turner's stages of frontier development in which he gives priority to the pathfinder, whom Cronon sees as a "an emissary from the metropolitan marketplace." For Turner, cities marked the end of the frontier. According to Cronon, Turner's stages of frontier development make more sense when read backward: the frontier began with the city instead of ending with it (51).

Today remnants of Turner's thesis have a new and different meaning in a world where revision in what we mean by an autonomous nation and a world marketplace has radically transformed Turner's idea of the frontier. The word *frontier* now carries a host of different meanings, from technological advances to imperial frontiers that result from nation-building. These acquisitions are analogous to Turner's idea of the frontier but engage a population that is culturally different (democratic rather than tribal), committed to outposts that nevertheless define us, as the frontier defined us for Turner. In an era following incursions in Korea, Vietnam, Iraq, Afghanistan, and elsewhere, we have created new forms of frontier reality by serving as the material source for a frontier hinterland that parallels Turner's open-and-then-closed frontier.

Such transformations suggest variations in meaning for Turner's frontier thesis and produce parallel changes in modes of literature. The priority in genre shifted after the closing of the western frontier, with the Western narrative mode giving ground to literary naturalism. The evolution of the Western is relevant to the agrarian-industrial feud. Initially, forces in play in the Western confronted forms of evil as they worked for good, an assumption challenged by literary naturalism with its persistence of more hostile forces. Once he was displaced, the Western hero—who had embodied rugged individualism and lived by a code of honor—gave way to the private detective, now operating in the morally ambivalent world of the city. Once naturalism had run its own course, it was transformed into a skeletal version of itself, or to forms of neorealism (involving naturalistic plots without naturalistic documentation), including literary and film noir, before yet another transformation yielded a version of postmodernism.

Despite the subsequent challenges to his frontier thesis, Turner's ideas carried the weight of his argument more or less unchallenged for nearly forty years, leaving an indelible imprint on western history. Both the historical and the literary response accommodated the transformation of American ideas (and ideals) as the country changed from a pioneer (frontier) nation to an industrial (global) empire. We have moved a long way from the Turner thesis, which included a deterministic system grounded in economic aspects of a sense of place. Today that sense of place has been extended to include environmental and ethnic matters that barely concerned Turner, including the fate of American Indians as well as immigration concerns. What remains after the process of multiple transformations is the residual belief that the West has an ethos and creative reality of its own, an illusionary mandate that informed a sense of individualism and a sense of destiny that awaited historical completion.

5

Historicism

Romantic Destiny Transformed

The idea of America depends on the historical assumptions we bring to defining that idea. The two most prevalent contexts involve romantic destiny as an anticipation of historicism. Romantic destiny assumes that history is infused with divine or supernatural meaning. Romantic destiny owes its being to a belief in American exceptionalism—that by 1850 America had become a superior nation, a New World nation unique in its origins and its future purpose. This conclusion owed much to the Puritan belief that America found a special calling in the wilderness—a calling that included being the people chosen to build the New Jerusalem.

Historicism assumes that history is the product of physical forces, subject to the laws of historical process, which depend in part on the organic workings of romantic nationalism or its by-products in culture to supply historical facts; such workings are then codified into laws that inform the meaning of an era such as the Italian Renaissance (cf. Jacob Burkhardt's *Civilization of the Renaissance in Italy*), or the meaning of an unfolding nation such as Germany (cf. Leopold Von Ranke's *History of the Romantic and Germanic People from 1494 to 1514*). There is a need here to clarify the difference between the "old" and the "new" historicism. The old is really a product of German scientism; the new owes its being to the structural assumptions of Stephen Greenblatt and is not really historicism at all. The main difference between the two is that the old historicism assumes that historical problems are built into movements and periods and unfold in causal and predictable ways.

The new historicism is really a form of structuralism and assumes that history is a constructed reality, the product of paradigms that the historian brings to the issues, where they are then superimposed to supply historical meaning. One method assumes that historical problems are real, the product of, say, economic forces; the other that they are constructed, fashioned out of tropes circulating constructed meaning, part of what Thomas Pynchon refers to as the "echo" system that accommodates the structural method. One looks out from a text to a historical (material) context; the other looks into the text and the realm of language treating the outcome as a hermeneutic (i.e., constructed) problem.

Historicism had its roots in nineteenth-century political transformations—especially the belief that the unified rule of nationhood had replaced the diversified rule of city-states. It involved the belief that each era or culture had an inspiring principle of unity, usually the product of economic or geographical determinism. Historicism assumed that history was a closed system, subject to the workings of physical laws (similar to the natural laws of gravity or entropy). Oswald Spengler predicted the decline of the West based on observing the workings of previous cultures: the assumption was that the realms of the past functioned according to natural law and that the same outcome would be repeated if the same historical conditions applied.

Historicism as an idea owed much to German romanticism, especially the Hegelian assumption that there was a "spirit of the age," a zeitgeist, a realm of the folk that celebrated language as a source of national unity, giving birth to an organic culture, the by-product of which was national identity. While romantic destiny and historicism are not one and the same, they do share common assumptions. The belief that such historical features as national unity were brought on by romantic destiny coincided with the political and social assumptions of historicism, reinforcing the theoretical belief that history also had unified meaning. While romantic destiny and historicism both emphasize a history infused with causal connections, romantic destiny suggests that such connections have mystical origins, while historicism relies on more scientific explanations.

Turner's wilderness thesis is an idealized abstract of the frontier. The best aspects are put forth as romantic destiny and later codified as historicism, or the attempt to impose empiricism on the process. (For a detailed account of how changes in the idea of history change the meaning of a discipline, see Klein 17.) The key to Turner's thinking is dialectic—the play between free land and settlement, savagery and civilization, individualism and community, egalitarianism and economic mobility, history and nature, West and East, and good and evil. But the terms are always weighted, and in these pairings Turner gave preference to the first option, to the thesis and not the antithesis, mystical and personal choice seemingly at one.

Karl Popper, the author of *The Poverty of Historicism* and *The Open Society and Its Enemies,* objects to the historical supposition that there is a deterministic pattern to history. He argues that such a belief contradicts "openness"—the right of choice, what amounts to a national free will—the freedom of a nation to will its future, to go beyond itself. Others resisted the claim to objectivity, insisting that historicism was as much a product of subjectivity as any other historical system. But despite their fundamental differences, both historical systems made claim to predictive powers and were in one sense aligned in purpose. Despite the contradictions, the historicist could on occasion accommodate the realms of destiny. This tended to happen with the idea of the West when looked at as the subject both of laws governed by the meaning of land and of the belief that the American moment was exceptional, aligned with historical purpose in its fulfillment of destiny.

Despite professional skepticism and despite the contradictions involved in accommodating romantic destiny, the historicists had a distinct historical perspective: they believed that the processes of history were material—physical and predictable. Seemingly nature and history are one: both depend on an organic or indwelling view of reality subject to expected outcomes that follow from causal happenings. The application of this view can be found in Vico and, with some shades of difference, in Toynbee; others would include Marx. But the more extended use of the methodology was seen in intellectual historians such as Oswald Spengler and economic determinists like Henry Adams, Charles Beard, and of course Frederick Jackson Turner himself. Turner, we know, was influenced by two economists who were important in their time but less so today: the Italian Achille Loria (1857–1943) and the American Henry George (1839–1897).

Loria believed that the scarcity of land led to the subjugation of those who worked it. The key to historical process was derived from the productivity of land in relation to the density of population: the larger the population, the greater the competition for land. The scarcity of land and the way it was worked led to predictable historical stages, such as slavery, feudalism, and sharecropping. Loria believed that the capitalistic process had come to a standstill on the American frontier because the workers lacked incentive: no laborers would work someone else's land when they could work their own land, acquired at no cost. Only when the population had grown to the point where land became scarce, and only when the land was worked to the point where available farmland was diminished, would landed capitalism be restored.

George's theory of economics also rested on the worth of the land. Advocating a single tax based on the value of land, he outlined his beliefs in an influential book, *Progress and Poverty* (1879), in which he argued that the land belonged to everyone and that wealth concentrated in land worked against the well-being of the population in general and was the main source of poverty.

The historians that preceded Frederick Jackson Turner were primarily conservative in their political outlook and amateur in their training. For the most part they concentrated on the European background of American history. George Washington Irving, for example, treated Columbus, Granada, and Alhambra before he gave his attention to George Washington. The same was true with Francis Parkman, also a romantic historian, who was influenced by Scott and the German idealism of Goethe, Herder, and Schiller. And even more of a romantic historian was George Bancroft, who was influenced by American transcendentalism as well as German idealism.

Bancroft was one of the early historians who broke with conservative ideology. He saw Washington struggling to free America from the influence of Europe, but this did not happen until the great interior basin of the Mississippi was settled. As a Democrat, he supported Andrew Jackson and was a foe of the Bank of the United States. These early historians needed to wrestle with numerous political questions—for example, they were conservative by nature but needed to account for a nation that had its origin in revolution; they prided themselves on the pastoral nature of America but also believed in the need for progress, creating the dilemma of how a people can progress when there is no need for change.

The romantic assumptions of these early historians were influential in helping to define the wilderness frontier, but they were transformed as the country moved from a pastoral to an industrial base. Romantic history pointed to the forces of fulfillment involving Protestantism and Democracy: the rise of the individual and the viability of a people's politics. Historicism adhered to the principle of an inner purpose that accommodated the more material forces that came with the impulse toward imperialism, the rise of a smokestack economy, the perpetuation of city political machines, and the moral imbalance of the gilded age when profits determined the means and end of business. The period between the end of the Civil War and the beginning of World War I (1865–1914) marked the years of the gilded age, sometimes stipulated as 1870 to 1910, the era highlighted by the writing of Mark Twain.

The common denominator between the historical modes of romantic history and historicism was force: a beneficent, spiritual force was at work in romantic history, while historicism could also accommodate the working of a more antagonistic, material force. Parkman, for example, considered the transformations in New England from Boston as village to Boston as an industrial city, with the spread of factories, the rise of tenements, and the influx of immigrants, "to whom liberty means license and politics means plunder" (qtd. in Hofstadter, *Progressive Historians,* 23). A similar transformation of beneficent force into a hostile counterpart took place when the idealized elements of the literary Western were transformed by literary naturalism. There was a sense of destiny at work in both literary elements, but one was supposedly moving toward a realm of progress, the other toward forms of degeneration.

While the course of American history cannot be totally reduced to any one historical mandate, historicism was making claims that transformed previous forms of historical explanation. In that context, Oswald Spengler's understanding of the rise and fall of past civilizations allows insight relevant to the rise-and-fall process of the nation state. Spengler's theory of history stems from a belief in the organic nature of society and is consistent with certain modernist theories of history, such as that of Toynbee, when he reduced each culture to a biological entity and saw its history as a matter of growth and decline.

Spengler discussed three cultures: the Apollonian, the Magian, and the Faustian; each culture is independent of the others, the product of German romantic belief based on the organic assumption that each era of history parallels a cycle of human development—maturity, decline, and death. According to Spengler, the process of decline took effect with the rise of an urban society. Destiny and countryside were at the heart of Spengler's theory—a national destiny and a vital countryside. As one moves away from the natural rhythms of the land, instinct gives way to reason, myth to scientific theory, and marketplace to abstract theories of money processed by banks. The physical presence of the land gives way to material influence far removed from the working of the land. When all this happens, a primitive sense of the past is lost to the dictates of a gilded age. Faustian man, with his desire for the infinite, gives way to the new Caesar and the realm of power and force.

Spengler's assumptions are fraught with cultural warning, especially when they are applied to his native Germany, where the dictates of business were supported by the power of the state, creating a fascism that was really a modern oligarchy. Hitler saw the implication of such transformations: he insisted that modern, urban civilization had interrupted a process of German destiny and that the rise of the city—with its heavy Jewish population—infringed upon an Aryan racial line. While left unsaid by Spengler, these ideas were factors in his belief that national mandates and a charismatic leader could save the state from the process of decline. Spengler believed that the urbanized state would inevitably become more powerful and extend its means of control. Such a state would reject economic activity separate from its own authority and thus reject theories of both nineteenth-century laissez-faire and communism. In theory, such a state would have an organic social order whereby the individual would find her or his place in the society based on ability. The new leader would exploit this new ideology in an order held fast by nationalism and militarism.

Spengler's sense of national decline is supported by historical events: Rome moved from a republic to an empire with the transformation of the landed realm under Caesar; France became an empire under Napoleon, Germany under Hitler. After the Civil War, with the advent of the gilded age, the contours of American power changed. The rise of an industrial nation saw the Dynamo spearhead technological transformations. The shift in power from the land to the city brought with it new forms of political power. The federal government became stronger, encouraging a stronger and more powerful presidency and the beginning of imperial design. Spengler believed that at this point a nation went into historical decline, marked by the loss of an idealized mission, an end to innocence. Before Spengler formulated this historical thesis in Germany, Henry Adams had witnessed an American version of the same historical experience.

Henry Adams was a mechanist: he believed that all natural process could be explained by physical causes, that reality was constituted by the way forces worked. For every action there was a reaction: we could not have wealth without poverty, health without sickness, strength without weakness. History operated in terms of laws: we do not create a national identity; we discover it. There is no order built into nature, only the illusion of order; but this illusion can organize and energize a society and determine its historical future. History was now destiny, mechanistic, not romantic, destiny: individual choice and desire were nullified by circumstance. In moving toward this idea, Adams was sharing belief with Carlyle, Tolstoy, and Spengler. Adams had come to believe that history had a momentum of its own, was now gaining force, and in the course of time was emptying old beliefs of their meaning. The past was now the repository of still-pursued but exhausted ideals (an idea he eventually shared with F. Scott Fitzgerald).

Adams's understanding of the gilded age anticipated the sense of force that the moderns (especially Pound, Eliot, and Fitzgerald) had to accommodate or repudiate. He believed in historical eras or periods, more or less self-contained and working themselves toward destined ends through the push and pull of inward forces that ultimately break down the country and dissipate its energy. Adams believed that history had reached a high point with eighteenth-century ideas of democracy. But he also believed that democracy had seen better days and that its gilded-age version was eventually doomed: its ideals were illusions, and forces within would destroy it. These are ideas he worked out in detail in his history of Jefferson and Madison and in his gold-conspiracy essay (*Historical Essays*, 1891), a work that shared sentiment with Ezra Pound. Adams's views on the gold conspiracy are best stated in *Historical Essays* and in (unpublished) correspondence with his brother, Brooks Adams.

Adams demythologized an era. He saw the Middle Ages preserving its sense of unity by refusing to see its own contradictions—by preserving an illusion, a saving illusion. William of Chapeaux and Abelard represented two extreme positions (realist and nominalist), both of which led to solipsism, pantheism, and heresy. Aquinas never healed this division. In fact, his own ideas were more pantheistic than he cared to realize. But the Virgin offered a way out: she (not the Christ of Eliot's *Four Quartets*) became the mediator, the source of a redeeming unity, between man and God.

Unlike a cultural commentator like William Carlos Williams, who believed in the power of the mind to recreate itself, Adams believed foremost in force, energy, and power. His "Dynamic Theory of History" became a credo. Out of this credo came stock figures of American culture: the fated idealist, the person of paralyzed will (cf. James, Eliot, Wharton), the symbolic power of illusion (anticipating Wallace Stevens), and the need for a redeeming imagination. Medieval man had the illusion of unity: he could accept the Virgin because he did not know the Dynamo—did not know the reality of uncontrolled, blind force. The same principle applied to Turner's frontier thesis: the idea of the wilderness frontier could control historical reality because the thesis ignored the transformative power of the industrial machine and the machinations of the gilded age: the illusion of truth outweighed its contradictions.

The historical assumptions at work today go far beyond the dictates of Spengler and Adams. We still have a historicism that relies on primary sources, but it does not academically prevail. The old historicism has been overtaken by postmodern assumptions—especially by a structuralism that relies mainly on paradigm, which in turn relies heavily on historical speculation, the realm of legend, or what Rob Kroes has referred to as "factions," the combination of fact and fiction (ix). Both historical procedures—the old and the new historicism—look for a context (e.g., the idea of a "usable past") to justify the historical process.

The desire to write a definitive cultural history of America stems from the assumption that one can find a context large enough to inform such a project. Early attempts by historians like V. L. Parrington, Van Wyck Brooks, and Randolph Bourne all looked to material culture and historical events; others looked to regional influence; others to key themes; and others to literary movements and the influence of genre. Each methodology involved a theory of historiography, the interpretive method changing from generation to generation. Regional study was best accommodated by the old historicism with its assumption that the historian could find in primary sources the basis for an inclusive history that informed the subject in a comprehensive way. The early attempts to find a material explanation of American literature was challenged by works like Lionel Trilling's *The Liberal Imagination,* which divided literary history into realms of "reality" and realms of "mind," giving priority to mind—that is, to an aesthetic rather than a social reading of the text.

Postmodern mandates take exception with some of Adams's assumptions, insisting that we create rather than discover history. Whether the frontier is a product of Turner's theory of land or of Limerick's theory of conquest involves speculation that takes us to very different conclusions. The choice of interpretation is often held in place by academic consensus, the product of academic hierarchy, a dominance that passes with each generation as one interpretive claim gains authority over another and becomes the prevailing opinion. Frederick Jackson Turner is an example of how such authority can come into being: his influential thinking about the frontier created a critical community; his presence dominated the University of Wisconsin Department of History; and his prestige facilitated his move from Wisconsin to Harvard.

Turner's influence reached down many academic avenues. For example, his thesis was influential in establishing the "myth and symbol" school of American studies, brought into being by two classic studies that had their origin as Harvard PhD dissertations in the American Civilization program: Henry Nash Smith's *Virgin Land* (1950), which depicted the literary side of the agrarian frontier, and Leo Marx's *The Machine in the Garden* (1964), which described the rise of an industrial frontier with its technological advances.

In *The Incorporation of America* (1982), Alan Trachtenberg transformed the "myth and symbol" method by substituting a multicultural approach, giving greater emphasis to racial, ethnic, and gender concerns. He did this by conflating the two frontiers, attacking the Turner thesis for matters better relegated to the industrial frontier. The works of Patricia Nelson Limerick and Richard White, both of whom continued to conflate the two frontiers, sustained his approach.

Almost all of the revisionists failed to see that the two frontiers were political mandates as well as geographical regions and idealized states of mind; they thus failed to see how the agrarian frontier, with its call to individualism and evangelical thinking, sustained neoconservative political ideology, while the industrial frontier, once reinforced by the rise of a labor force, better accommodated a liberal-progressive agenda.

Present authority in the field has passed to Patricia Nelson Limerick; in time it is likely that her authority will be contested by a new generation of critics, who will question her theory of conquest and her predating Turner's lapse of concern for ethnic, racial, and gender matters. Reading academic books written over several generations is like watching a parade go by.

6

The Urban Reach

There have been two major cultural revolutions in the history of the human race: the agrarian revolution, which led to the domestication of plants and animals, and the industrial revolution, which was a by-product of the Enlightenment with its dependence on science, technology, and investment capital, bringing the realm of material force to the implementation of produced goods. Feudalism was the economic system that promoted the agrarian revolution; capitalism (when investment money was privatized) or Marxism and socialism (when investment money involved public funds) empowered the industrial revolution.

Initially, people feared the wilderness and took comfort in the city. In time, people feared the city and took solace in the wilderness. The change came approximately in 1890, with the rise of urbanism and the assumptive close of the frontier. This transformation was at the root of a wilderness idea. A hunting and gathering society gave way fifteen thousand years ago to a herding and agricultural society. In both realms, a person was part of nature. Since there was nothing outside of nature, there could be no bias for what did not exist. With the advent of urbanism, city-dwellers were separated from nature. The city brought the wilderness into being, creating separate identities for life on the land versus life in the city, identities that then became the basis for an idea of self (Nash 1967, xiii).

With the transformation from hunter-gatherer to herder-farmer came a transformation in domain: having the advantage of keen eyesight, early humans felt more at home on the open prairie than in the forest. The pioneers burned the forest, transforming it into grassland. The same pioneers moved onward with greater security on the open plains of the West than in the deep forests of the East. As Roderick Nash has told us, one could better cope with the lion seen a mile away in the grass than with the lion concealed nearby in forest underbrush (1967, xvi). The transformation from forest to grassland expressed itself in both physical and verbal change: what was formerly referred to as "wilderness" was now a "garden."

The first industrial revolution occurred between 1750 and 1850 and was the product of machines powered by steam and by the creation of canals, railways, and new roads. The second industrial revolution began in 1850 and was powered by electricity and the internal combustion engine. Both revolutions saw the rise of factory-produced goods in an urban context, once power was no longer dependent on rural rivers.

The transition from an agrarian to a commercial-industrial system was not an easy one: on a personal level, the feud between Jefferson and Hamilton defined the differences; on a historical plane, the Puritan challenge to the king, the French Revolution, and the American Civil War promoted the shift from a feudal to a capitalistic-industrial world. While the wilderness frontier was primarily the product of an agrarian culture, the Northeast was essentially the home of the new technology, with 75 percent of industry located in that region.

Both the wilderness frontier and the urban realm were mythic ideals before and after they were political realities, and each left an intellectual residue when it was replaced or transformed. The wilderness frontier worked the "primitive" realm; the urban supposedly advanced the "civilized." The wilderness frontier celebrated the independence of the yeoman farmer, an independence that was lost once the nation was industrialized. The spiritual process of working the land inspired the yeoman farmer; the idea of a better tomorrow through technology, along with medical and economic advancement, motivated the industrial worker. The urban phenomenon was basically an industrial movement, working out of a belief in progress, bringing wealth and prosperity to an inspired few, infusing the culture with forms of new power and force (from the elevator and the new sky rise brought into being by the use of steel to the transcontinental railroad); but it was also the source of alienation for many displaced craftsmen, who had become mere mechanical links in the industrial process of a factory or the assembly line.

The two systems supported radically different ways of life, so different in their workings as to engage their adherents in civil war. What they held in common was the dark side of their movements: the source of labor. The agrarian life in the South depended upon slave labor, variously treated depending upon the slave owners; the industrial life in the North depended upon cheap labor and a work force that included women and children working in conditions that were often inhuman. When farming itself became mechanized, an industrialized America triumphed; an incorporated America was now dependent upon technology, investment capital, and the giant organization of mechanical factors, from the acquiring of raw material, to its processing, to its shipping to commodity outlets, now regulated by financial markets. A new reality had seized the day.

As earlier indicated, Max Planck told us that a new idea wins conviction when its opponents die and the idea has been taken over by a new generation. If Planck had been looking for an example, he could have found it in Turner's idea of the frontier. Turner first voiced his thesis in 1893, and it gradually attained a following. Turner died in 1932. The next year, Arthur Schlesinger Sr. published *The Rise of the City*, his rebuttal to Turner's thesis. For a generation Schlesinger's argument gained strength; it contended that the westward movement was as much an urban as an agrarian matter, that "the cities marched westward with the outposts of settlement" and that the frontier was never independent of urban influence (210). Then, literally a generation after Turner's death, Richard Wade extended Schlesinger's conclusions in *The Urban Frontier* (1959). Wade limited his discussion to the cities of the trans-Appalachian West (Pittsburgh, Cincinnati, Lexington, Louisville, and St. Louis) from 1790 to 1830. He argued that city-dwellers closely followed the frontier farmer and that major waterways—from the Ohio River to the Mississippi—supplied a tangible means of transporting goods from the East to the Mississippi Valley. These cities, though modeled after eastern cities like Philadelphia, left the eastern influence behind as they crossed the country. The Wade book renewed the Schlesinger book's impact and both undermined Turner's argument. But Turner's thesis lingered on, offering its appeal to those who wanted to preserve an idealized (albeit dated) past.

Added to the urban import were the influence of canal building and especially the implementation of the railroad. When the Erie Canal was completed in 1825, it supplied a direct passage from New York City to the Midwest—up the Hudson River, through the canal, and into the Great Lakes. The effect was symbiotic: the Midwest came into its own as a commercial region, and New York became the principal East Coast city. New York grew from only sixty thousand inhabitants in 1800 to more than eight hundred thousand by 1860, and once the railroad extended the canal, the city became even more influential to commercial and industrial interests.

As one can abstract from the Schlesinger and Wade books, the rise of a city was often the product of geography and technology—such as location on a waterway and the rise of the steamboat industry. This combination produced a marketplace and financial well-being. These factors explain the rise of a city like Cincinnati: founded in 1789 on the Ohio River, it owed its prosperity to steamboat transportation, becoming a center for pork packers. Similar factors explain the transformation of St. Louis, located at the junction of the Missouri and Mississippi Rivers and close enough to the lead mines in eastern Missouri to process the ore. Minneapolis was another example of the commercial success that was the fruit of geography and technology, once it was able to take advantage of the cheap waterpower at the Falls of Saint Anthony on the Mississippi River, enabling it to capture the wheat and lumber market and become the center for the flour trade. And then there were centers like Salt Lake City, which improved their condition by building a connecting line to the Union Pacific Railroad depot at Ogden, opening up the far West to industrial development as well as to a string of farms and ranches along the corridor.

After the Civil War, the country became fully industrialized, a transformation that introduced a realm of new forces and weakened the romantic view of reality. The new technology brought radical change and financial reward to a privileged few. Iron ore was turned into stronger steel by baking out the carbon content, facilitated by the Bessiner process and the open-hearth furnace. These procedures brought wealth to Andrew Carnegie, who set up refineries in Homestead, Pennsylvania, outside Pittsburgh. Along with steel, the invention of the elevator made high-rise building possible, so cities like New York could build upward when space became limited. The skyline created a new world, dwarfing a population, reducing the idea of self both physically and mentally. Petroleum oil replaced kerosene, a change that led to the fortune of John D. Rockefeller, who set up a system of oil refineries in Ohio. J. P. Morgan made his fortune through shrewd investments in the newly formed railroads and by buying out Carnegie's U.S. Steel.

Other fortunes were the by-product of new technology that changed or altered physical reality: the electric light, the telephone, the telegraph, the automobile, and the airplane were transformative inventions that occurred in rapid sequence. This new technology was either implemented or sustained by investment spending that led to the rise of a consumer culture, advanced in large part by the role of the railroad. The transcontinental railroad was a force unto itself: two railroads—the Central Pacific, starting in San Francisco, and the Union Pacific, originating in Omaha, Nebraska—met on May 10, 1869, in Promontory, Utah, where a golden spike was driven into a railroad tie, symbolizing the western completion of what was now a cross-country enterprise. The Union Pacific employed mostly Irish labor, the Central Pacific mostly Chinese. The enterprise was three years in the making, financed mainly by speculative money, and it involved twenty thousand workers who laid 1,775 miles of track. The railroad received from federal sources 23 million acres of land and $64 million in loans. In the 1880s as many miles of track were laid as in the forty-two years from 1828 to 1870. The reach brought new markets into being and collapsed space, reducing the time it took to cross the country from one month to one week.

Despite its impressive achievements, the industrial frontier diminished the effects of agrarianism and met resistance that brought with it the call for reform. First came the Populist movement from about 1890 to 1900, and then the Progressive movement from about 1900 to 1914. These movements were primarily in response to the industrial process usurping what had been the perpetual domain of agrarian life. As Richard Hofstadter has succinctly put it, "The American tradition of democracy was formed on the farm and in small villages, and its central ideas were founded in rural sentiments. . . . Rural life and farming as a vocation was [thought of as] something sacred" (1955, 7).

While the myth of the land and the idea of romantic destiny still had ideological presence, they exerted less real-life force and functioned to remind an industrial population of the benefits that were lost with the demise of pastoral existence. Vernon Parrington saw the transition from the optimism of Emerson, with its belief in free will, to the pessimism of naturalism, with its philosophical determinism. The naturalists saw the individual subject to the dictates of "environment or the social machine" as well as "heredity and the physical machine." Emerson gave us an idealized world subject to the human will: "The world is good, man is good. . . . 'Trust thyself.' [But] since Emerson's time a new world has been emerging. The old shadow is falling across the American mind. Determinism is in the air" (Parrington 214). Emerson's beneficent (transcendental) force was eclipsed by Henry Adams's more hostile (mechanistic) force. This transformation was compounded by the new economic and industrial order along with the rise of the metropolis with its interminable bureaucracy, which atomized the individual in a mass culture where fashions were determined by mass production and promoted by blanket advertising.

As Adams maintained, postwar America was the realm of the Dynamo, a realm of mechanistic force that he referred to as the source of a new culture of disorder and multiplicity. Adams's world breaks in two: there is the medieval world made up of the Virgin, religion, art, and feeling, characterized by a feminine principle; and there is the modern world consisting of the Dynamo, science, technology, and reason, characterized by a male principle. In the age of the Dynamo, the compelling illusion is democracy (Adams points to the doctrines of the Founding Fathers, Paine, and Walt Whitman). But, as he tells us in his novel *Democracy,* democracy cannot supply the controlling illusion for the nineteenth and twentieth centuries that the idea of the Virgin did for the sixth to the sixteenth centuries.

In *Democracy,* Adams depicts a George Washington–like figure, an eighteenth-century idealist named Carrington, whose views are doomed. Opposed to Carrington is Senator Silas Ratcliffe, who acts in the name of putative ideals: his ends are always defensible, but his means are corrupt. Adams concludes that ideals cannot remain pure in the face of corrupting political power. Senator Ratcliffe is not a sympathetic character, but he appears to be a realist; he is contrasted to Carrington, who is the voice of meaningless honor based on traditions of a dead past; he is also opposed to Madeline Lee, who is fascinated by power but shocked by how it works.

Adams came to believe that commercial forces determined the

workings of democracy, especially organized advocacy groups (today's lobbyists). Power structures rose and perpetuated privilege. Behind the noble ideas and principles of a democracy was blatant self-interest. Adams admired eighteenth-century idealists like Jefferson. But Jefferson, an antifederalist, was inconsistent to his own political philosophy; he did more to perpetuate big government (e.g., the Louisiana Purchase, his battle with John Marshall over the Supreme Court, his belief in the embargo) than any other president at that time. History was a realm of force, a more determining element than individual willpower. Adams came to believe that democracy marked the end of the modern era, which like the ocean (its symbol) was subject to its own inner forces, as the ocean was subject to the working of the tides.

As the oppositions of history—Federalist against Republican, America against Europe—became more pronounced, democratic ideals would give way to imperialistic mandates, augmented by military products that were the beneficiary of new technology. The struggle was between realms of historical forces: science, reason, and multiplicity would grow at the expense of religion, feeling, and unity. Adams developed these ideas in *Mont-Saint-Michel and Chartres* and *The Education of Henry Adams,* where he called attention to a transformation of national identity: the individual abandoned religion for science and art for technology and surrendered an inner sense of unity to an outerworld sense of force and multiplicity. The key metaphor here was Niagara Falls, where the particles (individualism) empty into a void (eternity) with energy (force) analogous to the Dynamo.

Adams had written a biography of Albert Gallatin and was researching his history of Jefferson and Madison when he was writing *Democracy:* he saw clearly stamped into time a process whereby history (the realm of impersonal forces) was more powerful than human effort. Gallatin's life was depicted as a struggle between an ideal and a corrupt vision, with the corrupt vision winning out. Adams came to believe in natural forces that operate mechanically through men. He believed that a fragmenting process was going on, an idea that he treated symbolically (once again with the Niagara Falls metaphor) in *Esther.* In his history of Jefferson and Madison, he argued that political ideals have no meaning until they have a force behind them, especially military force, which leads to imperial desire, increases the power of government, and diminishes the influence of the individual.

7

Populism

The Man behind the Curtain

I

After the Civil War, the American city expanded in unprecedented ways. But the influx of population was bringing with it urban conflict that in residual ways is still with us today. Two factions—one from rural areas, the other new immigrants—came to the city. The urban population multiplied almost seven times between 1860 and 1910 (Hofstadter 1955, 174); by 1910 more than 13 million immigrants were living in the United States, almost one-seventh of the population (177).

The history of immigration to America featured ethnic groups coming in waves. The colonial period saw immigration primarily from the British Isles, especially the Scotch-Irish. A second wave took place between 1820 and 1870, in which 7.5 million immigrants came from western Europe, about one-third from Ireland and one-third from Germany, with a heavy influx also from Scandinavia. From 1880 to 1914, more than 22 million people migrated to the United States. The number of farms grew from 1.4 million in 1850 to 4.0 million in 1880 and to 6.4 million in 1910, at which time the farm population started to decline; by 1920 the population of cities outnumbered that of farms.

The Scotch-Irish welcomed the newfound farming land and tended to scatter when it came to settlement. They were often restless and moved on, becoming the cutting edge of the frontier all the way to the Pacific. The Germans, more prone to staying put, resided in numbers in the Appalachian Valley. They were known for their elegant stone barns and their canvas-covered wagons, built on an old-world model at Conestoga, Pennsylvania. The Irish settled in East Coast cities (Boston,

New York, Philadelphia, and Baltimore) and, along with the Germans, in the Midwest, which had been opened by the completion of the Erie Canal in 1825. Many of the new immigrants were attracted by the call of American industry after the Napoleonic Wars. The large group that came from Ireland was fleeing the famine of 1845, while many Germans came to escape military conscription. The influx of Irish immigrants provoked a resentment that only increased when white-male suffrage reduced the influence of patrician politicians. The response to immigrants gaining political power was the rise of a nativist secret society, the Order of the Star-Spangled Banner, founded in 1849, later known (because its members denied all knowledge of their political agenda) as the Know-Nothing Party. They tried to exclude Catholics and immigrants in general from public office. Their influence was curbed when their northern and southern branches feuded over the slavery question.

In the decades after the Civil War, immigration benefited from steamships replacing sailing ships, and large numbers of immigrants came to America from southern and eastern Europe, including Italy, Greece, Poland, and other Slavic countries. Within this group were 2.5 to 3 million Jews, who prompted waves of anti-Semitism. The influx of immigrants at this time supplied the manpower needed to work the new industrial jobs in the steel, coal, textile, garment, and auto industries. But such large numbers of immigrants were not always welcome, and from 1920 to 1965, immigration was looked upon as a major social problem, culminating in the issue of several federal mandates against new immigration. The most serious was the Immigration Act of 1924, which curtailed immigration, especially from southern and eastern Europe. Some allowances were made for immigrants from Mexico and the Caribbean, with special provisions in the 1930s favoring those trying to escape Nazi Germany. In 1965 the immigration situation changed substantially when the Hart-Celler Act opened up immigration from Asia and Africa.

Within the unfolding history of immigration were dramas within dramas. Not only was there a great divide in ethnic matters nationally, but that divide carried over to the large cities themselves. At the turn of the twentieth century, two groups formally opposed each other in the newly empowered metropolis: those who had come to the city from rural America and those who had come as immigrants. While both factions were seeking a better life, they were doing it in totally antithetical ways. Their ambitions were similar, but their values and intent were remarkably different. The two factions embodied fundamental cultural differences, distrusted each other, and worked against the possibility of a community.

The rural population tended to be evangelical Protestants. The evangelical movement began in Great Britain in the 1730s and gained interest in America in the eighteenth and nineteenth centuries. The era from 1790 to 1850 was a period of American evangelism known as the Great Awakening, encouraged by the continued influence of Jonathan Edwards and based on revival meetings in western Massachusetts and newly settled areas of the Appalachians. The evangelical movement took the Bible, especially the Gospels, as its final authority, believed in the need of personal conversion (the assumption that we can be "born again" through the blood of Christ), and celebrated Christ's salvific words. The Puritanism that came out of this revival movement was different from the Puritanism of the founders of New England: it was more individualistic and a matter of private conscience in a realm that pitted good against evil, especially an evil that was supposedly infused in the wilderness. It was this version of Puritanism that moved west with the frontier, eventually encountering an Emersonian opposition that eradicated the idea of nature as the source of evil and supported the idea of nature as the source of all that was good, dramatically changing assumptions involving the way nature worked and the meaning of the wilderness.

Of the new immigrants, many brought Roman Catholicism from the Old World, especially the large number of Irish workers. A cohesive group, they were easily organized, and the postwar period saw the rise of the urban political machine, corrupt in its workings but attentive to the needs of the immigrants. Over time, every big city came to have its political ring, from James Curley in Boston to James Pendergast in Kansas City. In New York, the political organization that controlled the city was Tammany Hall. Tammany, founded in 1786, was a wing of the Democratic Party that politically exploited New York from 1790 to 1960. From 1872 there was an Irish boss of Tammany, including Boss Tweed up to 1876 and later Al Smith. Franklin Roosevelt was once an ally of Smith, but they quarreled and became rivals for the Democratic nomination in 1932. Once he became president, Roosevelt was one of many reformers who worked against Tammany. After 1960 the organization ceased to exist.

Smith was the Democratic nominee for president in 1928, running against Herbert Hoover. Smith grew up in the poorest of circumstances in urban New York. He dropped out of school at age twelve to work manual jobs, including a stint in the Fulton Fish Market. After working his way up the political ladder, he became speaker of the New York State Assembly. Beginning in 1919, he was governor of New York for four nonconsecutive terms and instituted a political program that anticipated the New Deal. Smith's run for the presidency in 1928 stumbled on his identity as a devout Roman Catholic along with his urban credentials. Hoover got 58.2 percent of the popular vote to Smith's 40.8 and carried the Electoral College 444 to 87. Smith lost every western state, including the normally liberal Wisconsin. The election of 1928 clearly illustrated the historical divide between an urban and a rural America—a divide that encompassed religious and political differences and turned on the supremacy of evangelical belief and the political fear of a larger role of federal influence.

II

But to see the immigrant movement as totally an urban phenomenon is clearly to distort historical fact. The prairie states of the Midwest, what became known as the Middle Border, accommodated many European workers who came in abundant numbers to the farmlands of America. The bulk of the immigrants settled in the cities, however, where the new industries were opening up jobs and other opportunities. The conflict in the city between its rural element and the immigrants stemmed mainly from the aforementioned differences in religious and political values.

Another way of thinking about the politics of geographical division involves a theory of Open versus Closed space. Those who live in Open spaces tend to resist the role of government as an unwelcome intrusion. Those who live in Closed spaces tend to welcome the role of government, especially when security is called for or assistance is warranted in times of need. According to the *New York Times,* 26 million Texans live in urban areas, and yet they think of themselves as rural inhabitants, rejecting the assumptions of Closed space and accepting the self-deluded myth of Open space ("Urban vs. Rural Values," A21). The point here has a larger relevance: the reason Jeffersonian agrarianism lived on beyond its need involved the same reluctance to dismiss the agrarian myth that the Texan has to dismiss affinity with the politics of Open space.

The threat to the old agrarian order, to the realm of Open space, brought Populism into being: Populism was a protest movement that tried to hold back the changes that came with the new industry, its urban reach, and its hoards of immigrant workers. The platform of Populism was mainly conservative, but inconsistently so: it opposed immigration but supported issues that gave more power to the people, including federal ownership of railroads and communication systems (telegraph and telephone), a graduated income tax, direct election of senators, presidential term limits, and abolition of government subsidies to corporations.

Populism brought with it the tradition of the frontier West, with its desire to restore individualism and a residual democracy, in opposition to a growing urbanism and its city bosses, corporations that were unscrupulous when it came to profits, the growth of government with its attendant bureaucracy, and the influx of a foreign work force. Such causes led to the Farmer's Alliance, an advocacy group that addressed the problems the farmers had with the railroads and the financial systems. Despite their reservations against big government, the farmers were sympathetic to the railroads reducing their rates by functioning like the federal post office, where the cost of mail to remote regions was offset by the aggregate benefit, "reducing the expense of all" (Postel 143). Such movements led to the People's Party of the 1880s. In 1890 the Populists won control of the Kansas state legislature. They merged with the Farmer's Alliance and the Knights of Labor. Their presidential candidate, James B. Weaver, won more than 1 million votes in the 1890 election, but the party lost momentum between 1892 and 1896 when they feuded and split over whether to become a nationalist as opposed to a regional party and merge with the Democrats.

The rural population adhered to the values of the old agrarian order, drawing upon their evangelical beliefs that gave priority to the individual and supported limited forms of government; salvation was a personal matter between the individual and his or her Maker. Despite the anachronism involved, the conservative branch of the Republican

Party still today advocates the politics of this agenda. The immigrants, in contrast, coalesced around the values they had brought from the Old World; supported each other, especially in fighting the bigotry that accompanied their presence; and benefited from the political machines and the largesse of the bosses who ran the city. They became a source of support for the New Deal in the 1930s and initially were faithful to the Democratic Party.

The two factions contributed to the modern-day two-party system, the ongoing basis of American politics. Between them the two factions generated conservative and liberal values ("liberalism" today referred to less pejoratively as "progressivism"). One faction opposed big government, relying on the resourcefulness of the individual for well-being; the other welcomed government assistance, believing that domestic needs often went beyond individual remedy and that government responsibility included the welfare of its population.

Thus the two-party system owed an element of its existence to frontier history, both its reality and its illusion, transformed as the two factions were over time. Even as the agrarian values long persisted, they did not carry their initial authority once they were weakened by the transformations that came with the passage to an industrial nation. In an industrial nation, there will always be more unemployed than there are jobs to be had; those left behind are at the mercy of the state and forms of welfare. As the nation became larger and more complex, the federal government was called upon to do what the individual did not have the capacity to do, and it implemented such benefits as Social Security, Medicare, the G.I. Bill, the interstate highway system, flood and dam control, farm subsidies, and federal investigative agencies with legislative authority. What often goes unnoticed in conservative ideology is that a nation builds upon itself. No one is purely an individualist in an urban-industrial society. The successful entrepreneur relies on an educated labor force to bring a product into being, on a transportation system to bring it to market, and on a federal monetary system for aid and financial security.

The idea of the rugged individualist had more romantic—and therefore more literary—appeal than that of New Deal politics. The literary implications of the bifurcation between agrarians and immigrants were important, as we shall see in more detail in subsequent chapters. The Western as a literary genre—with its spirit of rugged individualism, its witness to the feud between the ranchers and the farmers, and its personal sense of justice and spiritual redemption—owed its existence in great part to the wilderness frontier. Literary naturalism—with its depiction of tenement life, its concern over the financial scandals of an industrial America, and its insight into forces at work beyond individual control—owed much of its existence to the world of the urban frontier. When the wilderness frontier was closed (along the lines suggested by Frederick Jackson Turner), the literary emphasis shifted from the Western to literary naturalism. Westerns continued to be written, but they were now set in the old frontier world that no longer existed or existed as an idealized version of a former reality: the Western became the literary fiction of a historical fiction, while naturalistic novels like Upton Sinclair's *The Jungle* (1906) addressed the immediate social wrongs of the era and brought political response.

The political beneficiary of the new agrarian movement was William Jennings Bryan (1860–1925), the leader of the Populist movement, who turned landed interest into the basis of a political platform of the Democratic Party, eventually becoming its seemingly perennial presidential nominee. He ran unsuccessfully for president in 1896, 1900, and 1908 against McKinley and Taft. He ran for Congress from Nebraska, and he was secretary of state for Woodrow Wilson (1913–16). Raised as a Baptist and a Methodist, he later became a devout Presbyterian, supporting prohibition and opposing Darwinism to the extent of debating Clarence Darrow in the famous Scopes Trial of 1925 (he died five days after the trial ended). Like so much of the Populist agenda—and indeed like the western frontier movement itself—his political agenda was deeply conservative. Bryan supported agrarian causes and was unsympathetic to big government: he opposed the gold standard and the big banks, led the silverite movement, which was favorable to farmers, opposed federal largesse to the railroads, and opposed American imperialism and later involvement in World War I; he resigned as secretary of state when Wilson moved America toward war.

In 1896, at the convention in Chicago, Bryan gave his famous "cross of gold" speech, in which he enlisted the sacrifice (crucifixion) metaphor as he insisted that the prosperity of the country depended upon the vitality of the land, the priority of silver over gold, and the superiority of the farmer over the banker. "You shall not crucify mankind upon a cross of gold," he began. "The great cities rest upon our broad and fertile prairies," he continued. "Burn down your cities and leave our farms, and your cities will spring up again as if by magic; but destroy our farms, and the grass will grow in the streets of every city in the country."

III

Part of Bryan's lack of sympathy for the city stemmed from his belief that the city was indifferent to the agrarian movement, but another aspect involved his concern over the significant number of immigrants coming to America and settling in the large cities. Since a sizable number of the urban immigrants were Jewish, the Populist movement often revealed an undercurrent of anti-Semitism.

The western frontier prided itself on its Nordic superiority. As a racial type, Owen Wister's Virginian was a tall, square-jawed, blue-eyed, fair-skinned embodiment of Nordic heritage, an idealized composite of those Americans who came from northwestern Europe. They were a caste apart from the influx of immigrants coming from eastern and southern Europe. While it is true that most immigrants were attracted to the cities and industrial pursuits, the claim that the western frontier did not accommodate a wide variety of European immigrants was part of the misapprehension that made up the myth of the West. Authors like Willa Cather and Ole Rolvaag documented immigrant life in the West; in addition we know that between 1860 and 1890, Nevada had the highest percentage of immigrants born abroad and that the northern plains were close behind. Even more surprisingly, in 1900 the Census Bureau claimed that eight out of ten persons living in North Dakota were either immigrants or children of immigrants (Athearn 55–56).

Immigration promoted racism in America, a toxic phenomenon as witnessed by books like Lothrop Stoddard's *The Rising Tide of Color* (1920) and Madison Grant's *The Passing of the Great Race*. Stoddard grew up in Massachusetts, attended Harvard University, and graduated with both a BA and a PhD in history. He argued that Western civilization rested on the supremacy of the white race and warned that the rise of the colored races would end that civilization as we know it. He divided the white race into three realms—Nordic, Alpine, and

Mediterranean—each being superior to the colored races, with the Nordic race superior to the other white races. (Scott Fitzgerald had Tom Buchanan, a racist bully, voice Stoddard's argument in *The Great Gatsby*.) Both Stoddard and Grant were instrumental in implementing the Immigration Act of 1924.

The call to Populism found many forms of expression. Since the 1960s, critics have maintained that Frank Baum's *Wizard of Oz* (1890) is an allegorical embodiment of the main issues of the 1880s. The main source of this argument is an essay by Henry M. Littlefield, "*The Wizard of Oz*: Parable on Populism," published in the *American Quarterly* in 1964. According to Littlefield, Baum uses Dorothy's adventures to embody the Populist spirit. She is from the heartland world of Kansas, the physical center of America, and with the help of the good witch from the West confronts the wicked witch from the East. She is blown into a dreamlike parallel world by the transforming force of a tornado, which brings her into contact with three representative citizens: a scarecrow who lacks a brain, a tin man who lacks a heart, and a lion who lacks courage. Once the citizens are equipped with the necessary political attributes that they formerly lacked, the group is ready for its journey. In her silver slippers (ruby-colored in the 1939 movie), Dorothy leads her group down the yellow brick road to the Emerald City in the Land of Oz, where she discovers that a wizard hiding behind a curtain controls reality.

While there are some who maintain that the allegorical details are merely coincidental and that Baum had no special interest in Populism, Littlefield's reading does supply a list of possible correspondences: the tornado could be read as the political upheaval of the times; the tin man as workers displaced by industrialization without the zeal (heart) to find new opportunities; the scarecrow as the farmers whose fate has robbed them of the plan (mind) needed to find a way out of their bankrupt situation; the cowardly lion as William Jennings Bryan (who some felt was not adamant enough in the face of industrial opposition); the wicked witch from the East as the new industrial robber barons who control the bankers opposed to a bimetallic monetary system; the yellow brick road as a symbol of gold as the basis of the money system (raising the value of the dollar, limiting credit, and making it more difficult to repay agrarian loans); Emerald City as the urban center (the force that is opposed to agrarianism as well as the source of worthless greenback paper money); the wizard behind the curtain as the embodiment of hidden forces (such as lobbyists, who determine economic principles and control political reality). The allegorical elements here suggest the possibility of a play between gold and silver as the basis of a monetary system: the money supply was limited to the amount of gold in reserve and thus limited the number of dollars that could be printed. While the money supply was increased when more gold was found and mined, the amount of new gold did not remedy the plight of the farmers. The Populists wanted to change the financial components in favor of the farmers by adding silver to the system, equating sixteen ounces of silver to an ounce of gold; the added silver would increase the money supply and cheapen the dollar. Once added, silver would also increase the amount of money (credit) available for landed investment and cheapen the means of repaying agrarian loans, creating a monetary system that no longer worked solely in favor of the bankers. But despite the efforts of the Populists, the gold standard prevailed until 1933, when the monetary supply was equated with the gross national product rather than with the supply of precious metals. Present practice has gone beyond that and involves printing money as needed, increasing the national debt into the trillions of dollars ($17 trillion by 2013) and cheapening the value of the dollar while inflating the economy with each printing.

8

Progressivism

The Urban Crucible

I

Each imperial culture was distinguished by a capital city—Babylon, Thebes, Athens, Alexandria, Carthage, Constantinople, Rome, Vienna, Berlin, Paris, London—that testified to its high place in the history of civilization. As previously suggested, the Puritan revolution (1642-60), the French Revolution (1789-99), and the American Civil War (1861-65) all had the same historic function: each marked the transition from an agrarian to a commercial-industrial-urban culture. Defoe and Dickens observed this phenomenon in England, Balzac and Zola observed it in France, and Twain and Dreiser observed it in America.

In the Western world, the transition from a landed to an urban economy brought with it the rise of the middle class and a more centralized form of government. Cities grew for economic reasons: to serve as marketplaces for their region. The marketplace displayed new forms of money with new kinds of banks and credit theories that replaced subsistence (yeoman) farming and forms of feudalism before that. William Cronon makes use of S. H. Goodin's idea of the emerging city. Such cities (Pittsburgh, Cincinnati, St. Louis) are diagramed as concentric circles, described as self-contained and yet connected to (i.e., competing with) each other, all anticipating the drift westward to the next circle, satellites to the central city of Chicago (Cronon 1991, 39).

The rise of central cities was one in a series of evolutionary stages— political as well as urban stages—that brought about America as a nation. There was a Puritan America; a colonial America; a federalist America with an agrarian frontier and a federalist America with an industrial frontier; and an imperial America intent on its expansionist activity. Part of the imperial reach stemmed from a desire for new marketplaces, especially those realms that supply indispensable materials (such as oil) that fuel the industrial-capitalistic system.

The agrarian and industrial frontiers had points of similarity and points of difference. The Progressive movement admired the rugged individual, whether he was the new industrial baron or the independent rancher–yeoman farmer. But the Progressive element differed in its approval of the way the two movements accommodated the demands of democracy. The transformation from an agrarian to an industrial order created a great divide both within the nation and within the industrial order itself. The new industrialists were motivated more by the desire for profit than by the welfare of the community.

But industrial America was not culturally homogeneous. George Santayana shrewdly detected two cultures at work within industrial America: in gender terms, a masculine and a feminine state of mind were at work. Intellectually, America was standing still while it powered new forms of industrial development. The colonial mansion stood beside the skyscraper: the American Will inhabited the skyscraper; the American Intellect inhabited the colonial mansion. One was the sphere of the American man; the other was the domain of the American woman. "The one is all aggressive enterprise; the other is all genteel tradition" (16).

The rise of an industrial America took place in stages. At the beginning was a multiple-step method that produced goods in sequences: one producer would work thread into yarn; another would make the yarn into fabric; and a third would turn the fabric into clothes. The factory system was born when a producer realized that all three steps could be carried out under one roof: a product could be made from start to finish—and the profits multiplied—by consolidating the steps necessary to produce a good.

Intent on monopoly, corporate leaders resorted to the creation of the trust to maximize profits by persuading shareholders of various companies in a prime industry to transfer their shares to a board of trustees, a tactic that would minimize competition and increase profits, which would then be shared. The companies most noted for this practice were Standard Oil, U.S. Steel, American Tobacco, and International Mercantile Marine. The rise of giant corporations threatened the idea of democracy, especially when the process was pushed toward monopoly. When an oil company like Standard Oil cornered the market involving the supply of oil to be produced, we had a horizontal monopoly. When the same company controlled the entire process that turned oil into gasoline—the exploration, the drilling, the refining, the storage, the transportation to market, and the market itself—we had a vertical monopoly.

Supposedly the market—that is, supply and demand—controlled the price of the produced good; but by curtailing production and limiting the supply, a producer could create a shortage, which would raise demand and justify an increase in the price of the product. These practices were consistent with the profit motive and led to the abuses that attracted investigating journalists who sought to correct the dubious activity that had characterized the gilded age.

II

This new commercial and industrial order resisted regulation, becoming a form of righteousness unto itself and bringing the Progressive movement into being. If Populism saw agrarian values confront a newly industrial America, Progressivism saw the agrarian aspect of this experience diminish and the impetus extend to market abuses in general in what became an era of reform. The leaders in this movement were known as muckrakers, a pejorative term coined by Theodore Roosevelt based on a passage from Bunyan's *Pilgrim's Progress*. Roosevelt championed financial reform to a point, but when the reform threatened his own interests and those of his cronies, he withdrew his support. Despite his reputation as "trust buster," Roosevelt saw the rise of corporate America and with it the most influential source of radical change in the American character, creating a political as well as an economic system that transformed the idea of a democratic nation ruled by rugged individualists into a special-interest economy. The new America was the product of a politically controlled mass culture often impelled to work against its own best interests. A prime example is the scandal of the Crédit Mobilier.

The Crédit Mobilier and the Union Pacific railroad were one and the same: the Union Pacific used the Crédit Mobilier as its financial agent in charge of railroad construction. In work originating in Omaha, the

Crédit Mobilier supposedly (this information comes from its records) paid $27,500 per mile of track laid but was reimbursed at the rate of $42,000 per mile from the speculative money (stocks and bonds) invested in the railroad and from government loans.

Oakes Ames, a congressman from Massachusetts with ties to railroad executives, was offered a contract to construct 667 miles of track commencing at the one-hundredth meridian at a price ranging from $42,000 per mile for the first hundred miles to $96,000 per mile thereafter. Ames himself was a principal investor and large stockholder in the Crédit Mobilier. In order to get Congress to fund the Crédit Mobilier through loans and land grants, Ames offered stock to members of Congress for prices less than the stock was worth, in effect bribing the legislature. The congressmen involved included James G. Blaine and James Garfield, a future presidential nominee and a future president. When the details of this arrangement became public, the Congress censured Ames. Morally tarnished, he returned to his estate located on more than six hundred acres of land in North Easton, Massachusetts, and died two months later (Crawford).

Few know the story of the Crédit Mobilier, and those who do often forget to connect it to the origins of the railroad, which are romantically described in our major fiction. Many stories begin or are extended by memories of a railroad trip, such as Dreiser's Carrie's arrival in Chicago, or Fitzgerald's Nick Carraway's return to the Midwest from prep school in the East at Christmastime.

The story of the Crédit Mobilier involves both romance and scandal—and is representative of the Progressive era. From the perspective of the participants in the affair, the end justified the means. One cannot question the importance of the railway Oakes Ames helped bring into being: the transcontinental railway not only connected the West and the East; it also helped connect the Pacific with the Atlantic and Europe with Asia. It was one of the major achievements of the nineteenth century. But underpinning its construction were a series of illegal practices—implementing the future of the capitalistic system and brought into being by the misuse of that system—that included the fraudulent payment of thousands of dollars.

The story of the Crédit Mobilier was consistent with Frank Norris's account in *The Octopus*. Norris's novel actually extends the story, giving us the dark side of the railroad when it was completed and functioned as a giant corporation, with its arbitrary increase in storage fees and transportation rates and the morally dubious reclamation of farm and ranch land.

III

The Fourteenth Amendment gave the corporation the status of the individual—and the legal rights implied by that status. We have thus come full circle: Turner's frontier took pride in honing the rugged individualist. Now that status is given legally to the corporation. The transformation speaks for itself: what the frontier created with humans in combat with the environment is now given as a token of political preference to the corporation. We have moved from the realm of self-subsistence to the realm of institutional favoritism.

The idea of reform in the Progressive age went through radical transformation—a phenomenon that can be clearly seen when we contrast Frederick Jackson Turner's rural idea of frontier America with Richard Hofstadter's more cosmopolitan idea of America. In *The Age of Reform,* Hofstadter moved ideologically from 1930s liberalism to the more conservative strain of liberalism in the 1950s. He was less than sympathetic toward the Populist movement, lacking empathy with the farmers and claiming, among other charges, that the movement involved anti-Semitism. He was equally distrustful of mass sentiments (a view that was later seemingly justified by the rise of Wisconsin's Joseph McCarthy), which he believed anticipated American fascism. He was tolerant of the muckrakers' mission of challenging the social and economic irregularities of the Progressive-industrial era, but he came to believe that challenge was not broad enough: it attacked financial abuses but sustained the rural-agrarian-Protestant monolithic values of the Turner thesis.

Hofstadter believed there was a need to go beyond these matters and see the era in terms of an ethnic and social multiplicity that would call critical attention to American Indians, Jewish immigrants, and city-dwellers. There was thus a dispute over what it meant to be an American. What was the reality as well as the ideal of the frontier prototype? Hofstadter's definition moves us from benevolent to hostile force and parallels the similar ideological transformations in literature as embodied in the move from the Western to literary naturalism—the literary change paralleling historical change.

The city in which most of these transformations occurred was Chicago, what William Cronon referred to as "the gateway to the West." Chicago was the beneficiary of four natural and economic factors. First, Chicago is located on a fertile prairie, adjacent to rich farmland and its products. Second, Chicago is located on two watersheds—one to the east, the other a short distance to the west—as well as being on the Great Lakes and thus available from the East by the Erie Canal and from the West by the Mississippi. Third, Chicago is the center of railroads coming from the east, going to the west. Fourth, Chicago, like other western cities, became the beneficiary of eastern capital, initially invested in land and later in commodity markets, speculating in stored grain and other farm products once grain elevators made such warehousing possible.

But in Cronon's compelling account, Chicago's rise is only half the story: its fall is the other half. Chicago fell because it became too expensive to serve as a conduit for the new industrial goods. As with other gateway cities, land costs rose, labor became more expensive, and travel involving both human and industrial products became the victim of horrendous traffic. Soon other cities or regions overtook the functions that Chicago once monopolized: Omaha and Kansas City took over meatpacking, the Pacific Northwest took over lumber, and Minneapolis took over flour manufacturing. This cycle of rise and fall was destined to repeat itself, illustrated by the call to prosperity and the decline of St. Louis.

It all turned on power. In the eighteenth century, power resided with the landed elite. By the nineteenth century, intellectual spokesmen like William James and Thomas Carlyle thought that power (the driving force of history) was exercised through the will of an enlightened individual. So also the backward look of Turner's wilderness frontier depended on the will of the rugged individualist. But by the Progressive era of the nineteenth century, power resided with industrialists who had access to forms of new technology (those who had control of the technological advances from the printing press to the Internet had a wealth of power at their disposal) and with the corporation (working with lobbyists to control the economic-political system).

Power, in other words, had moved from that possessed by a social class, to the landed farmer, to the individual with access to new technology, to the new corporation with its political and economic reach. Power came and went with the job, not with the individual. (One who steps down from a position of power learns quickly that the power remains with the position, not the individual.)

Before the Civil War, the source of political power was mainly in the states. After the Civil War, the corporation exercised economic power, but the source of political power was mainly in the federal government. The federal government initially handled foreign affairs, and the states did get involved in domestic issues like slavery; but in general the states had more power before than after the war. The rise of a strong central government played a decisive role in transforming events on the frontier. Along with the reach of the federal government, the rise of corporate America brought new authority that curbed the spirit of individualism that had previously dominated the sense of frontier self. As the government became more powerful in relation to the individual, the corporation became more powerful in relation to the government. If one threatened the idea of individualism, the other threatened the idea of democracy. As Henry Adams told us, we moved from what might be justified as a democratic government to that of special-interest rule. We can once again cite Frank Norris's *The Octopus,* which drew upon literary naturalism to depict the rise of the railroad as a dominating corporate entity.

This transition brought about radical cultural and psychological changes. The human embodiment of Turner's world was a European peasant transformed into an American democrat; a product of the feudal system was morphed into a more autonomous being: optimistic in perspective, pragmatic in practice, inventive in disposition, and restless by nature. Such a character was the product both of the frontier environment and of a Protestant state of mind—a combination of commitment to the land and the willingness to work the soil as needed to bring forth a harvest and justify God's grace. In the industrial system, controlled as it was by the new corporation, the individual was reduced to being a cog on a wheel, engaged with other mechanized workers to create an energy (factory) system needed to produce consumer goods.

As part of this industrial process, the worker was atomized; the urban democrat was never fully able to shed his immigrant nature: his

European political beliefs often included socialist or anarchical thinking, his emotional commitment was to the immigrant community, and his religious beliefs—whether Catholic or Jewish—stemmed from his European background and differed substantially from the more rural-agrarian forms of Protestantism. While the Turner pioneer took the land as his task, the industrial worker was by necessity restricted to the city, often underpinning its political ring. In the human transformation from an agrarian to an industrial type, the spirit of rugged individualism gave way to a tolerance for community and government help. The spirit of Populism and Progressivism inevitably became the basis for the New Deal, at least until the first wave of immigrants was replaced by their descendants; and the following waves were transformed once more, giving us the era of Joseph McCarthy (with its fear of radical immigrant politics, be it communism, socialism, or anarchy) and eventually the Ronald Reagan years, with the political switch from New Deal Democratic to antigovernment supply-side Republican economics (in which the production side is favored in the production-consumer cycle).

IV

The transition from an agrarian to an industrial culture also brought a catalog of moral as well as economic and political problems. Over the years, there has been a tendency to see the reform movements, especially Populism, as anti-Semitic (and perhaps, when applied to the Irish, anti-Catholic as well). Such an argument can be made, but for more reasons than those often given. What was at stake here was often less a matter of religious intolerance and more a matter of different cultures and worldviews. As just enumerated, the agrarian value system, with its roots in the land, led to a far different state of mind than the industrial value system did, with its urban preference. The larger argument involves ideological differences based on a sense of place and a lifestyle accommodating that place. One must not distance behavior that is clearly racist. But while the difference between a basically Gentile and a Jewish state of mind suggests anti-Semitism is at work, this difference is only one of many lifestyle differences between these fundamental national types; the historical differences between the agrarian and the commercial-industrial character amounts to national rather than ethnic differences. While it did not lessen an existing bias, it nevertheless eclipsed what we usually mean by anti-Semitism.

Another significant change brought about by the rise of an industrial system was the shift in occupational training. It was now not enough to be the son of a farmer or a blacksmith or to apprentice with one; and the same was true with what was to become the more academic subjects. The conglomerates now depended on a corps of personnel trained in the new university. The days of amateur historians like Francis Parkman and George Bancroft were over: the amateur historian gave way to the university-trained historian, who was influenced by the German seminar system, grounded in historicism and influence study, working with theories of knowledge (like germ theory) in graduate programs throughout the country. Professionalism replaced on-the-job training. Professional schools proliferated: at this time the leading graduate-school program in history was at Johns Hopkins, which produced both Frederick Jackson Turner and Woodrow Wilson, scholars who were shaped by the training that they then passed on to other colleges—Princeton in the case of Wilson, the University of Wisconsin in the case of Turner.

The transition from Turner's frontier to that of an industrial America called for fundamental changes in the nature and function of government and in the idea of self. The idea of the rugged individual was now subordinated to the overpowering presence of the corporation; the trust in democracy had given way to a belief in capitalism and the laws of the marketplace. The yeoman farmer was now an industrial worker with a new state of mind; the myth of a spiritualized land had given way to speculation and agribusiness.

With the end of the wilderness frontier came the Progressive era—a time of reform that addressed the abuses that came into being with new forms of power: the increased power of government; the power of the new technology; the power built into political positions, whether executive, legislative, or judicial; and the power of the corporation.

Moreover, the rise of political power brought with it the desire for empire, especially when the executive function of the federal government exercised the power that presidents like Theodore Roosevelt claimed went with the job. At this point, the relative realm of innocence that permeated Turner's frontier was no more. If Turner's frontier had not actually closed physically by 1893, it had closed ideologically:

another state of mind—an urban reality—now replaced the agrarian vision of America.

V

The era of reform brought varied responses to the ways power was exercised and controlled. The rise of the giant corporation threatened the idea of American democracy and called the muckrakers into being as a corrective force. The leading muckrakers and their best-known books advocating reform were David Graham Phillips, *The Treason of the Senate* (1906); Ida Tarbell, *Standard Oil* (1904); Lincoln Steffens, *Shame of the Cities* (1904); Jacob Riis, *How the Other Half Lived* (1890); and Upton Sinclair's novel about the meatpacking industry, *The Jungle* (1906).

A popular literary device was to describe a dream vision in which a character is transported to another realm of time that can be compared to the present historical moment. Three of the most popular time-traveler narratives were Ignatius Donnelly's *Caesar's Column* (1890), Jack London's *The Iron Heel* (1908), and Edward Bellamy's *Looking Backward* (1888). The Donnelly and London fantasies treat the use and abuse of political power: Donnelly's points to abuses that might come from the proletariat, London's to abuses that might come from an oligarchy. Bellamy's fantasy is different; it is a utopian narrative about a time traveler who journeys one hundred years forward into the realm of an idealized socialist economy—a projected economy that works for the collective good and for the elimination of poverty. Bellamy is able to contrast the flaws in the present nineteenth-century industrial economy with remedies brought about by the dictates of a futuristic socialism.

There were few novels that took their characters to the realm of socialism found in London and Bellamy, but there were many novels—now mostly forgotten—that treated the abuses of the system. The plight of the working poor found expression in Elizabeth Phelps's *The Silent Partner* (1871), Thomas Bailey Aldrich's *The Stillwater Tragedy* (1880), Amanda Douglas's *Hope Mills* (1880), Mary Hallock Foote's *Coeur d'Alene* (1894), and Francis Hopkinson Smith's *Tom Grogan* (1896).

The speculative nature of finances was treated in Henry Francis Keenan's *The Money Makers* (1885), Charles Dudley Warner's *That Fortune* (1899), Garrett P. Serviss's *The Moon Metal* (1900), David Graham

Phillips's *The Great God Success* (1901), Robert Barr's *The Victors* (1901), Will Payne's *The Money Captain* (1898), and Harold Frederic's *The Lawton Girl* (1890).

And the corrupt nature of the system itself was the subject of Rebecca Harding Davis's *John Andross* (1874), J. W. De Forest's *Honest John Vane* (1875), Hamlin Garland's *A Spoil of Office* (1892), Henry Blake Fuller's *The Cliff Dwellers* (1893) and *With the Procession* (1895), and Robert Herrick's *The Gospel of Freedom* (1898) and *Together* (1908).

The most influential novelist in this era of reform was Mark Twain, who treated a host of social concerns in *The Gilded Age* (1873), which he wrote with Charles Dudley Warner. The novel tells of a plot of land, seventy-five thousand acres, owned by Silas Hawkins, who has bought it for speculation purposes in the hope of making his fortune. When he dies, his adopted daughter, Laura, travels to Washington, becomes a lobbyist, and unsuccessfully works Congress to purchase the land. Washington Hawkins, Silas's eldest son, gives up the land when he cannot pay the tax bill of $180. After the land is gone, coal is discovered on the premises. Twain wrote this section of the novel, which adds a potboiler subplot in which Laura is found not guilty of murdering her married lover and dies of remorse.

What Twain does superbly is to illustrate how capitalism creates a state of mind that leads to impulsive behavior: the system takes over the individual and not the other way around. He also convincingly depicts the close connection between capitalism and the political system: Washington politics are now inseparable from the marketplace. When not farmed, land is now subject to speculation—to be bought and sold for a profit.

The hazards of speculation are a theme continued in another Twain novel, *The American Claimant,* whose characters Colonel Beriah Sellers and Senator Abner Dilworthy are involved in a railroad bribery scandal. These novels were written in response to the political events of the times—the Crédit Mobilier scandal (1872–73) and the Homestead Act of 1862, which provided a grant of 160 acres of public land to anyone who would farm it continuously for five years. By the end of the Civil War, more than fifteen thousand homestead claims had been processed, although much of the land went to speculators; eventually the land accommodated agribusiness: larger farms in smaller numbers took advantage of the provision; very little of the land went to urban workers, who lacked the experience necessary to take up farming. By the end of the Progressive era (1914), we had come a long way from the subsistence farming on Turner's frontier.

Another literary work that takes most of these concerns for its subject matter is Mark Twain's *A Connecticut Yankee in King Arthur's Court* (1889). Twain's fantasy juxtaposes the cultures of the sixth and the nineteenth centuries. Such historical liberty allows a contrast of feudal and industrial realms, which parallel Turner's agrarian frontier and the Progressive era's industrialism. Turner's frontier is, of course, Huck's territory ahead, a realm of putative innocence beyond the corrupting reach of civilization. And Twain's industrial America demands that one accept the idea of "progress" that went with Progressivism.

But Twain also saw the dark side of the transition from one historical realm to the other (as we shall see in more detail in subsequent chapters). Twain is here telling us that technology (especially that involving implements of war) is only as good as the human nature that controls it, that human nature is flawed (sometimes because that is the way it is given, sometimes because we are the products of flawed institutions), and that he had little confidence that such technology would be used for good. Whether we inherited our flawed nature or were the flawed product of our culture, Twain saw that as a people we had come to the end of innocence. And with the end of innocence came the transformation of a nation.

Twain's response to the gilded age was the subject of Van Wyck Brooks's book on Twain, *The Ordeal of Mark Twain* (1920). Brooks was a part of a group writing for the *Seven Arts* magazine, a short-lived (1916–17) periodical of literary and political content; its life was cut short when its postal rights were canceled by the federal government in response to its antiwar sentiments. Waldo Frank was perhaps the most vocal member of the group (made up of Randolph Bourne, Gorham Munson, Frank, Brooks, and Lewis Mumford). As a group they were wary of the new industrial America with its capitalistic base. They did not turn to the ideas of Turner's frontier, but they did long for a more pastoral America modeled on garden cities, and they did look to an Emersonian idea of "soul" to implement cultural transformation. They were especially opposed to the Puritan legacy, believing that a subliminal materialism, along with a sense of evil both within the self and in the wilderness, cut humankind off from the Emersonian realm of beneficent nature, as did the rise of the Progressive movement. Despite such marginal efforts to recreate a semblance of the past, Turner's America was no more.

Waldo Frank's America picks up the elements that Brooks brought to the *Seven Arts*. Frank believed that America sprang from pure materialism, the pursuit of wealth. "No land," he proclaimed, "has ever sprung so nakedly from a direct and conscious material impulse" (1976, 120). The pioneering impulse stemmed from idealized motives that had become commercialized. Liberty involved the "right to make money"; freedom existed at the expense of regulation; political union meant the right to protect material (property) interests and ensure their power (120–21). The desire for prosperity—along with a hostile environment—turned the struggle inward. This inward pursuit was maligned by a persona like Jack London, who turned the impulse into an addiction for alcohol. Mark Twain created Huck Finn, the American "epic hero," who "expresses the movement of the American soul through all the sultry climaxes of the nineteenth century" (134). But Twain's idealized impulses are transformed by the genteel influence he encountered in the East.

The pioneer instinct eventually gave way in an industrial America: "The trail of the pioneer hardened into the Railway. Pioneering became Industrialism. Industrialism became a tool, not for production but for accumulation. Giants like Gould, Fiske, Rockefeller, Morgan, Harriman, with the consciousness and tactics of the stone-age, expressed America." Except for Lincoln, who embodied the emergence "from the materialistic culture of [industrial] America," the pioneer spirit was transformed. "What lives in Lincoln is the miracle of his achievement of spiritual values from the crude life about him" (Frank 1976, 144).

As Frank's essay reveals, the pioneer frontier—both as historical reality and as a state of mind—could not compete with a materialistic America or the impulse to control the new technology, with its capacity for force and power. The spirit of Lincoln emanated from Emerson and was carried on by Walt Whitman. But, as we shall see when we next consider Whitman, even that capacity could not endure.

9

Visions and Revision
Frontier Variants

I

Quest West can be reduced to six essential ideas about the evolution of the American frontier.

1. There were two frontiers: a wilderness frontier and an urban frontier.

2. The two frontiers supply different political agendas: the wilderness frontier better accommodates neoconservative thinking; the urban frontier, now that the liberal forces of labor have confronted the corporate realm, is more conducive to New Deal values.

3. The frontiers, especially the wilderness frontier, are as much states of mind as historical realities. They anticipate romantic destiny based on theories of nationalism—a destiny subject to revision when seen in the light of historicism.

4. The pursuit of frontier values became the pursuit of a lost vision: the pursuit of values locked into a past of transformed ideals.

5. The evolution of the frontier supplies the basis for a study of historical and literary interpretation: a changed definition of the frontier or a different theory of history can lead to a totally different way of conceptualizing a historical or literary event.

6. As the idea of the frontier changed, so did the idea of America—from frontier vision to imperial nation to the transnational assumptions of today.

II

So far our concern has been mainly with the workings of the two major frontiers, the wilderness frontier and the urban frontier. But we can also find in the historical past affinities to these movements. These affinities are three in number: the first is located in the idea of the Volk, the second is embodied in the agrarianism of the South, and the third is a national movement in which manifest destiny and the desire for imperial reach transformed the very idea of the frontier.

Romantic nationalism, with its theory of the Volk, was primarily a European movement that addressed the desire to move beyond the power of a divine-right king or of feudal lords, advocating rule from the "bottom up," not from the "top down." Such transformation of power was a key element of the romantic movement and the basis for a century of political revolution, from the French Revolution to the rise of nation-states.

One is born into a culture, not mandated by it; each citizen partakes of a nationalism based on cultural traits akin to the idea of the Volk. Included in this concern of folk culture are matters of race, language, art and literary expression, agrarian commitment, social purpose, and coherence of political and economic intent—all working in an "organic" (dynamic or living) way to give unity to the idea of a nation.

Reginald Horsman stresses the connection between language and race, arguing that the origins of racial theory stem from Indo-European language sources. Out of this tribal mix came the Aryan race, its Caucasian breed and its Anglo-Saxon language supreme. According to Horsman, "In Western Europe and America the Caucasian race became generally recognized as the race clearly superior to all the others; the Germanic was recognized as the most talented branch of the Caucasians, and the Anglo-Saxons in England and the United States, and often even in Germany, were recognized as the most gifted descendants of the Germans. . . . The Anglo-Saxons [including their linguistic heritage] were to become the final product of a long line of superior beings who stretched back through an Indo-Germanic cradle to Creation itself" (43–44).

Horsman's theory is consistent with the belief that the origins of the Volk movement were in Germany and arose from the desire to overcome Germany's national disunity. In the late eighteenth and early nineteenth centuries, Germany was a mosaic of principalities and duchies; along with Prussia and Austria, these realms composed the Holy Roman Empire, which gave way in 1806 to a loose confederation of German states in a desire for unity (the Habsburgs, a royal house of Europe, elected Holy Roman emperors between 1438 and 1740). Otto von Bismarck, working for national unity, proclaimed the Prussian king German Kaiser of the Second Reich in 1871—in what turned out to be a false effort for such unity.

A more substantial attempt at unity came from National Socialism, or the Third Reich, as a movement; it drew upon the ideas of romantic destiny as formulated by Johann Gottlieb Fichte and implemented by Anton Drexler. (The First Reich was the medieval Holy Roman Empire, 962–1806; the Second Reich included imperial Germany and the Weimar Republic, 1871–1918; and the Third Reich was a product of National Socialism, or the Nazi Party, 1933–45.) In its desire for national unification, National Socialism gave birth to beliefs in a common cause, especially belief in the superiority of the Aryan race as a basis for such unity. The original focus involved an antipathy to big business and capitalism, but these concerns were later downplayed and replaced by anti-Semitism and anti-Marxism.

The movement advocated equality of opportunity (known as "volkisch equality"). It sponsored a one-party state, outlawed strikes and lockouts, and extolled rural over urban life; especially celebrated was the return to the land and the values of living close to the soil, which encouraged a concern with the workings of nature, a belief that primary values had organic ("rooted") origins. The desire to return to the land encouraged territorial expansion (Lebensraum, or "living space"). The celebration of land, the praise of rural values, the dislike of the city, and anti-Semitism were all connected: the Jewish population was primarily urban, a product of cities, and remote from the land. Hitler took anti-Semitism one step further, arguing that Judaism and the hated Marxism were linked to the point where Marxism was a Jewish ideology.

Long before Hitler came on the scene, the volkisch movement had an extended influence in Europe. The idea of national unity took root in the eighteenth century in England and France, but by the nineteenth century—with the exception of Germany and Italy—the idea of a nation-state dominated European thinking. Eventually Germany and

Italy shed their belief in the diversity of city-state principalities and achieved unity in nationhood—Italy in 1870 and Germany in 1871. The belief in national unity had its side effects—especially its claim that national coherence brought with it unity of meaning, a unity of historical unfolding that was basic to belief in the old historicism.

In Germany, the idea of romantic nationalism took greatest hold, supporting the belief that the nation was endowed with a mystical nature, superior in racial matters, and inevitably blessed as the beneficiary of historical progress. The appeal was to feelings and intuition and not to reason. Romantic nationalism looked to past cultural glories, resurrecting lost epics (*Beowulf,* resurrected in 1871, is a case in point) and authenticating pre-Christian (pagan) religion, in both cases in pursuit of romantic ideals located in a distant past. The appeal was also to "blood" and to the "fatherland," the idea of "Blut und Boden," resulting in the belief that a member of the German (Aryan) race was endowed with a holiness and a special purpose not available to an estranged group of "others" (Jews, Marxists, socialists, homosexuals, gypsies, and the mentally and physically defective). Out of the romantic imagination came a toxic nationalism along with historical claims that led Germany into two world wars.

As previously suggested, German nationalism was firmly grounded in a German idealism that ran from Kant through Johann Gottfried von Herder and Johann Gottlieb Fichte to Hegel and was institutionalized in party movements like the Fatherland and the Nazi Party as sponsored by Anton Drexler. Joseph Goebbels repudiated capitalism on the grounds that it accommodated the Jews, but Hitler tolerated capitalism so long as it did not contradict the goals of the Nazi Party, with its claim to volkisch nationalism, its belief in Aryan racial superiority, and its romantic belief that nationhood is grounded in nature and is a living-organic process.

In its belief that meaning was imbued in geographical regions, the volkisch movement anticipated the assumptions of the wilderness frontier and American historicism. Though remote and physically disconnected by ways of implementation, the two movements nevertheless did share some common concerns. Both were grounded in the idea of national unity; both appealed to racist ideas of supremacy (Aryan in Germany, Nordic in the Old West); both heralded a return to the land and an antipathy to urban values, creating a network of "others" to strengthen the appeal to national and cultural unity; and both appealed to residual values (Turner's wilderness frontier to rugged individualism, National Socialism to coercive collectivism) as another source of that unity. In Europe, the desire for national unity thus found coincidental parallel in America, and Turner's wilderness thesis shared unintended similarities with the origins of romantic nationalism.

American romanticism shared with its European prototype an agrarianism, a sense of historical destiny, and a belief that its future legacy would be national well-being. America had analogues to the European idea of romantic nationalism. And the transformation of America into a corporate-industrial nation shared purpose with the second stage of romantic nationalism—the rise of a nationally sponsored capitalism, once removed from the fascism of National Socialism.

In 1935 Sinclair Lewis wrote a novel, *It Can't Happen Here,* depicting along lines suggested here the rise of Hitlerlike totalitarianism in America. But the dissimilarities between Hitler's Germany and a right-wing America are as important as the similarities. In America, the seeds of romantic nationalism were never planted as deeply as in Europe, perhaps because America did not have (with the possible exception of the South) a feudal past that it had to repudiate. The wilderness thesis had points of comparison with the European obsession for national unity, but the American quest for cultural identity stopped far short of the political policies that befell Europe, especially the genocide and other inhuman practices of Germany's Third Reich.

America, however, was not immune to the influence of various cult movements that functioned on the edge of the frontier. The most prominent of such movements was that of the Mormons. The origins of Mormonism go back to Joseph Smith, who was born in Vermont in 1805 and taken to western New York by his parents in 1815, settling in Palmyra. There he claimed that Moroni, a messenger of God, came to him and revealed a stone casket that held gold plates, the source of a legend inscribed in hieroglyphics, along with the magic lenses necessary to interpret them. The legend claimed that one of the Israelite tribes, the tribe of Lehi, came to America in 600 BC. There it split into two factions, the Nephites and the Lamanites. The former were white-skinned and the chosen of God; the latter were dark-skinned and the ancestors of the American Indians. The Nephites were destroyed by the Lamanites in the battle of Cumorah in AD 384. The prophet Mormon perished in this battle, but his son Moroni survived. The resurrected Christ then visited Moroni, authenticating the Book of Mormon and updating Smith to the presence of Christ in America.

Smith's claims were hostilely received, and he and his followers were driven out of New York to an outpost in Jackson County, Missouri, where they intended to build the utopian city of Zion. Subject once more to the anger of dissenters, they were driven to Kirkland, Ohio, and then to Nauvoo, Illinois, where in 1844 Smith was killed in neighboring Carthage by an angry mob. Brigham Young, who succeeded him, took the emerging flock to the Utah territory, where they settled in Salt Lake City. As for the connection between Mormonism and the frontier thesis, Mormon belief was more community-oriented than frontier individualism, and the two systems had little directly to do with each other. But they did have an indirect connection: each believed it had privileged status and that they were a law unto themselves, a product of a given destiny. Both flourished where only they could: outside the confines of an established community, in the realm of the wilderness frontier.

III

If one can find affinities between a wilderness frontier and right-wing romantic ideologies or nascent religions, one can also find parallels between the wilderness thesis and southern political ideologies. The source of the South's attempt at self-identity is in the 1930 composite of essays by twelve southern Agrarians, under the title *I'll Take My Stand*. Their explanation of why they considered the South superior to other American regions of the country, especially the North, rested primarily on its agrarian nature. Agrarianism in turn rested on the belief that rural values were superior to urban values and that an independent (yeoman) farmer in the Jeffersonian tradition was superior in occupation to a wage earner.

The best known among the southern agrarians were John Crowe Ransom, Allen Tate, and Robert Penn Warren. As a group they had an affinity with Vanderbilt University in Nashville, Tennessee, evolving there from a discussion group known as the Fugitives. They were politically conservative by nature, coupling their disdain for urbanism and industrialization to an isolationism grounded on resistance to national power and international involvement. While unanimous on their view of the South, they did not always agree on other matters of domestic and foreign policy. Seward Collins, for example, editor of the *American Review,* praised Benito Mussolini and Adolf Hitler for their anticommunism—a political leaning toward fascism that Allen Tate attacked despite its agrarian assumptions in the *New Republic.*

Despite their influence, especially in literary circles, the Agrarians met with resistance in both the North and the South. In the South they ran counter to social scientists like Howard W. Odum in his *Southern Regions of the United States* (1936) and Rupert Vance in *The Human Geography of the South* (1932). Both Odum and Vance saw southern traditionalism and the celebration of rural living as the problem and not the solution to southern decline. In the North, the New York intellectuals, whose hope for a futuristic ideal was inseparable from their belief in modern urbanism, picked up much of this argument.

A sense of progress involved looking toward the modern world of commercial-industrial urbanism; a sense of nostalgia involved looking backward to an agrarian past. The southern Agrarians had unlocked the past, bringing ideas of long standing to consideration, including John Locke's assumption, as stated in the "Second Treatise of Civil Government" (1690), that those who worked the land were its rightful owners. Locke's ideas had influenced Thomas Jefferson, who, in a letter to John Jay, wrote that farmers were "the most valuable citizens . . . most independent, the most virtuous . . . tied to their country and wedded to its liberty."

In Europe, one of the ideological ironies was that agrarianism lauded the rugged individual separate from the power of big government just as key European states were bringing megalomaniacal leaders into power. Robert Penn Warren saw this as a violation of the agrarian mandate, and in his novel *All the King's Men* (1946), Willie Stark is a rugged individualist who misuses uncontrolled political power. Warren's novel was an American cautionary tale—a warning to a Europe that had elevated Hitler, Mussolini, and Stalin to forms of uncontrolled power. Warren had said that at one point in his life he thought the agrarian life was irrelevant, but after World War II, he saw the need for the political values it encouraged.

The solution to southern cultural decline was supposedly a return to the past. As we have seen, many modernist authors saw the past as used up, a tabloid of exhausted ideas. But the southern Agrarians still located lost values in the past—values that may have been outdated but were nevertheless, from their perspective, real and worthy of restoration. The history of the frontier and the story of the South have much in common. An idealized world is transformed from within, and the perpetuation of that cultural ideal gives way to degeneration and decline.

Southern Agrarians took their agenda from the wilderness frontier as formulated by Turner and his disciples. They located frontier meaning in the "rooted" nature of the land, in agrarian stability and not thoughtless change. The two groups—the literary New Critics and the southern Agrarians—were composed of the same members with supposedly different intellectual agendas. But the connection between the Agrarians and the critics—the desire to live off the land and the desire to return to an unencumbered literary text—is not as remote as one might initially think. The missing link, the common factor and the shared concern, is a belief in the organic. The organic assumed a process built upon the living, dynamic, and developmental, which gave foundation to a common holistic purpose: a return to the fulfillment of working the land as an analogue to belief in the living autonomy of the literary text. The realm of the soil found its parallel in the realm of the autotelic text.

The idea of the organic justified the philosophical affinity between the southern Agrarians and the New Critics. Despite their difference of concern, we can find even more common ground between the Agrarians and literary critics by bringing the idea of literary excellence to poetic models that extend from the metaphysical poets to T. S Eliot. To the matter of literary tradition, the New Critics also brought the idea of textual autonomy to bear on the reading of literature that paralleled the organic nature of agrarian being. A belief in the power of organic development was the component that gave substance to both modern poetry and agrarian being—that is, the belief brought the agrarian social agenda and the literary cultural agenda closer together in both substance and mutual purpose.

Relevant to both the idea of literary criticism and the idea of a landed frontier are the novels of Thomas Wolfe and William Faulkner. Both examine the fated South in ways that anticipate the corresponding story of the closed frontier as told by Willa Cather and Scott Fitzgerald, among others. The South here is the West recast—an agrarian realm outmoded by the commercial and industrial changes on both regional and national levels that diminished, when not terminating, the way of life on the land.

IV

Like Fitzgerald and Hemingway, Thomas Wolfe (1900–1938) was published by Scribner's and edited by the famous Maxwell Perkins. Wolfe was the author of four autobiographical novels, two of which were published after his death in 1938: *Look Homeward, Angel* (1929), *Of Time and the River* (1935), *The Web and the Rock* (1939), and *You Can't Go Home Again* (1940). The novels deal with the same biographical experiences and thus duplicate one another. The novels also make use of the same themes: art versus life, the city versus the small town, and the search for a spiritual father. All of these themes are encapsulated in Wolfe's theory of time as a contrast between the river (time as flow) and the rock (time as intractable). Wolfe conflates two opposed traditions of literature. The first is a Whitmanian search for meaning on the road— that is, the search for a meaning by experiencing life. The second is a Joycean realm of art as privileged meaning, art as providing a unique perspective, as a coda to the meaning of life. The Whitmanian emphasis involves the search; the Joycean involves a way of seeing.

Wolfe believes that there is a confluence between the two forms of art: the search precedes the way of seeing. This takes us to what there is to be seen. For example, contrasts involve the difference between the city and the town, the North and the South, America and Europe. The young man in these novels becomes disillusioned with his natural father and rejects both his birth father and his provincial town. Unlike many southern writers, Faulkner for example, Wolfe reconciles himself to a transformed world and repudiates the longing for a lost South. He does this by taking us to the next evolutionary step—the journey to the city in search of a larger self. While the city is throbbing with life, the urban experience is a lonely one: people pass each other in the night; time is in flight; the romantic essence of life (what Wolfe refers to as the "unfound door") remains unfound, even as the search takes the seeker to far reaches. Like Joyce's young artist, Wolfe looks for the moment of epiphany, for the experience that will bring meaning to the search. Whereas a southern writer like Faulkner bewails the loss of an Edenic past, Wolfe commits himself to making sense of a time-bound reality as it unfolds with time past and time present as one.

The journey brings an encounter between two kinds of characters that make up what is essential in American life: the Babbitt figure and the hedonist. The Babbitt figure is the philistine who has reduced the meaning of life to material pursuits; the hedonist is the pleasure-seeking figure who wastes his time in debauched pursuits. Wolfe's protagonist finds little of substance to justify a choice between the two. At times the hedonist gives way to the aesthete, who reduces the meaning of life to forms of art. Wolfe's characters are often attracted to such a personality before they dismiss him as too intangible.

Wolfe defines these character types in *Of Time and the River*. Eugene Gant witnesses the Babbitt figure as he rides in the smoker of the train that is taking him from the provincial South to Harvard University and the urban East. Robert Weaver, whom he meets in Boston, embodies the hedonist. The two types offer extreme ways of experiencing life: one reducing it to an obsession with investment profit, the other to a mindless pursuit of pleasure, both to trivial ends. The aesthete, Francis Starwick, seems to offer more substantial possibilities. Eugene is attracted to him at first, but then he realizes that Starwick's pursuit of the beautiful is as empty as Babbitt's pursuit of money. Starwick wants to write the great American novel, structured on the Mississippi River, a region where he lived as a child. But he has lost contact with that world; indeed, he has lost contact with the land, that element that binds the southern imagination. He goes to Europe, adopts Continental manners and values, and repudiates America.

Starwick's fate ironically parallels the fate of George Webber (the Gant figure renamed) in Wolfe's last novel, *You Can't Go Home Again*. Here Webber comes to realize what was a truism for F. Scott Fitzgerald—that the past has been emptied of its meaning, that you cannot buy back the past, cannot resurrect past ideals once they are gone. The past is not a stable, solid block of meaning to which one can return at will. Present reality transforms the past. Because the past is constantly being emptied of meaning, "you cannot go home again," cannot go back to family, lost loves, old friends, familiar places. Once time has moved on, as Proust knew, past meaning both alters the present and transforms itself. To seek meaning in the past is to seek it in a realm that will never come again. Perhaps Wolfe's most genuine contribution to American literature was his ability to see that the ideals of the past have been transformed by a materialistic (commercial-industrial) society and that the antebellum world was lost forever.

V

In many ways, William Faulkner begins where Thomas Wolfe leaves off. Faulkner's world divides in two: events take on meaning depending on whether they take place before or after the Civil War. By 1865 the South was transformed; the old aristocracy was gone, and so also were the southern mansions, along with the land that brought the mansions into being. All was in a process of decline. The burden of this transformed time fell on a new generation, thrice removed from the war but still living with the legends that were passed down and trying to make sense out of a new social reality infused with the commercial and industrial being that the North imposed on the South.

Faulkner's world is heroically diminished, tragic in its fall from high to lower estate. A sense of decline sits heavily on the remains of the old aristocracy, whether it is Sartoris, whose sense of remorse is turned outward toward a life of self-destructiveness, or Quentin Compson, whose remorse is turned inward toward suicide. The decline has a mutant quotient, spawning Benjy, the idiot child of the Compson family, and James Bond, the deranged end product of the Sutpen line.

Faulkner's world is basically naturalistic, a realm in which heredity and environment have extreme influence; but it has been transformed into a modernist realm through the universalizing use of myth and the internalizing of historical time. In *Absalom, Absalom!* (1936), the Absalom story becomes a parable of the Civil War, with Thomas Sutpen's children turning upon him and on each other, as the fratricide element of the novel finds its equivalent in the war itself, which in turn is universalized in the Cain and Abel story.

Faulkner's heroic world has been turned upside down, leaving us in the realm of modern gothic. Faulkner's story of Temple Drake is a modern version of *Clarissa* (1748), by Samuel Richardson (1689–1761). The sublimity of the romance has been inverted. We are in the dying if not dead world of the father; the estate is in gothic decline; the world of the children is one of incest and fratricide. Romantic principles like honor have been played out and are now abstract ideals, dead to the living. The wilderness has given way to the wasteland.

Behind southern Agrarianism was the belief in property, at times breathtaking in its scale (Sutpen's "one hundred" refers to the one hundred square miles of land that he owned, along with its slaves, sharecroppers, and declining wilderness). Sutpen's decline has its counterpart in other cultures and repeats the stories of both Greek and biblical tragedy. The story of Sutpen is that of the aristocratic ideal emptied of meaning, leaving only its empty shell, rituals cut off from their origins, an ironic commentary on itself. The mind has been driven compulsively inward, looking for causal explanation (Quentin); women have become caricatures of southern maidens (Rosa Coldfield) or southern virtue (Temple Drake); property has replaced honor; money has replaced time.

As Faulkner inverts the heroic quality of the romance, he inverts the Christ story in *Light in August*. Joe Christmas incarnates hate turned back on itself. The product of Doc Hines and later McEachern's racial hatred, he is beyond redemption, whether the redemptive motherly love of Mrs. McEachern or the redemptive sexual love of Bobbie Allen. He is the product of miscegenation: the black pants and white shirt he wears symbolize his divisive black and white nature—a fact the novel presumes but never verifies, making his story a state of mind. Joe Christmas incarnates the modern South, its history turned back upon itself, the self in pursuit of its own destruction. In the center of Faulkner's Jefferson is the courthouse, on top of which is the town clock, ironically centered, as is the jail beneath. Thus in the center of Faulkner's world are both the clock and the jail, time as a prison. "All was is," Faulkner tells us. There is no escape from history, the past now infused with the present in a kind of Bergsonian bond that plays itself out as Spenglerian decline.

The events leading to the end of the wilderness are recounted in the collection of stories that make up *Go Down, Moses* (1942), including perhaps Faulkner's best novella, *The Bear*. Sections 1 through 3 of *The Bear* tell the story of Ike McCaslin, who grows up in Mississippi after the Civil War. From the time he is ten, he goes on bear hunts with his cousin Cass Edmonds and the leading citizens. This part is an initiation story. When he is sixteen, Boon Haggenbeck and the mongrel dog

Lion kill the bear. Chronologically, the next section of the story takes place in section 5, not 4. It is two years later; he is now eighteen: Ike has come back to the wilderness to find it no longer wilderness. The lodge is gone, hunters have disbanded, and the lumber company has moved in and is cutting what remains of the forest. In section 4, three years later, Ike is twenty-one: he has come into his inheritance at the same time that he discovers that his grandfather, Carothers McCaslin, has seduced one of his slaves and later has a child by the girl (his own daughter) who was born of that union. Ike repudiates his legacy, becomes a carpenter suggestive of the Christ story, and lives a hermetic existence. The novella closes with the train, now carrying its load of lumber, snaking its way through the diminished wilderness, symbolic of the serpent in the garden. The New Testament links the fall in the garden to original sin. Faulkner links the fall of the New World garden to miscegenation, often coupled with incest, his proxy for original sin. In one instance, the garden has given way to the imperfect world of humanity; in another instance, the garden has given way to the lumberyard.

Faulkner's is an agrarian world in the process of industrial transformation. Much that is evil in Faulkner's world has come down the railroad tracks from Memphis, roughly fifty miles to the northwest, and tainted the town. The New South in great part was embodied by the Snopes family, who came mysteriously from the North, infiltrated the town through Frenchman's Bend, and is now in the process of claiming possession of the town in the name of greed. What takes place in Faulkner's world is seen mostly through the eyes of the town, and much of that involves a process of decline from the world of the old aristocracy. The story of the town, with its transformation of the old aristocracy and the rise of the Snopes family, is told in a trilogy made up of *The Hamlet* (1940), *The Town* (1957), and *The Mansion* (1958). The three novels compose a sustained story of the loss of honor and chivalry. Yet such a loss was destined: the present empties the past.

As we move in Spenglerian terms from an agrarian to an urban realm, we move from harmony to disharmony, from one value system to another. We move through the heroic, the tragic, the romantic to a fallen world in which the capacity for action is gone. We are left with Flem Snopes, whose world is now overlooked by Gavin Stevens, the man of paralyzed will. Change transformed Faulkner's postwar world, and yet the seeds of this change were planted long before, when the idea of property was extended to those who oversaw rather than those who actually worked the land—when the land became equated with money rather than with work. The prewar South prided itself on chivalry and honor, now overtaken by materialism and greed. The sins of the fathers have been passed down to the sons, one of the many biblical themes that universalize the meaning of Faulkner's world. Faulkner plays out a Spenglerian legacy that he shares with such other moderns as Pound and Fitzgerald. Once the wilderness is gone, once the land has been transformed, once the pursuit of money replaces the rewards of work, Faulkner's world is taken over by the same process of decline that we have repeatedly witnessed in this study of the Turner frontier wilderness. The past is emptied; the ideal has failed and left us with lost innocence; and the historical promise has given way to a legacy of decline. Despite the differences, the worlds of Fitzgerald and Faulkner have shared elements, especially the Spenglerian belief that we are locked into a past, the ideals of which we continue to pursue even after they are long gone.

VI

This has been a study in transformations. Transformations involve the ability of literary and political reality to alter ideological content. Transformations usually involve generational change, but in every case they involve seeing older visions through new ones: the revisions displace status quo authority and open up the subject for new ways of thinking and talking about it. Such change creates alternative explanations of history; there is a need to know why the primary view was transformed, an obligation to see how newer interpretations are extrapolations of older ones, and a need for the newer vision to make clear how it is building upon or changing an original view.

A new America arose from the transformed values of an older America. The drive for empire, for example, rested in great part on the religious need to bear the white man's burden. Max Weber saw how religion and economics came together when Protestantism (especially Calvinism) moved the country toward a less cohesive society, putting the emphasis upon the individual to engage in personal enterprises through trade and investment wealth. Despite an increasingly rationalized (bureaucratic) society, the country witnessed the end of collectivism, with its sense of tradition and normative standards, and the rise of a norm-less individualism that presumed a disharmony between the individual and the community. This transformation involved the movement from community to narcissism.

Theodore Roosevelt was concerned with men and battles and the winning of the West. Frederick Jackson Turner, in contrast, looked to institutions as the source of historical change. But the two did share common ground: they both were aware that the frontier was a meeting ground for the primitive and the civilized, and they both were convinced that the frontier mentality prepared the country for the next historical phase—the reach of empire. A major transformation was the movement of America from an isolationist to an imperialist nation. The move from frontier to imperial nation was inevitable, especially when one believes the right to accumulate land is a matter of destiny. The move to extend the frontier by imperial acquisition was in the air at the end of the nineteenth century. As we have seen, Frank Norris anticipated an imperial America when he gave consent to the belief that the direction of modern civilization was moving along a western frontier, from Europe to America, and from America to the Pacific: as proof of America's extended engagement, he cited Dewey's exploits in Manila and the participation of U.S. marines in China during the Boxer Rebellion.

Nineteenth-century historians were constrained by the idea of *nation:* each country had its own boundaries and its own laws and was subject to its own institutions and culture. Variations of life might exist within the nation as a whole (the western United States reflected a ethos different from that the northeastern United States), but each area was subject to the authority of the federal government and its laws. Turner's frontier thesis was the product of such nineteenth-century thinking, with roots in the idea of nation. His frontier was composed of rugged individualists who supported principles of democracy and advocated national expansion, validated by a willingness to go to battle or to war against American Indians or foreign countries.

In America, this expansion-isolation issue was a nineteenth-century matter. The imperial reach created a sequence of new frontiers. The American Southwest was a frontier product of the war with Mexico; Puerto Rico, Guam, and the Philippines came to the United

States as bounty from the war with Spain—Cuba also, before receiving its independence in 1893; Hawaii's connection to America came via a settler's coup that led to independence and eventual absorption as an American colony and later as a state in 1959; and parts of the Northwest were acquisitions from the struggle with England. Each region (or "section," as Turner phrased it) had a character, if not a culture, of its own and functioned as a frontier appendage to the body politic.

Today we have gone beyond the constraints of nationhood and live in a world of flexible borders. As a result, we have on a global level a parallel to the nation-frontier dictates that preoccupied Turner. We have, analogous to the American Union, world powers that tend to meld into each other (including Russia now that we have gone beyond the Soviet Union and the Cold War), with third-world countries made up mostly of tribal Arabian (Near East) states (as Spengler actually predicted).

This new frontier is supposedly ambivalent to the call of democracy and militant to the extent of demanding institutional and political corrections. Today culture, not borders or citizenship, separates the global powers and their subsidiaries. Turner's thesis today is subject to revisions based on a changing idea of nation as well as a change in what is meant by marketplaces. We now live in a global city, where Bombay and Beijing are part of our economic order and their populations part of our labor supply. The idea of borders that separate us from other nations is eroding. While immigration practices may still be a matter of law, it is law often more broken than enforced. We still have a frontier situation—only now with global nations as protectors of third-world countries. Transformed by global reach and a different cast of characters, Turner's frontier is a lost vision, a historical scroll relevant to another world, to another moment of time.

10

The Dark Side of the Way West

I

A major theme in American literature involves the idea of an American Adam. The play of a mythic Adam and a real-life innocent characterizes much of the literature. The mythic Adam is a man outside time, an abstracted phenomenon who embodies pure idea—nature, the wilderness, or the call of space or open land. The American innocent stands alone; he has no past, follows no tradition, has little or no sense of history; he is a creature of his own making, the product of the frontier, outside the realm of town and civilization, more likely to be found in the literary Western than in other narrative forms; he tests his strength against both natural and manmade forces.

There are, of course, two Adams: the innocent Adam before the fall and the sinful Adam after the fall. The American Adam is usually thought of in terms of the former, the embodiment of innocence. But both are present in the American experience—the first in anticipation of the New World, the second as participant as well as witness to its transformation. In literary naturalism there is an opposition between the will of a character and the forces of a prevailing environment. The American Adam is the product of his innocence; he lives in a realm where free will and extrinsic forces tend to reinforce rather than contradict each other. But his innocence is subject to transformation: he desires—but never quite succeeds—to remain outside the domain of evil.

The elements that compose the myth of the American Adam are to be found in Hawthorne's *The Scarlet Letter,* especially in the duality between the wilderness and the town or community. The wilderness is the realm outside of time; the town or community is the historical realm within time. The wilderness involves the element of passion: the sex between Hester and Dimmesdale; Pearl, who is the product of this passion, finds herself strangely free in the wilderness; so does the evil Chillingworth. The wilderness is outside the law. Hester lives between the town and the wilderness, and the scenes involving her and Dimmesdale all take place in the wilderness. If Cooper takes us to the limits of the New World garden (the garden that represents the wilderness tamed), Hawthorne takes us to the limits of the wilderness. Dimmesdale has lost Adamic innocence: he is Adam after the fall. His redemption is not in the wilderness but in the village. It is in the town, on the scaffold, that Dimmesdale is redeemed, when he confesses publicly that he seduced Hester and is the father of Pearl. Here he escapes the hold of Chillingworth and is welcomed back into the community.

Hawthorne's tale includes the components of the two frontier theses: its essential elements involve an exchange between Turner's frontier and the city. One is the realm of individual pursuit, the other of communal reunion; one is the product of nature, the other of society; one works within the realm of time, the other outside of time. What happens in the wilderness reveals Adam in a state of innocence; what happens on the scaffold reveals the fallen Adam in the process of redemption. Hawthorne's American Adam is the product of Puritan belief—sinner in the realm of nature, redeemer in the realm of the community—where lost innocence is made stronger by the fall.

Melville reverses this sequence of events. One of Melville's key themes depicts the city as a fallen realm. In *Moby-Dick,* we first see Ishmael leaving New York, which has become for him an unnatural realm; he goes to Nantucket in search of lost innocence, the purity that might be found at sea. Ishmael steps out of history into nature, just the opposite of what Hawthorne's Dimmesdale does. But once on the sea, he realizes that it also can be transformed by the way it is observed, as when Ahab superimposes an evil residual in nature onto Moby-Dick and, by extension, onto the mystery of the sea.

Once Ahab sees evil as a part of nature, he becomes obsessed with destroying the wilderness (now embodied in Moby-Dick), despite the human cost—a theme Melville treats in *Typee* (1846) and *The Confidence Man* (1857), as well as in *Moby-Dick* (1851). In *Typee,* Tom, the narrator, jumps ship at the port city of Nukuheva, on one of the foreboding Polynesian islands in the Marquesas chain in the South Pacific. He is picked up by the Typees, the native tribe known for its cannibalism (limited to the dead of enemy tribes). Despite such practices, Tom is impressed by their culture, which involves working the land and living in harmony with nature. Tom comes to the conclusion that the primitive life is superior to the civilized life, that the city involves a process of decline rather than a mark of progress. Tom steps out of historical time when he reverts to the life of the Typees and then back in time when he returns to the port city with the realization that, as a product of the modern world, he cannot escape the influence of the city.

We can find still another version of the fall from innocence in *The Confidence Man*. A group of diverse passengers board the *Fidele*, scheduled to make its way down the Mississippi from St. Louis to New Orleans, plying a course on the edge of the open West. In a novel that contains narratives within narratives, we meet Colonel John Moredeck, the son of a pioneer woman who has lost three husbands to attacks from Indians; he is with her when she is attacked once again, along with his brothers and sisters. Surviving while his family is exterminated, Moredeck becomes her avenger, going in pursuit of the last attackers and killing twenty who made up the band. Instead of satisfying his desire for vengeance, this experience only whets his appetite for the extermination of more Indians.

Like Captain Ahab, Moredeck becomes obsessed with destroying what is for him the embodiment of evil, the reality that impinges on his desire for the reign of innocence. Like Ahab, he believes he can, through the strength of his will, destroy all elements of evil that work in the wilderness. In Ahab, Melville takes us to the edge of insanity, to runaway obsession that challenges the moral limits of the Enlightenment: the belief that nature can be transformed and the primitive turned into a realm of innocence. For Hawthorne and Melville, the American Adam discovers how fragile such innocence may be.

Turner's pioneers were a step ahead of Melville's characters: they were the product of the wilderness, subject to its transformations—and the transformation into the American Adam was one of them. This figure finds his identity in the Western in the character of Shane or the Virginian. We see him as a loner or an independent individualist, find him on the edge of civilization; he is usually homeless, thus often on the move, a man with a mysterious past who believes in action more than words, who, like the sheriff in *High Noon,* has recourse to the gun when all else fails. In this context, *High Noon* is a derivative of *The Virginian.* In both there is a woman; in *The Virginian* she is Molly, the schoolteacher from Vermont, who embodies eastern or more traditional values, especially those involving justice. Despite the presence of the sheriff and a judge, when the Virginian hangs Steve in the name of frontier justice, more vigilante than traditional justice is at stake; it is thus a moral as well as a romantic conversion that prevails when Molly accepts the Virginian (and presumably his western code) after he wins the shootout with Trampas.

The pioneer's more peaceful origins can be found in Cooper, Emerson, Thoreau, and Whitman. And with selective reference to the above characteristics, we can find semblances of him in our major literature in such characters as Huck Finn, Jay Gatsby, Holden Caufield, Augie March, and Raymond Chandler's Philip Marlowe, the private detective in Los Angeles. With the exception of Huck, these characters have no direct contact with the wilderness, but they do share some of its values, especially the sense of self-reliance.

The wilderness thus offers a remote legacy of what these characters held in common, shaped as they were by its lost mold, their fates in quest of or beckoning back to a reality long gone. What we mean by civilization, especially as it is confronted by the wilderness, is a topic that lies deep in the literary imagination of America and remains to be addressed here.

II

Mark Twain's works tend to develop in bunches, with one work anticipating its sequel. For example, *The Gilded Age* was followed by *The American Claimant; The Adventures of Tom Sawyer* (1876) was followed by *The Adventures of Huckleberry Finn* (1885), *Tom Sawyer Abroad* (1894), and *Tom Sawyer, Detective* (1896); *The Prince and the Pauper* by *Pudd'nhead Wilson;* and *The Innocents Abroad* (1867) by *Roughing It* (1872).

Despite the sequential nature of the compositions, Twain's works are not always thematically in sync with each other. For example, his depiction of human nature sometimes changes radically. There is the assumption that Huck Finn acts out of an innate sense of innocence, while the inhabitants of Hadlyburg are morally flawed and appear to be innocent only because their virtue has never been tested. The community, often presented as the small town or village, is the most commonly flawed and the source of lost innocence. Huck seems to realize this intuitively, which explains his desire to stay ahead of the encroaching territory. Twain's views just before his death—perhaps influenced by the deaths of his wife and children, his own illness, and his skirmish with bankruptcy—are even more pessimistic; they are documented graphically in "The Mysterious Stranger" and "What Is Man?"

If for some the rise of civilization means the end of the wilderness, for Mark Twain something like the opposite prevailed, confirming his belief that if prototypical American characters begin as innocents, they soon lose their pristine being to the corrupting environment. Mark Twain was among the last to see the possibility of a new beginning in the American experience, but by the end of the Civil War—despite his fascination with science and the new technology—he realized that the ideal had given way to a destructiveness that came with the new technology and to the rapaciousness of a new capitalism.

Twain confronts the new capitalism in various ways. One of his major themes is the need for a new culture to go beyond the dictates of the medieval world, controlled as it was by the Catholic Church and feudal institutions. He treats this theme in *The Prince and the Pauper* and in *A Connecticut Yankee,* where he contrasts the sixth century with the nineteenth and the feudal South with the industrial North—that is, where the difference between feudalism and capitalism is both a chronological and a spatial matter. Time and war erased the evils of feudalism only to replace them with the abuses of the capitalism he and Charles Dudley Warner depicted in *The Gilded Age.* There was no residual innocence to which the country could return. Even the ideal of the West was problematic, given the debased human nature that the pioneers brought with them. Civilization contaminated rather than freed man; rapaciousness delimited generosity. The new man was bent on controlling the wilderness, turning the power of nature into forms of (destructive) wealth.

Twain's most incisive depiction of the contrast between innocence and degeneration was *Huckleberry Finn* (1885). Huck tries to preserve his sense of innocence and freedom against the fallen nature of humanity and encroaching forms of "civilization." We see the worst in human development embodied by Huck's drunken father, a stultifying religious mentality on the part of Widow Douglas, the senseless family feud between the Grangerfords and the Shepherdsons, the runaway honor of Colonel Sherburn and the cowardice of the mob, and the outrageous fraudulence of the king and the dauphin. All of this is contrasted to the genuine human affection between Huck and Jim—an affection that springs from a natural innocence that defies prevailing conventions. Like Henry James, albeit with a totally different set of characters, Twain questions the moral center of his story: Pa and Widow Douglas embody discredited or questionable values, while Huck's sense of right and wrong is authentic: humanity is located in the outcast, while morality stays a step ahead of "sivilization."

Twain takes us to the American great divide—to the Mississippi and the promise of what lies beyond, to "the territory ahead" that will also become the concern of Cather, Fitzgerald, and Nathanael West. But what he is looking for beyond the Mississippi and what he will find are two different things. *Huckleberry Finn* is a novel in which we can begin to see America losing its innocence (or at least a claim to innocence) as Huck's heart wins out over conscience and a lost individuality triumphs over community. Twain in his novel depicts a society gone astray; Twain in his other writing depicts a foreign policy equally remiss.

After *Huckleberry Finn,* the idea of community had to be rethought, and the major American authors eventually came to the conclusion that America had taken the wrong path. Spiritualism was more a state of mind than a religious reality. The American experience took us from hope to doubt, from the belief in a new beginning to the realization that national ambition—the commitment to policies like manifest destiny and later imperialism—was simply the repetition of a dubious mandate, the call to runaway power.

The work in which Twain most directly takes on these questions, including concerns over the moral aspects of human nature, is *A Connecticut Yankee* (1889). Here he depicts modern technology creating a new materialism that increases the power of the military. But before he gets to the topic of misplaced technology, he takes on what he considers the wrongs of the Middle Ages. He satirizes the medieval idea of chivalry and the romantic idea of the Middle Ages as depicted by

Sir Walter Scott. The novel is one of the earliest to make use of time travel: Twain was aware of Edward Bellamy's *Looking Backward* (1888), which anticipates William Morris's *News from Nowhere* (1891) and H. G. Wells's *The Time Machine* (1895). Morris's *News from Nowhere* was written in response to Bellamy's *Looking Backward*. Morris's libertarian socialism was offered as a corrective to Bellamy's state socialism. Morris postulated an agrarian society that had similarities to Turner's wilderness frontier. Unlike Turner, Morris eliminated the monetary system and other public institutions, replacing private property with common ownership. But like Turner's wilderness, Morris's fantasy was based on the workings of an agrarian society and the absence of big cities with their commercial institutions. In this world individual mandates had priority over institutional mandates.

In Twain's *Connecticut Yankee,* the time traveler is Hank Morgan, the superintendent in a Connecticut arms factory. Hank gets in a fight and is knocked unconscious by a blow to the head from a crowbar. When he regains consciousness, he finds that he has been transported to King Arthur's court in the sixth century. This narrative device gives Twain the ability to contrast the flaws in medieval feudalism and in modern industry. One is the product of authoritarian rule: the monarchy and the Catholic Church as well as the dubious rituals of chivalry; the other is the product of the new science, with the often betrayed potentiality to influence the human situation for the better. While Twain prefers the age of technology over the age of chivalry, he is quick to point out the flaws in both systems, stemming from man's flawed human nature.

Hank uses the new science to overwhelm his medieval hosts by predicting a solar eclipse, by rigging electric devices that blow up Merlin's tower, by establishing a network of factories throughout the country that produce modern tools, by restoring running water to a holy fountain, and by persuading King Arthur to abandon the practice of slavery. But while such matters, with their corresponding technology, can work for the good, Hank goes beyond the beneficent and creates a technology that takes him to the killing fields. Armed with a Gatling gun, electrifying a minefield, he literally buries himself under the mountain of dead that he slaughters.

Twain is telling us that technology is only as good as the human nature that controls it and that he has little confidence that such technology will always be used for good. If Huck Finn acts out of innocence, and if on the raft he does what is right intuitively, Hank seems more the product of the Progressive era, more the beneficiary of a transformed America with a more militant agenda. Hank, we remember, worked in an arms factory in his modern incarnation, at a time when arms were at a premium to fight the wars that needed to be fought to sustain America's new imperialist policy—a policy that Twain abhorred. Modern man's technological achievements are indeed impressive, but they are morally no better than the human nature that employs them.

Twain believed that human nature was determined by and a product of culture. There is a Rousseaulike quality to his thinking about the nature of man. We are born innocent and then transformed by the institutions and ideologies of our culture. We can begin to see the transformation at work in Tom Sawyer, who gets his ideas from romances and already adheres to the dictates of chivalry. Huck manages to stay in the realm of natural innocence by staying ahead—that is, by remaining outside of—the constricting realms of society. By implication Twain was telling us that there is a residual innocence in the "territory ahead," ahead of civilization, in what in effect is Turner's wilderness frontier. Short of the frontier, innocence is a perishable product. When Twain looks from medieval man, the product of chivalry, to modern man, the product of the industrial revolution, he finds much to question in each cultural system. As different as they may be, they both determine the nature of one's motives. In each age we find elements of the heroic, but we also find a moral constant that questions whether human nature is programmed to function beyond a nascent innocence.

Twain's meaning has its origins in the interpretive assumptions we bring to his narrative. But criticism can differ on what is central to literary interpretation. In the Norton edition of *Huckleberry Finn,* we have a series of essays that speak to each other. Each essay brings a different meaning to the novel. Leo Marx, for example, believes the novel is about achieving the ultimate freedom for Jim. Richard Adams believes the novel is about the state of romance that Tom and Huck bring to their respective idea of adventure. For Marx, the ending that has Jim as a prisoner on the Phelps farm is irrelevant: the novel has already ended when Huck sets Jim free. For Adams, the episode on the Phelps farm continues the exchange between Tom and Huck and is central to the conclusion of the novel. Each reading depends on an interpretive starting point: Marx's is the idea of freedom; Adams's is the idea of romance. What follows are different interpretations of the same novel. It becomes difficult, if not impossible, to say that one interpretation is better than the other, so long as the controlling context, what amounts to an interpretive starting point, remains a matter of opinion.

The point here is charged with meaning relevant to critical theory in general and is pertinent to the meaning of this study. The way the frontier was defined determined the way we viewed America. The frontiers as depicted are the subject of superimposed interpretations: each definition anticipated a given conclusion. The wilderness frontier brought with it the realm of rugged individualism. The urban frontier brought with it a sense of industrial community. Each starting point offered a coherent meaning of its own, each a variant America, each the by-product of a thesis that led to a different conclusion.

III

More than his contemporaries, Walt Whitman was writing with a spirit that has long been lost in America. There is a great divide between his world and ours. In the abstract, what is lost is a state of mind; in the concrete, what is lost is a belief in America as a realm of new possibility. That sense of historical possibility—of destiny—came from many sources. One emerged from the myth of the land, discussed above, the belief that there is an essence, a destiny both personal and communal, connected with the nation. Out of this sense of quest came the thrust of Whitman's poetry and the tradition inherited by those who followed, such as Thomas Wolfe and Jack Kerouac.

The pioneer movement was based on a state of mind, based on blind faith that a more glorious moment was up ahead. But such faith failed to recognize the great divide in American culture, in which an agrarian idealism found itself contested by the rise of an industrial society that negated the Jeffersonian vision. With the rise of finance capitalism, the new republic found itself bending to forms of power that negated the idea of pure democracy. After Whitman's generation, agrarian destiny was transformed, even to the extent that as a state of mind Scott Fitzgerald believed it marked a time that would never come again. There was a loss of innocence because there was nothing to take the place of the mythic ideals that generated Whitman's sense of the One, the sublime, the heroic, and the mythic. The quest was eventually a mirage (as the modernist demonstrated). But it powered a frontier movement and the literature that went with it. Whitman wrote his poems when he believed in the promises of an America that went beyond the poem—promises that faded, even for him, as we see in "Democratic Vistas."

Whitman began to doubt his easy optimism when he read Thomas Carlyle's "Shooting Niagara; and After" (1867), in which Carlyle questioned the meaning of American democracy in the face of government by popular vote and herd rule. He also questioned the wisdom of three hundred thousand white men dying in order to give the vote to 3 million blacks. Whitman's initial response to Carlyle's harangue was anger, but the more he considered democracy as the product of mob rule controlled by special-moneyed interests, the more his doubts took on substance. Whitman's view darkened as he worked himself through "Democratic Vistas," which began as a revision of three previous essays—"Democracy," "Personalism," and "Orbic Literature"—that he had tacked together and then moved through a series of drafts over a period of four years, concluding with the belief that if America continued in its current direction, it might well end up "the most tremendous failure of time" (1950, 461).

Whitman had opposed slavery in the free states, but he had serious reservations about the ability of whites and blacks to live together harmoniously. Whitman's racial views were long seeded. In a *Brooklyn Daily Times* editorial in 1858, he had raised the question, "Who believes that Whites and Blacks can ever amalgamate in America? Or who wishes it to happen? Nature has set an impassable seal against it." Whitman's growing concerns about the future of America were intensified by other racial matters, specifically his dislike of immigrant Catholics, especially the Irish, who were transforming New York. Such matters confirmed his belief that the future of the American city was in the West.

But even the hope of the West was qualified by the effect of the new technologies like the Atlantic cable and the expansion of the railroad—activities that reduced democracy to investment money and threatened national purpose (the democratic One). The federal government and big business were getting stronger as the people were getting weaker. The National Banking Act (1863), the charter of the Union Pacific and

Central Pacific Railroad, the Fourteenth Amendment, which gave corporations the same legal rights as the individual—all worked against the hope of an ideal democracy.

In "Democratic Vistas," Whitman lamented the change: "The spectacle is appalling.... The depravity of the business classes of our country is not less than has been supposed, but infinitely greater. The official services of America, national, state, and municipal, in all their branches, except the judiciary, are saturated in corruption, bribery, falsehood, maladministration and the judiciary tainted. The great cities reek with respectable as much as non-respectable robbery and scoundrelism" (1950, 467). Whitman spoke for his generation: from faith in the soil to industrial doubt, a vision of an inspired America had come and gone.

IV

Willa Cather intensifies the Whitmanian sequence of hope giving way to doubt as she takes the "idea of the West" theme to the prairies of Nebraska and to the resolute people who turned the limitless land into a way of life. Some came before the Civil War, but many were attracted by the "free land" available after the war. The Union Pacific Railroad was completed in 1869, and the Burlington Route entered southern Nebraska in the 1870s, bringing thousands of settlers to the midlands prairie.

In her novels, Cather makes use of four landscapes. The first is the prairie and its farm; the second is the town, once removed from the land, where life becomes a bit more conventional; the third is a city like Lincoln, even further removed from the land, the seat of a midwestern university and a source of prairie culture; and the fourth is New York City and Cambridge, Massachusetts, the opposite of the land and the location of a great eastern university that can educate the remnants of pioneer stock, transforming them culturally so that they can take their place in corporate America.

The wilderness thesis maintains that the development of modern America involves progression from land to city. But Cather insists that the prairie soul, a product of the land, will be transformed, carry an agrarian stamp, and be both different from other regions and better because of it. This is the main theme of *My Antonia* (1918), the story of the Shimerda family. Mr. Shimerda could never reconcile himself to this new world, and his loneliness and homesickness for Bohemia led to his suicide. His daughter Antonia perseveres, sustains her husband in a way her mother could not sustain her father, and is the source of stability until a second generation is in place. The story is told from the point of view of Jim Burden, who, like Antonia, is a product of the land, even as he leaves Nebraska for a Harvard University law degree and eventually the corporate world of New York. The road has taken him in a circle, and although he has moved far beyond the realm of Antonia and the land, the two share a beneficently determined past. As Jim tells us at the end: "I had a sense of coming home to myself. . . . For Antonia and for me, this had been the road of Destiny. . . . Whatever we had missed, we possessed together the precious, the incommunicable past" (272). But much of this is sheer nostalgia for a lost world. Cather realized that the frontier experience was over, was now in the moneyed hands of men like Wick Cutters, who had lost contact with the land and whose obsession for money proved self-destructive.

Cather treats a variation of this theme in *A Lost Lady* (1922), a novel that had indelible influence on F. Scott Fitzgerald's *The Great Gatsby*. Captain Forrester, who came to the plains after the Civil War and was instrumental in building the railroad, embodies the meaning of the frontier. His spirit is carried on by his young wife, Marian, who becomes for Niel Herbert, the moral presence in the novel, a force for good. Frank Ellinger and Ivy Peters, both of whom have lost contact with the land and in turn corrupt Mrs. Forrester, embody the force of decline. The novel ends on a note of loss: Niel "had seen the end of an era, the sunset of the pioneer. He had come upon it when already its glory was nearly spent. . . . This was the very end of the road-making West. . . . It was already gone, that age; nothing could ever bring it back." But ideals die hard: Niel cannot forgive Mrs. Forrester for betraying the past, the spirit of the frontier, now a lost ideal that has been overtaken by a material realm, no longer the incarnation of innocence, a realm emptied of possibility. It is this theme that Fitzgerald brought to *The Great Gatsby*.

Cather again offers a choice between an idealized (lost) past and a diminished present in *The Professor's House* (1925). The contrast here is drawn by setting the primitive Cliff City (modeled on Mesa Verde, on the border between Colorado and New Mexico) against Washington,

DC. Dug out of rock cliffs, the lost city may have had a population of as many as seventy thousand. As it became more civilized, it became less militant and was probably destroyed by a less advanced tribe. Tom Outland finds the city, but he fails to get the federal government to declare it a national monument.

The professor's study of the Spanish conquest—a story of military victory, not defeat—establishes a thematic contrast to the story of Cliff City. The professor has come to the end of a distinguished career and feels that he has little to live for. When his family is away, he almost dies when the wind—as if facilitating his self-destructive wish—blows out the stove's gas pilot. The professor survives, thanks to Augusta, who arrives in time to save him from asphyxiation. Augusta—the devoted family servant, the Antonia figure in the novel—embodies the spirit of willed life.

The novel contrasts two states of mind: a modernist desire to control the land in pursuit of material goods, and a pioneer desire to live in harmony with the land. The latter ideal is embodied by Augusta and by the inhabitants of Cliff City; it also supplies a source of new meaning to Tom and the professor. The latter can now better reconcile the contradictions between the present and the past and can now commit himself anew to life. Cather ends this novel on a positive note, but the import of her total corpus was not so sanguine and anticipates the theme of historical decline. She depicted in fictional terms what Frederick Jackson Turner documented in historical terms: the frontier was gone and with it the land as the redeeming source of life's meaning.

V

In *The Great Gatsby*, F. Scott Fitzgerald draws heavily upon romantic assumption, especially the romantic idea that we seek an idealized (a Keatsian) moment. The moment is transformative, creating a realm of time, an eternal presence, to be perennially sought as an order of identity necessary to complete the idea of self. In 1917, on a moonlit evening in Louisville, Kentucky, an eighteen-year-old girl gives herself to Jay Gatsby ("flowers," as the text has it) to create a resplendent moment and a love to which he afterward strives to return. The lovers come from different classes, but their social differences are concealed for the moment by the leveling power of Gatsby's army uniform, which transforms even a poor farm boy from the Dakotas. That moment is a "becoming" transformed into the elusiveness of romantic "being." Five years later, Jay Gatsby is still reliving that experience in memory, not realizing that those five years have transformed the moment from the realm of epiphany to empty promise, from romantic wonder to physical loss.

Put differently, Gatsby embodies the true romantic by engaging in the godlike activity of self-creation. And what Gatsby creates on the personal level finds an equivalent on the historical level in Frederick Jackson Turner's pioneer. One could argue that the narrative elements in *The Great Gatsby* parallel those in Turner's frontier thesis. Gatsby's pursuit of pristine love finds its parallel equivalent in the pioneer's pursuit of a new beginning. They both have known the ideal, have the imagination and the will to pursue the tangible moment; not finding it, they share a sense of loss.

Nick tells us his (Gatsby's) story is a story of the West. But it is the West whose inhabitants (Gatsby, Nick, Tom and Daisy, Myrtle and George Wilson) have come east. Fitzgerald's novel is the story of America once the West has been transformed and the East is now the nation's center of gravity. It is to the commercial-industrial East that the westerners have ventured. No longer is the land the center of meaning. In fact, the land has given way to the valley of ashes—the remains of an industrial hell. The promise of the New York skyline has taken the place of agrarian promise, and it is to this world of James J. Hill, Carnegie, and Rockefeller that Gatsby and the Buchanans venture. Gatsby's America is the product of the new capitalism and the second industrial revolution (the era of the combustion engine and electricity)—a world that looked back nostalgically to the agrarian ideas of Thomas Jefferson, a realm of history to which Nick (falsely?) believes he can return at novel's end.

Besides the celebration of self-creation (a form of heightened individualism), besides the claim to romantic destiny (on both a personal and a national level), and besides the theme of the West (with the novel's ending on Nick's return west in search of a lost ideal), there are other elements that Turner's frontier thesis shares with *The Great Gatsby:* it may be coincidental—but it is nevertheless uncanny—that Gatsby's father is a German farmer, true to the myth of the land and possibly volkisch trust in national destiny (cf. his aligning the fate of Gatsby and that of James J. Hill).

The death of the frontier, with its emphasis on the romantic nature of heightened individualism, finds a parallel of sorts in the fate of Gatsby himself—from the promise to the betrayal of self-creation. Gatsby, the product of farm life in the Dakotas, is a creation of the wilderness frontier: his teenage imagination is intensified by reading Western and dime novels by authors who never went west of the Mississippi; he owes his being to that realm of illusion, to the fiction that created an ersatz self and a desire for a romantic West or its equivalent. The "idea" of Gatsby, along with the idea of the wilderness frontier, dies on the plains, mountains, and deserts of the West with the closing of the frontier.

The urban transformation of Turner's frontier is embodied by Tom Buchanan in the novel: he is the product of enormous Chicago wealth, a graduate of the eastern Ivy League (Yale, 1915), and a successful Wall Street broker, specializing in bonds. As Turner's frontier world gives way to the city, so does Tom's base of power, when he moves from Chicago to New York. He is the embodiment of urban force, and his whole person suggests a realm of power. As Nick tells us, his "pack of muscle" reveals "the enormous power of that body. . . . It was a body capable of enormous leverage—a cruel body" (Fitzgerald 1957, 7). Tom, like the city itself, is the incarnation of force, the human equivalent of Henry Adams's Dynamo.

Both Gatsby and the wilderness pioneers are transformed by their respective environments, which work in mysterious and not fully understood ways. Fitzgerald's city and Turner's frontier both reside in a twilight zone between reality and fantasy, their call pervasive and transformative. One went to the city to realize a heightened self, a potential readiness, as one went to the wilderness to satisfy a rugged individualism, a desire for adventure. In America, a youth in the realm of Jefferson would seek fortune in the wilderness frontier; ninety years later, a youth in the realm of Theodore Roosevelt would seek fortune in the city. Urban reality had replaced the agrarian call.

Both Fitzgerald and Turner ponder what made the West the West, what gave it preference over other regions. For Turner, the answer involves the land; for Fitzgerald, the answer involves a state of mind that distinguishes between the anonymity of the East and the intimacy of the West. The idea of the West dominates the novel in ways seldom discussed: "I see," Nick Carraway tells us by way of conclusion, "that this has been a story of the West, after all" (1957, 177).

A story of the West: the phrase takes on meaning in the historical context in which Fitzgerald was writing. In 1920, five years before Fitzgerald published *Gatsby*, Frederick Jackson Turner published his *The Frontier in American History*, a collection of essays and the reworking of his famous frontier thesis about the West. In 1922, Van Wyck Brooks reinforced the Turner thesis in *The Ordeal of Mark Twain*, in which he distinguished between the meaning of the East and the meaning of the West in America. Brooks argued that the frontier reality Twain had brought from the West was gentrified when he came east under the influence of his wife and his friends, such as William Dean Howells. The frontier spirit that had dominated the land was transformed by the genteel influence of eastern wealth and the manners that money perpetuated and sustained.

Brooks's thesis has application to *Gatsby*, where the major characters come from the West and then are transformed by the money-world of the East. Brooks's thesis, as we have just seen, finds illustration in the character of Tom Buchanan, who comes from the Midwest and is transformed by Yale and Wall Street. The difference between East and West was not simply a geographical distinction but involved different ways of life, two different value systems. And central to any discussion of the West was the myth of the land—the belief that land was an idealized entity, a spiritual realm rightfully claimed by the people (consistent with a transplanted theory of the Volk) to which their fate was coupled, as was the destiny of the nation.

America was a product of the land before the land was transformed into urban reality. Gatsby intuits the shift in America away from land to city. Despite his romantic reading, despite his idealized version of the West, despite the legacy of James J. Hill and the illusion of frontier wealth, Gatsby realizes that his fate is connected with the East: he rejects the (Jeffersonian) life of his yeoman father and finds in Wolfsheim the substitute father who introduces him to the resources of the urban underworld, with its illegal drugstores and circumspect brokerage houses.

Gatsby embodies the end of the western frontier, which he endows with symbolic meaning even as he abandons it as a lost vision. He models himself on Dan Cody; the name suggests the careers of Daniel Boone and William "Buffalo Bill" Cody: the first is a man who enters the wilderness even before it has become a frontier, the second a man who comes at the end of the frontier and turns the whole experience into a commercial Wild West show. Daniel Boone and William Cody represent the beginning and the end of the frontier: they were the bookends of the pioneer movement—one initiating it, the other overseeing its close.

America is a land caught in a transformation that has radically revised the yeoman agenda. Gatsby is quick to take advantage of the new opportunities. Nick tells us "the city seen from the Queensboro Bridge is always the city seen for the first time, in its first wild promise of all the mystery and the beauty in the world" (Fitzgerald 1957, 69). Gatsby's city is a realm of pure possibility: here a Dakota "roughneck" becomes the heightened embodiment of his imagination, the product of that mysterious process in which fantasy transforms reality, linking Gatsby to Oxford and the Kaiser and much more. But urban promise comes fraught with the unexpected, and as Nick crosses the Queensboro Bridge, the splendor that is New York is undercut when a dead man in a hearse overtakes his car.

Like the Turner frontier thesis, *The Great Gatsby* is a story of the land. The New York skyline is a monument to corporate America; the hinterland with its valley of ashes is a wasteland result of that same world. Gatsby's "becoming" is a product of the land; his destiny is a product of the city. The novel is based on a series of contrasts—agrarian versus urban, ideal versus grotesque, wonder versus wasteland, myth versus reality—but none more important than East versus West. From Nick's perspective, the East is cold, impersonal, and anonymous, while the West is warm, personal, and intimate. In the West the houses are named after families: the Ordways, the Herseys, and the Schulzes, as opposed to the anonymous house in the East that emerges from Nick's surreal fantasy. The West carries boyhood memories for Nick: the pleasure that came with the train rides that took him through farmland and brought him home from school at Christmas, the glance of snow-covered terrain from coach windows, the "sleigh bells in the frosty dark and the shadows of holly wreaths thrown by lighted windows on the snow" (Fitzgerald 1957, 177).

The myth of the land evolved from the worship of the land—with its European origins in the romanticism of Herder and Fichte and its American expression in Jefferson; its literary expression could be found in Whitman, Norris, Cather, Steinbeck, Pound, Faulkner, Dos Passos, and Fitzgerald himself. But by the time the modern writer engaged this theme, it was superseded, relegated to a lost past. As we have seen, by 1920 there were more people living in American cities than on American farms. As urban presence filled agrarian space, the transformation encouraged an overwhelming nostalgia for the landed past. The Agrarian critics, who gave us the New Criticism, argued in *I'll Take My Stand* (1930) that the agrarian life was superior to the urban life and that southern values were superior to northern. (Fitzgerald recognized his own southern origins through that of his father, who migrated to the Midwest from the mid-Atlantic states, and through family connection to Francis Scott Keyes, after whom Fitzgerald was named.)

And just as Fitzgerald gives us an inverted sense of the West in his description of the urban East, he uses the narrative formula of the Western to depict Gatsby's fate in the East, inverting the novel of the West, turning the classic "Western" into what might be called an "Eastern." In the traditional Western, the hero comes from the East and goes West; he encounters conflict between civilization (often embodied by the city) and the wilderness (embodied by the land); his biggest problem involves a villain who opposes his frontier agenda, including his love for a woman who is reluctant to see him in such a duel; the difficulties are removed when he triumphs in a shootout that resolves the conflict and opens up a new future. Out of this experience comes the myth of the pioneer-cowboy, perpetuated as we have seen by novels like Owen Wister's *The Virginian* (1902), which carried on the tradition of Fenimore Cooper's Natty Bumppo novels, works of imagination that created a West that neither author knew firsthand. *The Great Gatsby* reverses every one of these narrative elements, including the subtext of the Western, which involves confronting the land, imposing one's will upon it, and turning that control into wealth. Gatsby comes from the West and goes East; he confronts a villainous Tom Buchanan, who wins not only the girl but the shootout (of words) as well, opening up the future for the villain and closing it for Gatsby. The narrative ideals are inverted, and the narrator is left returning to the West in pursuit of the past now emptied of the lost ideal.

The novel establishes this theme of the Western when Gatsby's father appears from the Dakotas at the end of the novel and confirms Gatsby's interest in the Western when he pulls from his pocket Gatsby's copy of Clarence Mulford's *Hopalong Cassidy,* in which Gatsby had written the Benjamin Franklin–like resolves that governed his adolescence. (Gatsby has dated the page September 12, 1906, an impossibility because that specific title was not written until 1910.) Fitzgerald took historical liberties with Mulford because the Mulford novel gave historical reality to myth—underlying the way a sense of illusion perpetuates the novel as a whole. Even though he never went west of the Mississippi, Mulford created a myth, a faked realm of the West. He did this by building upon the myth-of-the-land story, superimposing romance onto myth and entrenching the belief that the West had a meaning of its own—even if what he brought to that meaning was pure fiction. *Hopalong Cassidy* and *The Virginian,* despite the remote connection of their authors to the frontier, build upon a fictional idea of the West, with its code of chivalry, honor, and the land as spiritual reality.

Fitzgerald also builds upon this narrative tradition. As we have seen, the culmination of each novel involves a confrontation, deadly in *The Virginian* and no less so in *Gatsby* despite the absence of guns. The "shootout" in *The Great Gatsby* comes in the Plaza Hotel, where Gatsby is undone, not by bullets, but by an explanation from Tom about the sources of Gatsby's money. The meaning of the West turns on physical experience; the meaning of the East turns on a hierarchy of social values and a set of manners. Whatever ideals Gatsby brings to the East die with him. The rest is left to Nick, who at the end returns to the West, reasserting what is left of the value system the novel has just emptied.

Like the chthonic gods, whose response to human behavior controls the land, Gatsby's death coincides with the transformation of the land. Gatsby brings his sense of promise to the city in which he will die. As we have seen, the splendid buildings that make up the New York skyline find a counterpart in the valley of ashes. The infertility of the valley of ashes embodies the fate of the land. Fitzgerald describes it as "a fantastic farm where ashes grow like wheat into ridges and hills and grotesque gardens, where ashes take the forms of houses and chimneys and rising smoke and finally, with a transcendent effort, of men who move dimly and already crumbling through the powdery air." Now grotesque, the land brings forth ashes worked over by "ash-grey men [who] swarm up with leaden spades [i.e., pitchforks] and stir up an impenetrable cloud which screens their obscure operations from sight" (1957, 28).

Fitzgerald's city functions symbolically between the promises of a heaven and the tortures of a hell. As an ending point, the valley of ashes is an analogue to Turner's closed frontier. The background for the valley of ashes is the biblical Gehenna, the wasteland realm on the outskirts of Jerusalem in the valley of Hinnom. There, Israelite apostates sacrificed by fire their children (by concubines?). Gehenna is thus the demonic land of the wicked—a place of torment and of expiation.

Gehenna takes on several roles: wasteland, sacrificial site, and realm of hell—all end products of one process or another. Fitzgerald seems to see it as a hell for those damned to failure, a realm for those whose life has burned out, and are now ashes. The valley of ashes is located on the rail line halfway between West Egg and New York; thus, anyone entering New York from West Egg must pass through a vestibule of hell. The city offers salvation or damnation, depending on whether one succeeds or fails. Those who fail are assigned to the valley of ashes. The skyline of New York beckons to the saved; the valley of ashes calls to the damned. Fitzgerald's world appropriately turns on contrasts: Faustian expansiveness finds limits; romantic destiny gives way to the entropic; the heavenly promise of the New York skyline finds its counterpart in a grotesque hell, worked over by demons who oversee the failures in life such as George Wilson.

George Wilson is the custodian of the valley of ashes. A failed idealist, he has come from the West with the hope of succeeding in the East. He is the product of middle-class America (his garage is on what the novel calls Main Street). His journey, like Gatsby's, takes him to failure and death. It is one of the many ironies of the novel that the agent of Gatsby's death is fated to be Wilson, who is the custodian of both the valley of ashes and his own dead dream. (In his depiction of Wilson, Fitzgerald was suggesting another, historically larger, fated idealist, Woodrow Wilson, whose defeat over the League of Nations led to his demise. There is also a connection between the failed presidency of James Buchanan and the failed morality of Tom Buchanan. In his use of historical names like Wilson and Buchanan, Daniel Boone and Buffalo Bill Cody, Fitzgerald builds his novel on a historical base and extends historical reach.)

In the valley of ashes, the majestic has given way to the grotesque;

heaven has found its hell. Along with Wilson, this degenerate realm is overseen by a godlike figure who is blind, symbolized by the nearsighted eyes of Doctor T. J. Eckleburg, which brood dimly over this wasteland, or the myopic eyes of the owl-eyed man, an American Tiresias. Fitzgerald has depicted an inverted world: not only is the novel an inverted Western, but nature is working in an inverted way: wheat fields bring forth ashes; God is blind; the act to be redeemed (Myrtle's death) never touches the guilty. The forces that lay claim to the grotesque—the Buchanans and their moneyed institutions—are also responsible for the valley of ashes as they turn the land into a hell.

The Great Gatsby parallels Turner's frontier thesis as it takes us from an idealized realm to its demise. *The Great Gatsby* is rich in reference to theories of history, including historical process that supplies an understanding of this phenomenon. One such view of how the processes of history work is found in Oswald Spengler's *The Decline of the West*, a theory of history as a force both romantic and entropic. As it applies in *The Great Gatsby*, Nick Carraway observes New York becoming more diverse, less culturally homogeneous, less grounded in nature, more the product of manipulated money—factors that accommodate the move from Spengler's idea of culture to civilization, initiating a process of cultural decline. The city harbingers great promise (the "wild promise of all the mystery and beauty in the world" [69]), while another reality moves toward death (the death of Gatsby, Wilson, Myrtle) and death roams the street ("a dead man passed us in a hearse" [69]). Hope and promise, decline and death merge in this novel. Gatsby brings his sense of promise to the city in which he will die; the splendid buildings that make up the New York skyline find a counterpart in the valley of ashes.

Faustian man with his desire for the infinite gives way to the new Caesar—just as Gatsby gives way to Tom Buchanan, the frontier to the new city, radical individualism to new forms of power inseparable from money. Fitzgerald's novel is more than the story of the rise and fall of radical individualism; it is also a story of the rise and fall of Faustian culture—the limits that new urbanism brought with it. Once more we confront the novel's central truth: Faustian expansiveness finds limits—romantic history gives way to the entropic.

Spengler's philosophy of history, like individual human development, moves us toward realms of decline. Nations are like living (and dying) plants. Such theory stems from a belief in the organic (life-infused) nature of society and is consistent with romantic theories of history. As we have seen, decline resulted from abandoning the land. Destiny and countryside were at the heart of Spengler's theory—a national destiny and a vital countryside. As one moves away from the natural rhythms of the land, a theory of the soil gives way to abstract forms of reason, scientific theory, and institutionalized money processed by banks. When all this happens, the spiritual sense of nature is lost.

In *The Great Gatsby,* Fitzgerald suggests that the American West was still connected (at least in an illusionary way) to the myth of the land, the source of spiritual roots that still had conviction on a personal level. While the West had moral superiority over the East, the East embodied the future of America. As we have seen, Fitzgerald brilliantly portrayed the idea that key American ideals have been used up, located now in a dead past. This is a realm in which the world of the father has broken down. Gatsby's natural father has been repudiated. Dan Cody has given way to Meyer Wolfsheim—to a realm of bootlegging, "bucket (crooked brokerage) shops," and extortion. Wolfsheim's world is an ersatz version of Tom Buchanan's—the brokered world where money makes money. Back in the Dakotas is Mr. Gatz, Gatsby's father, whose yeoman existence put in motion his son's dream for an ideal that has already been consumed.

In an early draft of the novel, Fitzgerald concluded chapter 1 with the following words: "[S]o we beat on, boats against the current, borne back ceaselessly into the past." He moved those words from the end of chapter 1 to the end of the novel when he realized that the sentence summarized the meaning of his novel: that an idealized America—a lost innocence once located in the idea of the West—better existed in the past than in the present. At the end of the novel, Nick seeks this lost ideal—and returns to the West. Nick's words to Gatsby—"[Y]ou can't repeat the past"—are words that he fails to apply to himself as he heads west in search of a lost ideal. Fitzgerald thus ends his novel on a note of ambiguity: what Nick will find in his return to the West remains a matter of speculation. He will be rid of Tom, with Tom's arrogant sense of privilege that goes with money, but he is unlikely to find a redeeming ideal in his father's hardware store.

Nick's return is to an America that has been changed by time. It is a continued pursuit of an Enlightenment dream that brought with it the belief that one could create oneself out of imagination and remain true to that creation. Gatsby comes close to fulfilling that dream, but Tom is the impediment—the instrument of defeat. What Nick must learn next—as Fitzgerald demonstrates in *Tender Is the Night* (1934) and *The Last Tycoon* (1941)—is that the spirit of America now turns on money rather than an informing imagination.

In *Tender Is the Night* the Spenglerian element is even more pronounced. Here Fitzgerald made conscious use of the European setting. He depicted the breakup of the European aristocracy following World War I as that class was replaced by a new-money class embodied by the Warren (war end?) family. The Warrens ruled by virtue of their money; they were grand consumers: trains crisscrossed the county carrying goods to satisfy their desires. All of these elements have Spenglerian reference. Just as Greek culture gave way to Roman civilization, Pericles marking a historical beginning, Alexander a turning point, and the Caesars a terminal point, so in modern history Charlemagne marked a beginning point, Napoleon a turning point, and the new Caesars (moneyed and military) a terminal point. In each sequence, the turning point came as control passed from a landed aristocracy to an urban money center (it is no accident that Dick Diver's final decline took place in Rome, against a backdrop of decadence).

When Dick leaves Rome, he is a defeated man, and his defeat anticipates the appearance of Tommy Barban, the new "barbarian" who comes with the end of every civilization. As in Eliot's *The Waste Land*, Fitzgerald makes use of "the falling tower" theme when he superimposes one period of time upon another—the modern upon the ancient. As the West (Europe and later America) lost its vitality, a new threat came from the East: the fall of Rome anticipated the fall (i.e., the decline) of London, Paris, and New York (each city was marked by decadence or brutality, such as the brutality of Abe North's death in New York).

The fate of both Abe North and Dick Diver embodied the fate of America after the Civil War. Fitzgerald believed that American cultural values divided with the advent of the war, a Jeffersonian agrarianism giving way to a Hamiltonian industrial society. In an earlier draft of the novel, Abe North was named Abe Grant, suggesting his connection to both Lincoln and Grant and to both prebellum and postbellum

America. Fitzgerald filled in the details with the help of Spengler's historical formula. Grant paralleled Napoleon; 1865 in America was the equivalent of 1815 in France; the new capitalism and technology transformed both landscapes; Paris and New York were now systematically interchangeable.

In "My Lost City" (1932), Fitzgerald projected success and failure onto New York and created two cities: the city of his prep-school dreams of success and the city of his postwar experience working in advertising and living in a drab room in the Bronx. Once again Fitzgerald's world divided in two, with the excitement of expectation giving way to the disappointment of reality. America embodied this division: "[B]ehind much of the entertainment that the city poured forth into the nation there were only a lot of rather lost and lonely people" (28). Here Fitzgerald tells us that New York, with its romantic potentiality and its realistic squalor, had limits. Where New York stopped, America began: one could never escape the larger destiny that contained the city itself; beyond the romantic city was provincial America, founded on a Puritan legacy that incorporated both God and money, a religious and secular state of mind.

In his early novels and short stories, Fitzgerald showed how difficult it was to create the romantic self in the face of this Puritan legacy. *This Side of Paradise* (1920) takes on this theme directly. Princeton becomes the safe harbor that supplies a buffer against the outside world, softening the contradictions that are built into a money economy grounded on religious belief, anticipating the ideals that lead to disillusionment with a war that supposedly preserved such ideals. *The Beautiful and Damned* (1922) picks up where *This Side of Paradise* leaves off. Adam Patch is a product of the post–Civil War period when the subsistence values gave way to materialistic values and the country was remade in an image that could no longer accommodate what both Amory Blaine and Anthony Patch felt were necessary components of their identity.

Fitzgerald's last treatment of entropic history comes in *The Last Tycoon* (subtitled "a Western") (1941), which once more deals with the man of romantic aspiration caught in the materialistic culture that defeats him. Monroe Stahr, the last of the Faustians, is counterpointed against a former Hollywood czar, who commits suicide at the "shrine" of Andrew Jackson's Hermitage: it was Jackson who fought the rise of the national bank in the name of yeoman culture. The novel demonstrates how far America has moved from the landed, cohesive culture of its origins, and the defeat of Stahr and the suicide of Schwartzman suggest the destructive nature of this change.

The entropic process was so swift that it called into question the ability of the romantic hero to function in modern America. The attempt to create an idealized self was more difficult. Added to a Puritan legacy that betrayed its spirituality were a series of power custodians from the corporate realm (Spengler's new Caesars) intent on material pursuits. The vitality that Gatsby displayed in holding together his romantic sense of self is so greatly altered in *The Last Tycoon* that the necessary contrast between the romantic impulse and the degenerative process is diminished. Fitzgerald's America was a far more power-driven place, a "top-down" realm, when he was writing *The Last Tycoon* in 1940 than when he was writing *The Great Gatsby* in 1925. The material aspect of American culture may be a given, but the idea of creating oneself out of imagination was not. In fifteen years, the idea of romantic opportunity met powerful resistance, and the idealized hero with belief in romantic destiny would founder even more quickly on the shoals of institutional power.

VI

Nathanael West's *The Day of the Locust* (1939) is still another novel that can be read as a commentary on Turner's frontier thesis. A throng has come to Los Angeles in pursuit of ideals as compelling as those that attracted Turner's pioneers. Los Angeles beckoned to a new life, a new beginning. Hollywood reinforced the idea, promising a realm of glamour and affluence to those within and a realm of excitement and allure to those outside. Much of what happens in the novel is consistent with urban pursuit and turns on money, from Homer Simpson's attempt to buy Faye Greener's love to the Greeners' attempt to find prosperity in Hollywood. In West's world, youth and beauty are commodities for sale. Tod Hackett, the narrator, observes the frustration connected with the selling of self. Characters pursue and are pursued in a round-robin of activity in which each is subject to a centrality of force, a situation not unlike the realm of change that comes with adaptation to the frontier.

West's novel is a study in transformation. The Greeners are transformed by their desire for success. Earle Shoop, the cowboy, is transformed by the city and becomes, in a mechanical way, the first of the urban cowboys. And Tod Hackett's moral intelligence is transformed by his own inability to resist lust and violence. The novel turns on the transformation of a beneficent force into a hostile one. A surface placidity gives way to violence: the violence of the cockfight anticipates the violence of the fight between Miguel and Earle. The commonplace gives way to mayhem. The desire to create oneself anew that went with the frontier leads instead to mob rage and a rampage, turning the ideal of the Western into a naturalistic display of hostility. The New Jerusalem gives way to apocalypse.

The culmination of forces at work here has a historical equivalent. The Enlightenment celebration of individuality—the ability to create oneself out of imagination—has been transformed by history: Napoleon at Waterloo lost his romantic individuality as well as a historical battle. The novel suggests as much when Tod Hackett watches a filming in which a makeshift Waterloo set comes apart, tumbling the cast harshly to the ground. The collapse of the set is a metaphor for the novel itself, for that moment in history when the Enlightenment call to historical promise came to an end. The resulting sense of emptiness fuels a rage that is seemingly atavistic, as if all restraint has been abandoned in the final push west.

West's novel depicts the dark side of the journey west, the pursuit of an abortive destiny. The journey began in Plymouth on the Atlantic coast and ended three thousand miles west on the Pacific shore. It was a journey through history in search of both personal and national ideals—a journey, despite its ending, that was fraught with purpose and hope. Ending aside, the journey involved a belief in national destiny unique in its promise—a promise that the land can no longer sustain. The themes of the West and the end to innocence come to completion in *The Day of the Locust*. West saw that as expectation moved west, it carried with it a sense of hope, of renewed promise, of serial new beginnings. But once this state of mind reached land's end, it hit a terminal point: the promises connected with the idea of the West gave way to transparent disappointment. The situation became worse when a new order of experience connected with the making of films and the glamour that went with movie stardom created a new kind of expectation, the product of Hollywood as a new order of frontier. It would only be a matter of time before hope in both fabricated senses of the word was seen as fraudulent. When this happened, a whole population would rise in protest, their disappointment now a continued state of frustration, their frustration the basis for anger, and their anger the fuel for the riot on which the novel and the promise of romantic destiny rest.

Tod Hackett comes to realize that his world is a combination of forces working against one another. The force can explode without direction, as it does in the ending of the novel, or it can be controlled and organized politically, as was the case in 1939 in Hitler's Germany. With prescience, Hackett sees the modern city as an energy system working toward destruction or totalitarian ends. The Enlightenment city, like the wilderness frontier, had offered new promise on both sides of the Atlantic. But the last of that hope vanished in America, on the outer edge of another continent.

VII

Like West, Steinbeck sets his fiction in California. Steinbeck's novels often treat the desire for fulfillment that the Turner frontier promised. Most often there is the desire to own enough land to be independent and self-sustaining, the yeoman embodiment of the Jeffersonian vision. But the dream is now outmoded, still a dream but realistically out of reach.

Of Mice and Men (1937) is one of Steinbeck's early treatments of this theme. The novella tells of two migrant workers, George and Lennie, who dream of owning their own land. But there is always a serpent in this dream garden; here it is the dementia of Lennie and his attraction to soft, cuddly objects, be they rabbits, puppies, or young women. As might be expected, Lennie accidentally kills the wife of the owner's sadistic son, and George "saves" Lennie from a lynch mob by taking his life. There is not much in this story that is not predictable. But most predictable is the expectation of finding a homestead—an expectation that can never come to be.

Steinbeck treats the theme of "westering" as a part of the heroic past that is now gone. Like so many other novelists who write about the pioneer world (Cather, Fitzgerald, Faulkner, West), Steinbeck treats the idealized past as a mirage. The dream lives on, always tempting, never again realized. In chapter 4 of *The Red Pony*, "The Leader of the People," Steinbeck celebrates the heroic past of the protagonist's grandfather, who led a wagon train west. The grandfather becomes a spokesman for Turner's pioneers. As he tells us in a summary of the idea of the West, "It was a movement and westering. We carried life out here and set it down the way ants carry eggs. . . . Then we came to the sea, and it was done." As these words reveal, the closest Steinbeck's characters come to the Turner frontier is either as a vision of expectation or as nostalgic remembrance of the dream now lost.

Another of Steinbeck's works that treats the theme of the frontier as mirage is *The Pastures of Heaven* (1932), a collection of twelve interconnected stories about the Monterey Valley that recount its founding by a Spanish corporal and its settling by generations of occupants. Like Émile Zola, who wrote a series of novels about two peasant French families (the Rougons and the Macquarts), Steinbeck traces his pioneer families through the lineage of the Monroes. The dream, the expectation of a new life, lures the Monroes and their offspring on—but toward disaster and loss. Fate delivers a way of life far different from Turner's wilderness experience. Ideal expectations turn into grotesque reality. The valley, as its name suggests, beckons to pioneer opportunity, only to deliver its opposite. The people who come to the valley bring dreams of transformation, only to see them negated by forms of insanity, sickness, or death. Like so much of the way literary naturalism portrays frontier experience, expectation exceeds achievement. As with so many stories of pioneer expectation, Steinbeck's stories take us to a hostile ending, a realm of illusion that creates a counterfeit reality.

Perhaps the most forceful portrait of the lost frontier involves the fate of the Oakies in Steinbeck's *The Grapes of Wrath* (1939). The Joad family lose their farm to bank foreclosure; they default on their loan after the drought destroys their crops. They head for California and the promise of work in the orange groves and orchards, even the possibility of free land. The novel develops two major themes connected with the idea of the West: the theme of the mythic frontier, the belief that prosperity awaits in the West; and the biblical theme of the New Jerusalem, with the journey from Oklahoma to California paralleling the Israelites' migration from Egypt to Canaan.

The journey is fraught with difficulty: the grandparents die; others desert the family. In California they find that the big agricultural corporations have bought up the land and have overpowered the unions. The call to work from California has brought a flood of bankrupt farmers from the Midwest, creating an oversupply of labor. Except for a settlement camp, the benefaction of the New Deal, their situation is discouraging. When they become involved with strike-breaking, the agents of the corporation murder Jim Casy; and when Tom Joad avenges his death, he becomes an outcast, a fugitive wanted for the agent's death. Tom takes flight from the family, fully resolved to fight oppression. Despite their travail, the family moves on, motivated by the will of Ma Joad.

The novel describes two journeys: a physical journey from Oklahoma to California and a spiritual journey motivated by the power of illusion—the belief that hope and help lie ahead and the endurance to act upon that expectation. The Joads are elevated beyond the lost frontier to a biblical level and a symbolic reality paralleling the Israelites' errand in the wilderness. Modern man can take strength knowing that his plight has been tested at the highest plane of historical reality. The reality of the frontier is dead, but its illusion lives on, if only as a remnant with the power of a myth, and the journey becomes testimony to a lost past.

Steinbeck felt that he treated the theme of the West most successfully in *East of Eden* (1952). Adam Trask comes from Connecticut to farm in the Salinas Valley in California. He learns from his half-brother that his father has left them a legacy of fifty thousand dollars each, money that he uses to buy his ranch. Adam marries Cathy Ames, a mentally unbalanced woman who has killed her parents by setting fire to their home. Even after giving birth to twins—Caleb and Aron—she continues her violent ways: tries to murder Adam before she takes flight from the family; always on the edge of society, she eventually becomes a prostitute in Salinas.

Life goes on: Caleb pursues farming; Aron studies for the priesthood; and Adam becomes involved in a scheme that includes using refrigerator cars to send fresh produce east—a sensible idea but an adventure that nearly bankrupts him. Caleb works to restore his father's lost fortune. But when Adam rejects Caleb's gift of money, Caleb in a fit of jealousy takes his brother to the house of prostitution and reveals that Kate (as she is now called) is his mother. All of this happens between 1900 and 1914, the outbreak of World War I, the war that claims the life of the disillusioned Aron. Adam dies of a stroke at the news of his son's death. The novel clearly makes use of another biblical theme, here the Cain and Abel story, with the modern Cain surviving to render homage to an idealized, but now lost, past.

Steinbeck's literary world is a product of naturalism on the way to a transformed modernism. His characters are primarily the product of heredity and environment in a world that is perpetually deterministic. Like Faulkner and Joyce, he superimposes a symbolic reality such as the Cain and Abel story or the journey to a New Canaan on a sequence of otherwise secular events. But when Faulkner and Joyce resort to symbolism, it is to universalize the story, to heighten the narrative, while Steinbeck resorts to biblical parallels to seal his characters into predictable realms of time—into what is now foretold. One could not find a better example than Steinbeck to document a major transformation in literary mode. With the closing of the wilderness frontier, the options available to the new pioneer were more limited: the representation of that reality was changed in literary terms when the Western was transformed by literary naturalism.[1]

11

Literary Transformations

I

Narrative forms are changed or transformed as they depict varied historical realities or give way to different encroaching narrative modes. Darwin's theory of adaptation (1859) anticipated William James's theory of pragmatism (1907), which accommodated the idea of literary realism—just as Emerson's belief in nature as the source of spiritual energy (transcendentalism) anticipated, when inverted, the forces of literary naturalism. As we have seen, the common denominator between Emersonian transcendentalism and literary naturalism was a belief in natural force, only the Emersonian force was beneficent, while the naturalistic force was hostile (with some exceptions, such as the germinal force of the wheat in Norris's *Octopus*) or at least more indifferent to human needs.

As literary naturalism grew out of environmental and historical conflict, so did the Western as a literary type. Like literary naturalism, the Western has a history of its own. It may owe some of its narrative elements to the medieval romance. In both modes we have a heightened figure—the knight in the romance, the gunfighter in the Western—who is the product of a moral code: that of chivalry embodying courage, dignity, and courtesy in the romance, and that of honor and integrity in the Western. In each genre, there is the fight between good and evil, right versus might, with the difference clearly defined. In each, the principal character usually embodies the law but can sometimes be on the verge of or outside of the law, when the law is the product of dubious and often-corrupt authority (Robin Hood is proudly outside the law, and so is Joesy Wales). In each, there is an antagonist to confront or a quest (such as the search for the holy grail) to fulfill. In each, there is a call to arms. In the romance the call is to the defense of the nation: King Arthur fights the Roman and Germanic invaders along with the barbarians; Robin Hood opposes John when he tries to usurp the throne from King Richard, who is off fighting in the third crusade. In the Western, the call is more immediate: the Virginian confronts Trampas, who is an individual threat to the order. In the pursuit of virtue in both the medieval romance and the modern Western, the narrative tone is one that presumes well-being in the future—at least as long as a frontier mentality is sustained.

The Western persisted because there was a need for the nostalgia of a romantic past. But as Wallace Stegner has noted, there was a change from hope to bitterness when the wilderness frontier gave way to the urban frontier. In literary terms, this shift prompted the transformation within literary naturalism to accommodate elements of the Western. The transition was not that difficult, because there were naturalistic elements (e.g., the Darwinian need to adapt to the terrain or environment) already present in the Western. Frank Norris believed this narrative coupling marked the end of the Western, an idea that was reinforced by his contemporary Emerson Hough (Athearn 163). But as Hamlin Garland's *Her Mountain Lover* (published serially in 1901) suggested, along with Zane Grey's novels and Frederick Remington's illustrations (e.g., *A Desert Romance,* published in *Century Magazine* in 1902), portraits of the romantic West still found their many outlets.

According to John Cawelti, the Western owes its greatest debt to Turner's frontier thesis, especially the belief that the frontier was the meeting ground between savagery and civilization. As the frontier pushed on, it left the transformations of civilization in its wake. Once idealized, the cowboy accepted the burden of redeeming the realms of savagery (Cawelti 68). The redemptive aspect here brings to the surface the Puritan (i.e., Calvinist) belief that we live in a world informed with evil. In the Western the reincarnated cowboy confronts such evil (Turner's "savagery") wherever he finds it, especially in its forms of lawlessness. Leslie Fiedler's *The Return of the Vanishing American* (1968) is a variation on the Cawelti theory, narrowing the source of evil primarily to the conflict between the transformed cowboy and the hostile Indian.

The romance had a long and involved history, undergoing a number of transformations. As just noted, in its application to the Western it made direct use of Turner's wilderness thesis—a connection best illustrated by reference to Owen Wister's *The Virginian* (1902), a novel written by a Pennsylvanian about a Virginian in Wyoming. If Turner could trace the movement of democracy west, Wister could superimpose on that democracy a southern chivalry. Wister's hero is the Virginian who brings the courtly values of the South to the West. He also brings to the West the values of another Virginian, Thomas Jefferson, who sustained the belief in an inspired democracy, based on yeoman farming and worked land. The Virginian embodies a Nordic racial type and a Protestant ethos. He epitomizes the virtues of individualism, masculinity, resilience, endurance, and an ability to adapt to the landscape and its hardships.

In Wyoming, the Virginian dedicates himself to these ideals, but he is frustrated in his pursuits by the novel's villain, Trampas, who stands opposed to all that the Virginian holds sacred. As in the prototypical Western, this conflict can be resolved only by a personal confrontation or shootout. The Virginian not only wins the shootout; he wins the converted love of the novel's heroine, who seemingly abandons her eastern sense of righteousness when she accepts the Virginian's western code. The novel guarantees that the Virginian will triumph and so will his values, which now have their roots in the West. The perpetuation of those values perhaps best explains why the Western came into its own at the end of the nineteenth and the beginning of the twentieth century. At this time the prevalence of an industrial America created a desire to keep the spirit of the wilderness frontier alive, and the Western had the means to do so. Wister's novel in particular satisfied nostalgia for the idealized frontier. It stayed at the top of the *New York Times* bestseller list for six months in 1902 and within three years had sold three hundred thousand copies.

Another romantic version that kept the West alive was the novels of Zane Grey (1872–1939), especially his *Riders of the Purple Sage* (1912), which became an ongoing best seller. Cooper's *Leatherstocking Tales,* Wister's *Virginian,* dime novels, and the idealized illustrations of Frederic Remington's West influenced Grey's works. *Purple Sage,* set in southern Utah, gives us the story of Jane Withersteen's battle to escape persecution by the Mormon Church—and later the story of her conversion to that church. A second plot deals with Ben Venters, a gunman with a grudge against Mormons, and his escape into the frontier wilderness. Part of Grey's appeal was his unpredictability: in 1925 he published *The Vanishing American,* a defense of the Navajo Indians.

Another popular writer who helped create the myth of the West was Clarence E. Mulford (1883–1956). Mulford was born in Strator, Illinois, and moved with his family to Utica, New York, and later to Brooklyn, where he wrote a series of stories about the Bar 20 Ranch for *Outing Magazine.* In 1907 these stories were collected into a book, *Bar 20,* and the Hopalong Cassidy legend was born. Modeled on Wild Bill Hickok and James Wesley Hardin, Cassidy was a Texas rancher who lived by the code of the West. The legend became so popular that Mulford wrote twenty-eight novels in this series alone and then went on to write more than one hundred more. Wister and Mulford turned a formulaic plot into popular lore.

In the Western the conflict is often between ranchers and farmers, or between the individualist and the forces of conformity that threaten his independence. *The Virginian* and Jack Schaefer's *Shane* each treat the Johnson County war in Wyoming, but the Virginian sides with the ranchers, while *Shane* sides with the farmers. In each novel the principal character is a law unto himself and thus the source of what is good and evil, as the Virginian and Shane stand on different sides of frontier values.

One of the best modern Westerns is a novel by Edward Abbey, *The Brave Cowboy,* adapted for film by Dalton Trumbo with the title *Lonely Are the Brave* (1962), starring Kirk Douglas in the lead role. The film depicts the remnants of Turner's frontier wilderness, the last of the rugged individualists, consistent with the values of pioneering, true to principles of self-reliance (a by-product of Abbey's libertarian values), embodying the western code of personal honor. The film graphically portrays how the rigidity of the frontier mind, with its throwback to the heroic, is doomed to be destroyed in an industrial world becoming more mechanical and bureaucratic. There is no better depiction of what was lost when Turner's frontier wilderness and its state of mind came to an end.

Despite the brilliance of selected Westerns, a complaint often brought against the genre is that it lacks the continuity of a past, has no historical tradition to build upon (see, for example, Westbrook 73–85).

As opposed to the South, with its code of chivalry, and the Northeast, with its legacy of Puritanism, the West tended to lack a core meaning that could be used to sustain a tradition. But while the West may have lacked an extrinsic source of history, it had an intrinsic source that it often enlisted—namely, the western movement itself as a state of mind, the desire to move across the country informing "savagery" with "civilization" and reason with intuition, imbuing the present with a meaning that was a worthy counterpart to the lack of historical continuity.

A physical terrain generates its historical assumptions. But the physical terrain of the West is so immense, and the "center" of such terrain so vague, that it is easier to think of it as a state of mind than as a specific physical place. That state of mind usually includes the reality of a beneficent nature worked by a rugged individualist who lives intuitively by a code of justice and a belief in the priority of democracy. But writers like Walter Van Tilburg Clark invert these values, opening up the West to a different reality. His *The Track of the Cat* portrays a mountain lion as a source of the inimical: the animal embodies the hostility of the land, suggests the killer instinct built into and indwelling in nature, and depicts the inevitability of death. His *The Oxbow Incident* describes a mob manipulated by a man whose claim to being a rugged individualist stems from a desire for power, in a narrative that questions the workings of justice and democracy.

As the Clark novels reveal, the Western is not always set in a pristine and idealized world. Besides ideological variations, the Western often contains ethnic stereotypes. As we saw, the wilderness frontier was confined mostly to white, Nordic, Protestant settlers. It is thus not surprising, as Delbert Wylder has pointed out, that Emerson Hough's novels contain elements of racism when dealing with ethnic diversity, especially in their treatment of Indians, blacks, and Jews (Wylder 111–17). Similarly, John R. Milton argues that Vardis Fisher's representative character in *The Testament of Man* is unable to control the harsh land and his own animality. According to Milton, Fisher's character is "without tradition, without a legitimate place on the frontier, because he has brought almost nothing with him, and it is already too late to carve an empire out of a frontier which has vanished" (130). Another example of the belief that limits are built into the wilderness frontier is Donald Stewart's claim that A. B. Guthrie depicts a vanishing America, sees the settler carrying the seeds of destruction as he crosses the country.

Guthrie's principal character in *The Big Sky* (1947) "fled a corrupt civilization" while he carried "the corruption of the civilization he escaped with him" (Stewart 139). With the settlers "the land is enclosed, cattle replace the once plentiful buffalo, wolves, and antelope which either get exterminated" or confined (141).

On one level the Western owes its existence to forms of conflict built into the frontier. On another level the Western owes some of its narrative elements to the historical and medieval romance. At times a subgenre in one country finds its equivalent in another: Kipling's *Captains Courageous*, an example of the British novel of imperial adventure, found its counterpart in the American Western. As in the Western, where there was a need to impose one's will on the land, the fishing banks of Nova Scotia tested one's strength and courage. In both literary modes, the heroic was embellished and made romantic: the cowboy and the seaman were thematically interchangeable; once transformed by nature, both were depicted as rugged individualists, independent of spirit, dedicated to the land or the sea and its physical and moral transforming powers. The Western was transformed once again when it was taken over by science fiction: *Star Wars* is in narrative essence a Western in space.

The romance transformed did not stop with the Western: novels like those of Rider Haggard were revised until they reached the realm of apocalypse that one finds in Pynchon or in more popular forms such as the James Bond novel, where the protagonist must combat the antagonist who desires to conquer and/or destroy the world. The transformation led to a comic-book reality, good surrounded by evil, a kind of archetypal situation reduced to cartoon expression: one can find it in such popular mass-market products as *Star Wars*, where Darth Vader is the source of evil, or the Harry Potter novels, where Voldemort fulfills that function.

Nineteenth-century forms of the romance tended to merge with forms of myth, often enlisting the supernatural, looking toward distant meanings of the universe and universal truths that lie buried in the remote past. Postmodern forms of the romance moved in the opposite direction, toward suspended meaning, the emptiness of the past, or the implausibility of universal conjecture. Built into the postmodern romance is the inverse use of myth that robs it of heightened meaning. Whereas modernism puts the emphasis on individual consciousness, on what might be called "perspectivism," postmodernism collapses consciousness (the product of ideological influences, such as the workings of advertising or political campaigns or op-ed journalism) into the culture itself, where it becomes a state of mind, where culture thinks us.

II

The Western went through many narrative incarnations, but the most significant was its transformation by literary naturalism. Literary naturalism is characterized by plots assuming a dichotomy between man and both natural (cf. London's "To Build a Fire") and mechanical (cf. Zola's *La Bête Humaine* or Norris's *The Octopus*) forces. In each case, the human burden involves adapting to the force rather than being destroyed by it. The individual in combat with a force is analogous to the individual on the frontier in combat with the environment, and thus literary naturalism was a perfect literary mode to accommodate narratives of the frontier—and to pick up where the Western left off. Along with a theory of force, naturalism was the product of the radical shift in cultural meaning that came with the transition from an agrarian to an industrial society. The naturalistic novel examined in detail the fate of the farmworker (the peasant in France) who was now being displaced from the land, moving to the city to find work in the new factory system. In the Western, the characters had a certain control over the environment; in literary naturalism, the environment controlled the characters. When the character reached the city, the control (or lack of it) over the environment depended on the character's ability to fathom how the urban institutions work (cf. Dickens's Inspector Bucket or Conrad's Inspector Heat with Chandler's Philip Marlowe) and to work the urban system accordingly.

Naturalism emerged as a response to romanticism and as a product of ideas taken from Charles Darwin and Herbert Spencer. The romantic element supplied the ideal that most naturalistic characters seek, and the Darwinian-Spencerian element supplied the forces that they must confront. There is thus a romantic dilemma at the heart of a naturalistic narrative: naturalistic characters pursue an ideal that puts them in motion, even though the ideal is not achievable. The ideal lures them on, but the material force holds them back: we can find this plot element in novels that range from Norris's *McTeague* to Dreiser's *An American Tragedy*. The literary situation owes its depiction to the historical situation: the frontier in its various versions supplied an ideal that called for militant pursuit in the face of restraining physical obstacles.

As in the Western, the naturalistic plot usually unfolds chronologically, the story building upon itself; there is a character whose experiences are repetitive, suggesting a determined sequence of events, and whose behavior is predictable. The character in the literary Western is formulaically predictable, but perhaps less so than in literary naturalism—less the product of biological and economic forces and more the product of an abstract process, such as good confronting evil, with good often defined in terms of chivalric ideals.

Primitive forces in the Western and literary naturalism work in the same way, as agencies that bring about transformations. The primitive works to transform the physically weak character into a physically strong and self-sufficient individual. Both the rise of the British empire and the settling of the American frontier gave rise to ideologies that found expression in narrative subgenres and in turn literary movements such as literary naturalism. The connection between literary naturalism and the wilderness theme has not been well understood. The novels of imperial adventure and the Western helped to dissect these historical and literary experiences, often depicting the transformation of a character from a weakling to a rugged individualist by a frontierlike experience.

Kipling's *Captains Courageous* (1897), for example, portrays the transformation of Harvey Cheyne, weak and sickly, who falls overboard from an ocean liner on which he is traveling to Europe with his millionaire parents. He is picked up by Disko Troop, the fishing captain of *We're Here* and is transformed by the rigorous work and hardship he must submit to aboard Troop's ship. Harvey learns the value of hard work, self-reliance, and disciplined living; and when he is united with his parents, the boy has become a man who can now carry on in the spirit of his father, who came from poverty to conquer the West by confronting the Indians and transforming the land by running a railroad over it. In a plot that has become formulistic, Harvey moves beyond the soft, civilizing world of his mother, becomes his father's son, and can now carry on the task of claiming the West in the name of progress. Kipling is not too far removed from the wilderness assumption to believe that each generation of white men must renew this primitive sense of strength, must be challenged by the rudiments of nature itself, if they are to sustain the demands of manifest destiny. Kipling's novel is only one of many—for example, there are naturalistic novels like Jack London's *Sea Wolf* and romantic novels like Frank Norris's *Moran of the Lady Letty*—that depict the transformation from an overly civilized weakling to a rugged individualist able to carry on physical tasks demanded by the dictates of the West.

Naturalism as an ideological movement comes the closest of the narrative modes to depicting the historical and mythical assumptions of the frontier movement. Henry Adams's discussion of the movement from the idea of the Virgin to the idea of the Dynamo expresses symbolically the nature of this transformation as well as the argument of this book. From the idea of cultural unity (symbolized by the Virgin) to the fragmenting power of force (symbolized by the Dynamo), Adams traces the theoretical transition from the medieval to the modern. Jack London kept this spirit alive with his interest in the frontier wilderness. Frank Norris took us beyond the wilderness into the frontier movement itself in novels like *The Octopus*. Stephen Crane adds naturalistic dimension to the theme of the West when he redefines the code of the West.

Literary naturalism keeps coming back to one or another version of force, whether it be a life (vitalistic) force like that of the wheat that pushes life ahead of it, or the mechanistic (physical) force like the railroad that has its origins in human invention. In Frank Norris's *The Octopus* (1902), the two forces work antagonistically, and the characters define themselves by the way they align themselves with one force or another. On the side of the wheat are the wealthy farmers; on the side of the railroad are its executives and agents; a mediating link between these forces is the poet Presley, whose understanding of the situation leads to an epic vision of conflict. Vanamee is the character most in tune with the forces of nature. He is the Hebraic shepherd, mystic prophet, biblical visionary, whose mission is an errand in the wilderness. He incarnates the spirit of the land, can hold his flock of sheep in place or call to others by the power of mind. He mourns the death of Angele, whose rape led to her death in childbirth, even as he believes her spirit lives on in nature and is as alive as the wheat that bursts from the land each spring. This spirit is the force that drives the novel, a source of the corrective to the injustices the novel depicts. When Presley returns for the last time to the ranch, Venamee tells him that evil has no permanent status, is only a transitory phenomenon, ultimately subject to counterforces that "work together for good" (Norris 1958, 448).

Despite the ending of *The Octopus,* Norris takes us to the end of innocence. Although his sympathy was with the ranchers, they were equally corrupted by money. In *The Pit* (1903), Norris indicted the speculative economy, because it substituted a market economy for a landed culture. The value of wheat was measured by abstract concerns that were matters of speculation: it all turned on whether the price would rise or fall and had nothing to do with working the land to produce the wheat. Moreover, such markets could be manipulated if one had the means to buy up future wheat in abundance and then hold it off the market, depleting the supply and inflating the eventual cost.

Norris's novels found their counterpart abroad in writers like Knut Hamsun (1859–1952). His early novels, such as *Hunger* (1890), are marked by romanticism; his later novels, including *Growth of the Soil* (1917), show the influence of a Norwegian neorealism. All of his novels portrayed life in rural Norway, often from the point of view of an itinerant observer, who becomes the town's mysterious stranger. His interest in rural life, especially the life dependent on working the soil, is a narrative element that connects him with Turner's American wilderness frontier. Another Norwegian writer of significance was Sigrid Undset (1882–1949), whose *Kristin Lavransdatter* (1920–22) is set in the fourteenth century and depicts Kristin's growth, concentrating on her sexual history. A convert to Catholicism, Undset idealizes the medieval world in ways similar to Turner's idealizing the frontier: she glorifies a Christian past rather than the secular present.

Hamsun and Undset provide a literary model for an American Norwegian, Ole Rolvaag, who depicted the immigrant experience in America in *Giants in the Earth* (1927), a story of Norwegian immigrants working the Dakota territory from 1873 to 1881. Their experience was the product of government homesteading, in which a plot of 160 acres of public land was available to those who worked the land for five years. Along with the literary influence of Hamsun and Undset, Rolvaag's depiction owes much to his own and to his family's experience as they adapted to the land. The process of adaptation was not an easy one; surviving from season to season required overcoming such hostile forces as winter blizzards and infestations of insects in the summer. Per Hansa meets these obstacles with fortitude, unlike his wife Beret, who cannot adapt to the new world and longs to return to her native Norway; her experience is similar to that of Antonia's father in Cather's novel. Ironically, it is Hansa—and not Beret—who dies in a prairie blizzard, bringing the novel to a tragic resolution. True to naturalist assumptions, both Rolvaag and Norris showed how the element of force often worked in a hostile way. With the closing of the frontier, the working of force changed: the forces that had generated life on the land were now depicted as more antagonistic or as the product of commercial-industrial pursuits.

One of the main themes behind the myth of the Western was the assumption that moral imbalance can be corrected, that "right" will eventually overcome "might," and that justice will prevail. The Western hero lives by strength in a society of illusions, which upholds absolute justice and Christian restraint while the forces of greed, trickery, and self-interest work with cunning and corrupting force in deadly combat out of view. A lone crusader like Shane, or the Lone Ranger, or larger-than-life projections of the Western epic like Clint Eastwood, or John Wayne, or Gary Cooper, or other products of film fantasy embody residual justice and are the agents of moral change. With the exception of *The Octopus,* literary naturalism challenged this heroic view of mythic reality and gave us a more turbulent and less mystical view of the way west. Once again we are in the realm of transformation. We move in the Western from the wilderness as open frontier to the wilderness transformed by the power of human work that underlies a code of righteous pursuit.

But once the land has been worked, it is turned into property; and once it is property, it is subject to a legal system. That move takes us from the realm of the primitive (the wilderness unworked) to the realm of civilization (the land subject to the laws of property). It also takes us to the end of innocence—innocence giving way to the complexity of social mandates and law. Both Natty Bumppo and Huckleberry Finn tried to stay ahead of such restrictions. Once the wilderness is used up, its energy gives way to legal institutions that work to the advantage of those who have the means and the shrewdness to manipulate them. This takes us beyond the Western (which sometimes functions outside the law) to literary naturalism and the force of the new corporation or trust such as the railroad, or the force of cosmic whimsy that works against romantic destiny. Frontier work eventually becomes entangled with forms of natural, human, and cosmic force, so that literary reality (representation) gives way to a material process and to philosophical determinism.

We can see the transformation from the Western to naturalism in stories like Stephen Crane's "Blue Hotel," set in a Nebraska hotel, where stereotypical characters (each defined by his name: the easterner, the cowboy, the gambler, etc.) confront the Swede (the foreigner), who has been reading too many dime novels, is obsessed with what he feels is the lawlessness of the wild West, believes he is going to die as a victim of Old West violence, and then goes about promoting such a fate. The point of the story is not that he becomes the victim of Old West codes but that each character acts according to his temperament and the combined result is inevitable: what is predictable, indeed determined, is more consistent with the dictates of literary naturalism than with the spirit of dime-novel reality, which is being recast here. Crane takes us into literary naturalism and revises the mythic codes of the West.

Harold Kaplan, who has analyzed the nature of the stereotypical in literary naturalism, has shown how literary naturalism moves from the personal to the abstract, from human instincts (most often grounded in sex and money) to forms of political allegory in which sex and money, social status and physical display, operate subliminally and become the determining element, the power and the force working beyond human will and understanding.

A book that anticipates the connection between the closing of the frontier and literary naturalism is Mary Lawlor's *Recalling the Wild*. In her discussions of Frank Norris, Jack London, Stephen Crane, and Willa Cather, she sees a hardening of literary assumption. What she might have added to her argument is that the transformation from the Western to naturalism came simultaneously with the compulsive interest in the working of power and force, especially as those elements are abstracted from the theories of Darwin and Spencer and reified into a legal system that favors corporate entities, property, or other capitalist interests that became the forces that often controlled the narrative of naturalistic fiction. Naturalism replaced the Western: the two literary modes portrayed two different social realities. When the wilderness frontier ended, the problems of the urban-industrial frontier were still dominant, making naturalism (that frontier's literary mode of representation) more immediately relevant than the Western to this era.

But literary naturalism was later transformed by hermeneutic changes. There are two orders of literary textuality: one is the product of mimesis, the belief that literature imitates the realms of nature; the other is the product of the constructs a critic brings to the text. The mimetic view looks out to a physical and historical world; the constructed view looks inward to a consciousness that stems from the assumption that reality works like a language system with all time available simultaneously. When the constructed view is applied to a work of literary naturalism, it erases the historical aspect of the text, negates cause-and-effect progression, and produces a second realm of literary naturalism. In our discussion of postmodernism, we will see how the difference in critical assumption leads to different interpretations of Turner's frontier thesis.

III

There are essentially two traditions of meaning at work in premodern American literature. Walt Whitman and William James take us to a historical divide. Whitman takes us to romantic Oneness and to transcendental reality; James to literary realism, out of which came literary naturalism. Whitman's optimistic poetry arises out of the romantic myths involving the land and a frontier vision—a romantic vision that proved inadequate to cope with the new commercial-industrial complex. What emerges is another America, which Whitman begins to see too late. A major theme in this new vision was the end of innocence.

The transition from naturalism to forms of modernism involved what I have called elsewhere "an inward turn," the move toward narrative subjectivity or impressionism. A major influence here was Walter Pater's preface and conclusion to *The Renaissance* (508–12). Impressionism oversaw the transition from an objective to a subjective reality. The distinction between descriptive detail and impressionistic detail is objectivity on the way to becoming subjectivity. Joseph Conrad was the benefactor of Pater's theory, and through Conrad Stephen Crane, and through Crane Ernest Hemingway. Hemingway's is a naturalistic world transformed by a Paterian prism, with consciousness overriding naturalistic elements.

The connection between traditional forms of realism, the Western, and literary naturalism was only one in a series of steps that took us from forms of narrative romance to neorealism. Neorealism is literary naturalism without the naturalistic documentation. Dos Passos's *USA* (1937) trilogy, for example, depicted characters caught in the realm of force, but the source of force now was primarily historical, the product of the ups and downs of the capitalistic system. The result was a novel devoid of hereditary and environmental commentary. Another example of this kind of transformation is James M. Cain's *The Postman Always Rings Twice* (1934), which also moved away from naturalistic theory, presenting a naturalistic story without the racial or inherited background—without, that is, the documentation that previously made it naturalistic.

Another literary legacy in the transformation of naturalism into neorealism is literary and film noir. Jeff Jaeckle gives us a useful summary of the common ground between literary naturalism and film noir. He points to the constraints that characters in the two movements share: "[T]hey are poor, unemployed, or work unsatisfying jobs; they are trapped in failed relationships or marriages of convenience; they have powerful yet culturally inappropriate urges; and they are surrounded by characters who are better off, better educated, and happier." They are obsessed with a "desire for gold, wealth, and fame; crave sex or infidelity; are consumed with jealousy; and are drawn to violence and destruction. Like the naturalist novel's plot of decline, these characters succumb to their urges and wind up imprisoned, dying, or dead." Christopher Orr also believes that film noir developed out of literary naturalism and points to the common use of destructive women and to characters who are the victims of forces beyond their control (Jaeckle 483–84; see also Orr and Hirsh).

The transformation here depends more on the mix of narratives than on the influence of any one text. A significant debt is the noir reality produced by "hard-boiled" novelists like Dashiell Hammett, who established the prototype with *Red Harvest* (1929), *The Dain Curse* (1929), *The Maltese Falcon* (1930), and *The Glass Key* (1931). Hammett portrayed a corrupt world, usually embodied by the modern city with its shady alliance among business leaders, political bosses, elected officials, and corrupt lawmen. Into this world steps a putative redeemer (Ned Beaumont, Sam Spade, the Continental Op), a private or agency detective. He is not naive enough to believe that the city can be changed or unrealistic enough to believe that it can be redeemed. Its corruption is simply given, creating the determining force that works its way in noir in a manner similar to the working of hostile forces in literary naturalism. In both modes, we are in the realm of inevitability. The plots thicken around a young woman whose situation is an extension of the corrupt city; she is addicted to drugs or cult religions or suspected of murder or other crimes. Her situation constitutes the story; her fate its unfolding. Attempts at forms of redemption are unsuccessful because, like the city, she cannot be changed.

Hammett's detective is a modern embodiment of Sisyphus; he rolls the rock up the hill knowing it will roll down again. Such a disposition of mind marks a narrative difference from literary naturalism, especially when the protagonist brings moral understanding to a world that he cannot change—a world that includes the corrupt institutions that are at the source of what is all-determining. To this extent, he is more aware of the forces at work than is the traditional hero of literary naturalism, is more willing to live with the gratuitous element than is the naturalistic persona. The task itself becomes its own reward. He plays out a corrupt reality because that is all there is to play. He accepts and brings rare understanding to what literary naturalism gives us at its worst.

Hammett takes us to Raymond Chandler and a similar vision of urban control as portrayed in the sleazy world of Los Angeles that we find in *The Big Sleep* (1939), with its blackmailing component, bootlegging, pornography, and illegal gambling. An extension of Los Angeles, *Farewell, My Lovely* (1940), takes Marlowe into the equally corrupt world of Bay City, Chandler's fictional depiction of Santa Monica. The emphasis in these novels is less on the meaning of character, with perhaps the exception of Marlowe, than on the operation of a sordid city—a city that has come into being as an idealized product of western resolve but has given way to the perpetuation of the morally dubious, conditioning those who fall prey to its operations.

Chandler's city is a secular Eden, once bright with the promise of an idealized past, now a darkened, fallen realm. Its history is duplicated by General Sternwood, who embodies the lost promise of the past and vulnerability to its now corrupt workings, along with the truncated legacy (as perpetuated by what is representative in his wayward daughters) for any kind of future. As in the Western, Marlowe brings a chivalric code to bear in his pursuit, but it fails him. As in literary naturalism, the environment, now corrupted, controls both the workings of the city and those who take the city as their task.

The formulaic quality of these texts was reinforced by the publication of Hemingway's *To Have and Have Not* (1937), a work that followed most of Hammett's novels and preceded the novels of Chandler. Once we have a novel like *To Have and Have Not,* we have endowed yet another realism, the transforming power of "hard-boiled" narratives that reverses traditional plots like the Western. In the Western, good and evil are demarcated, with the protagonist on the side of "good," the antagonist on the side of "evil." In noir fiction, these terms are reversed: the noir character, whose perspective dominates what and how we see, works outside the realm of good—that is, the noir character is most often the antihero, such as Hemingway's Harry Morgan; instead of embodying the values of society, he lives outside the law, on the edge of community.

The women in noir literature and film are femme fatales; like Margo Macomber, they have no desire to settle down or raise a family. Their presence is destructive: when not out to destroy a man, they demand the dominant role. At the center of a noir plot is the assumption that everyone is degraded: nobody is innocent; good and evil blur as moral choices; redemption and betrayal are one and the same.

The noir novel with its antihero takes us to the edge of a democratic society, to the antithesis of Turner's frontier thesis, to a realm opposite that of the Western, to marginal men and women living by their wits. Once they are further socially removed, they will become the drifters in the novels of James M. Cain, the seekers in Kerouac, the homeless derelicts in Nelson Algren and William Kennedy, and the family outcasts in Joyce Carol Oates.

The movement from Wister's Virginian to Chandler's Philip Marlowe paralleled the transition from the wilderness frontier to the urban frontier. Hemingway depicted characters that embody the reality of both wilderness reality and its reformation in the ills of the city. In effect, Hemingway bridged the connection between the cowboy and the detective, the transition from Gary Cooper to Humphrey Bogart. While the influence of *To Have and Have Not* on literary noir is demonstrable, his other works carry on the other tradition of modernism and give us a neorealism version of the Western code hero: the individual defined by conduct in the arena in works whose values he brought to his depiction of Africa and Spain, to war in general, to the bullfight, the big-game hunt, and the deep-sea encounter.

Further transformations in the Western—and in the attributes of its hero, who embodies the values of the wilderness frontier—await additional discussion of literary modernism and its postmodern reformations.

12

Realms of Interpretation

I

The philosophy of history (historiography) deals with history as a system of meaning and looks at the questions history asks, the answers returned, and the assumptions involved in understanding the way such interpretation works. When applied to historicism, historiography assumes that history is subject to physical laws of a closed system (as opposed to the modernist response that history is not a closed system—is not a system at all—and that there is no principle ordering its being or dictating its meaning).

In this study, we have witnessed two forms of change: one was a physical change in the transformation from an American wilderness to an urban frontier. The other was changes in the idea of history as we moved from the assumptions of romantic destiny to the principles of historicism. In both cases we are dealing with the idea of America based on changing concepts of history—one involving physical changes, the other involving conceptual changes.

At one point in pursuing the historical record, we accommodated the theoretical concern involving the difference between history as conflict and history as consensus. Beard and Parrington thought of "conflict" as the linchpin of history. Richard Hofstadter went along with this assumption until 1945, when he substituted the idea of "consensus" for conflict as the fundamental issue for historical study. The consensus historian believes that there are issues that prevail in each era, around which conflicting parties take sides—that is, there is agreement over what are the basic issues but disagreement on the meaning of the issues themselves. The emphasis is on partisan response to the issues rather than a study of an issue in isolation—for example, the Civil War as a conflict involving multifaceted concerns, especially the transference of power from South to North, rather than an ideological conflict over the slavery issue as the main or total concern.

Perhaps the most transformational historical concept involved the desire to create a "usable past," a desire to retrieve what might stand for an idealized past, to bring to the historical surface a sense of tradition upon which the historical and literary imagination could build. Emerson supplied such a cultural construct, both in his insistence upon self-reliance and by redefining nature in ways that released it from Puritan restraint. Emerson wanted a cultural product that was American in its roots, and he supplied the basis for such a vision that was carried on by Walt Whitman, Hart Crane, and William Carlos Williams. The *Seven Arts* authors, especially Van Wyck Brooks (1976), discussed the need for such historical unfolding. In its own way, Turner's frontier thesis can be added to this list, because it brings a sense of what is unique in American experience and points toward historical and intellectual reality and beyond to the idea of the West.

The reality of Turner's frontier is superseded only by its legacy. Turner's frontier is the basis for many transformations in the realms of American education. As previously suggested, his thesis was the foundation for two major works in American studies: Henry Nash Smith's *Virgin Land* (1950) and Leo Marx's *The Machine in the Garden* (1964). Both were begun as dissertations in the American Civilization Program at Harvard. The first validated the reality of the frontier, based on documentation from the dime novel and the Western; the second documented the evolution of pastoral America from agrarian to industrial (technological) pursuit.

Along with Harvard, Johns Hopkins University, in which Turner was enrolled as a graduate student, played an important role in his intellectual development. Hopkins modeled its program on the German seminar system, was sympathetic to Kantian idealism, and inculcated the idea of the Volk, with its belief that the working of the land was key to national purpose. At Hopkins, Turner studied under the supervision of his mentor, Baxter Adams, whose pedagogical preferences leaned toward historicism, another product of the German system. Turner owed more than he acknowledged to the German educational system; much went unacknowledged because he firmly believed that what started out as German influence was transformed by the frontier experience into an indigenous American product.

Turner rejected much in the Hopkins approach in his desire to portray an indigenous America. The desire to write a definitive cultural history of America stems from the assumption that one can find a context large enough to inform such a project. Early attempts by historians such as V. L. Parrington, Van Wyck Brooks, and Randolph Bourne all looked to material culture and historical events.

The influence of Puritanism became a dominant concern in Perry Miller's *Errand into the Wilderness* (1956) and Sacvan Bercovitch's *The Puritan Origins of the American Self* (1975), as well as Bercovitch's *The American Jeremiad* (1978).

Puritanism shared interest with regional matters in Perry Miller's *The New England Mind* (1939) and W. J. Cash's *The Mind of the South* (1941). Hamlin Garland's *Main-Travelled Roads* (1891) was a collection of short stories dealing mostly with midwestern agrarian life, and his *A Son of the Middle Border* (1917) was an autobiography of westward expansion. The history of the far West found popular expression in Wallace Stegner's autobiographical novel, *The Big Rock Candy Mountain* (1943), and his account of the exploration attainments of John Wesley Powell in *Beyond the Hundredth Meridian* (1954). Bernard DeVoto's work involving the far West is best represented by his studies of Mark Twain and his *Across the Wide Missouri* (1947).

Regional concerns in turn gave way to the study of key themes—such as the idea of an American Adam or the loss of national innocence as conceptualized in R. W. B. Lewis's *The American Adam* (1955). I have already mentioned Smith's *Virgin Land* and Marx's *The Machine in the Garden,* one depicting the literary benefits of the agrarian frontier, the other of the industrial frontier. A more controversial working of themes can be found in Leslie Fiedler's discussion of an American affinity for interracial homoerotic experience (Huck and Jim, Queequeg and Ishmael, Natty Bumppo and Chingachgook) along with an expression of racial and ethnic concerns and a defense of American Indians in *An End to Innocence* (1955), *Waiting for the End* (1964), and *The Return of the Vanishing American* (1968).

The interest in key literary themes was supplemented by the study of such cultural phenomena as the rise of the city in Richard Lehan's

The City in Literature (1998), or as an interest in generic movements such as the literary Western or literary naturalism in Lehan's *Realism and Naturalism: The Novel in an Age of Transition* (2005), or the transformative power of modernism in Lehan's *Literary Modernism and Beyond: The Extended Vision and the Realms of the Text* (2009). Earlier (from the late 1930s to the early 1960s) the major critical movement involved Agrarians or New Critics, who in works like Cleanth Brooks's *The Well Wrought Urn* (1947) shifted interest from a historical and generic context to the individual work itself, claiming that each work was "autotelic" (or self-contained, an end unto itself), with its own independent meaning and formal integrity.

A major shift in the critical landscape came a generation later, with the rise of structuralism—the belief that paradigmatic changes opened up the meaning of history and supplied the authority to justify a "constructed" reality, moving the source of historical meaning away from primary sources to the consciousness of the critic or the unconsciousness (as in a language system) of meaning latent in the text. The rejection of transhistorical mandates led to a revised aspect of structuralism and to the poststructuralism we find in works such as John Irwin's *American Hieroglyphics* (1980), a deconstructionist study.

Quest West has concerned itself with a number of theoretical problems as they relate to the study of history, including the just-mentioned role of historicism: the belief in a system of historical laws that bring coherence to a historical process. As we have seen, the story of the West has been told from many historical perspectives, each perspective creating its own interpretive realm. Some endorsed the Turner thesis (Billington, Jacobs, Curti, and Bogue); others rejected it (Wade and Schlesinger); others transformed it (Hofstadter, Cronon, Limerick, White, Nash, and Klein).

Turner aside, others concentrated on such adjunct activity as wild-West exhibits and the tendency of the western code to be trigger-prone (Slotkin); others restricted themselves to the more historical aspects of the movement (Walter Allen's *Urgent West*), or to its unfolding by explorers such as John Wesley Powell (Wallace Stegner's *Beyond the Hundredth Meridian*). Still others related the benefits from commercial pursuits (Gerald Nash); others found benefits in the commercial lapses that accompanied the decline of myth (Robert G. Athearn's *The Mythic West in Twentieth-Century America*). Each book had both content and context: Turner's thesis dealt with the content of wilderness in the context of the frontier, while Patricia Limerick's book dealt with conflict as content in the context of the West as a realm beyond frontier.

II

Quest West is a study of national origins as well as the frontier as a region. Regionalism includes the belief that each region creates a culture of its own; the working of its environment creates a state of mind—a regional consciousness—that distinguishes it from other regions. There is thus a crucial difference between frontier and region. The frontier is the spearhead of, say, the movement west: it is the geographical realm beyond established borders, occupied by pioneers and settlers who define themselves in relation to the wilderness. The region is that geographical realm behind the frontier best defined by established borders, economic and political leanings, and cultural traits. The region takes much of its being from a dominant city within its borders: New York in the East, Chicago in the Midwest, Atlanta in the South, Denver in the Rockies, San Francisco in the Pacific Northwest, and Los Angeles in the Pacific Southwest.

Turner adhered to the difference between wilderness and region, as did Charles Beard. The distinction became the basis for an assumption that led to what became known as progressive history. The movement was taken over at the University of Wisconsin, where, under the influence of Turner, the history department followed in his footsteps, as we can see by examining the careers of such distinguished practitioners as Merle Curti, Ray Allen Billington, and Allan G. Bogue. There was both continuity and difference between the historians of each generation. As for continuity, Merle Curti wrote his PhD dissertation at Harvard under the supervision of Turner, who had joined the Harvard faculty in 1910, and Richard Hofstadter wrote his dissertation under Curti at Columbia.

In 1955, a generation (twenty-eight years, to be exact) after Turner recorded his frontier thesis, Earl Pomeroy published an influential essay, "Toward a Reorientation of Western History: Continuity and Environment." Pomeroy redefined the frontier, insisting that the frontier began in Europe and was not a purely American experience: America was Europe's West. Pomeroy's enlarged version of the frontier reasserted the earlier claims by Walter Prescott Webb, who in 1952 published *The Great Frontier*. Webb and Turner are often compared: Turner saw the West as a moving frontier, subject to constant change; Webb saw it as a more fixed environment to which the pioneers had to adapt (see West 2004, 38–39).

The West took on added interest with the rise of environmental and ethnic studies. It was not surprising to find a revised idea of the frontier, more consistent with the global nature of America, after World War II. Once more a transformed America accommodated a changing idea of the frontier. Pomeroy went beyond Webb when he claimed that the West was more a colonial outpost—a capital, technological, and political dependency. The West became a settlement dependent on the East, rather than a separate, independent geographical region, an interpretive strategy that negated the West as the determinant of its own fate.

Another major break in the transition between generations occurs with the work of Patricia Nelson Limerick, who in *The Legacy of Conquest* (1987) gives us a new interpretation of the West by changing the terms of the discussion. Turner's idea of the frontier was based on Anglo-American participation in an agrarian process, with the frontier ending when the population of a region had reached two persons per square mile. Limerick substituted a different conceptual construct for Turner's idea of the frontier: a construct grounded in forms of power, especially the use of militant force, rather than Turner's agrarian idea of a community based on the working of the land by yeoman farmers. Limerick does away with the idea of a frontier altogether, substituting "conquest" for frontier, "occupancy" for process, and an "unbroken past" for Turner's receding (evolving) west.

Limerick argues that Turner's thesis offers no continuity for the transformation from an agrarian to an industrial world, that a region might be coming into its own (and not in a process of decline) when its population increases, and that the history of the West—from the displacement of the American Indian to the extermination of the buffalo—is a matter of conquest, of change produced by forms of power, most often militant but sometimes legal. She refers us to the popular Western writer Louis L'Amour's satisfaction with the passing of the buffalo, because with the buffalo gone, the land could be used for raising grain. It turns out that L'Amour's sense of progress that came with the passing of the buffalo was not consistent with his response to a utility company's proposal to build a 345,000-volt power line in proximity to his own land. Progress, it turns out, was a relative matter, and the success and failure of lawsuits, along with more militant forms of power (what Limerick calls "conquest"), determined who ruled and who defined what the frontier was to be. Limerick makes further inroads into Turner's thesis when she argues that Turner modeled his idea of the West on Portage, Wisconsin, the small town in central Wisconsin where he was born and grew up. Almost three generations after Turner explained his frontier theses (eighty-four years, to be exact), Limerick tells us that her hometown of Banning, California—on the edge of the Mojave Desert, part of a trail west—was equally part of western history, extending the mandate of the idea of the frontier.

In another book, *Something in the Soil*, Limerick extends her attack on the Turner frontier thesis. Focusing on Turner's claim that each generation rewrites the story of the frontier from what is uppermost in present concern, she questions whether one can focus historical concern so readily, claiming that the historical present is equally as complex as the historical past and not so easily reduced in meaning. She argues that Turner's thesis is the product of his own racial, class, and gender beliefs (white, middle-class, male perspective) and that historians will always be influenced by the prejudices they bring to the historical equation. She insists that Turner's belief that the present and the past clarify each other is demonstrably simplistic and fails to do justice to the complexity of history.

Limerick's revision of western history brings with it expanded concerns about what is the West. Her books give us another way of thinking about the West as they build upon Pomeroy's assumption that the frontier was more a colonial outpost, a conquered realm, than a realm of open and free land. Where Pomeroy viewed the East-West controversy from a national perspective, Limerick viewed it from a western perspective, as both a deviation from and a continuation of the Turner thesis.

The main arguments of both Pomeroy and Limerick over the supremacy of the East are qualified in *The American West Transformed* (1985), by Gerald Nash, who believes that in 1945, at the end of World

War II, the West was liberated from eastern dependency; moreover, because the West was part of the sunbelt, the western-eastern roles were reversed, and the West became a "pacesetter" for the nation, autonomous and independent of eastern control. Under the influence of this revisionist thinking, the West takes on a plethora of new meanings.

Still another revisionist interpretation along the same lines is Robert G. Athearn's *The Mythic West in Twentieth-Century America* (1986), which depicts the weakening of the most potent myths of the West—such as the myth of the Golden Age and the belief that the West embodied the Promised Land: myths that depict the wilderness experience as unique, producing a new breed of man and an idealized reality, the character of which has been transformed by the rise of modern-day civilization. Athearn's book describes in detail the way the romantic West gave way to a process of decline brought on by drought and depression. As he put it himself, "even the die-hards among Old West fans had to admit that, indeed, the land of their dreams was no more. The American dream had become an illusion as the myth of unlimited possibility had run aground on the reality of drought, depression, and agricultural desolation" (104). Athearn points out by way of conclusion that Turner's wilderness West died, to be resurrected into a tourist attraction and a realm of entertainment, the product of popular songs by Gene Autry and Roy Rogers or blockbuster-superhero movies featuring John Wayne and Clint Eastwood, displaying romantic images of the frontier cowboy long lost to anything like historical reality. (As products of the wilderness frontier, it is not accidental that both Eastwood and Wayne supported right-wing causes that infused wilderness ideology.)

The most radical revision of the Turner thesis came in books by Richard White and Richard Etulain. Richard White's *"It's Your Misfortune and None of My Own": A History of the American West* (1991) challenges the Hollywood wagon-train version of the way west that played off the Turner thesis. He gives credence to ideas that never engaged Turner, especially the claim that the way west was conflicted by racial and ethnic matters. He argues against the assumption that the white man destroyed an environment that the Indians had preserved, insisting that the Indians altered the land by living off it.

Richard Etulain, in his *The American West: A Modern History, 1900 to the Present* (2007), brings the discussion of the West up to the present and tries for balance between the older ideas of Turner and the new ideas involving ethnic concerns. Under the influence of the radical social changes of the 1960s, it was not surprising to see the focus change from rugged frontier individualism to the victims of the pioneer movement, especially the American Indians.

A series of books that confirms and extends the White and Etulain theses are by Richard Slotkin: *Regeneration through Violence* (1973), *The Fatal Environment* (1998), and *Gunfighter Nation* (1992). Slotkin's trilogy treats the fate of the American Indian, the frontier as depicted in the dime novel, Buffalo Bill's Wild West show, and Hollywood films. He also discusses the way the rise of an industrial America transformed our perception of the wilderness frontier. Slotkin's view of the frontier is ultimately different from prevailing commentary. He sees the West as a powder-keg region prone to forms of violence, adding that the myth of the West kept alive a state of mind that that has expressed itself in racism, imperialism, and wars such as the Vietnam War (and later conflicts such as those in Iraq and Afghanistan), as well as the violence that has provoked the mass murders we have witnessed in Littleton (Columbine High School) and Aurora, Colorado, and in Newtown, Connecticut. Guns kill more than eleven thousand persons each year in America, far more than in any other country in the world, justifying the epithet "gunfighter nation." As we have seen, this tradition of violence was built into the American frontier; and Slotkin seems justified in seeing it encouraged more by war-minded imperialists such as Theodore Roosevelt, whose belief in manifest destiny is acknowledged in *The Winning of the West,* or romance-prone novelists such as Owen Wister in *The Virginian,* than by Turner's critique of the frontier.

Still another revisionist reading of Turner is William Handley's *Marriage, Violence, and the Nation in the American Literary West* (2002). Handley begins with Turner's depiction of the frontiersman as self-reliant, idealistic, and egalitarian, above all individualistic and male, and often prone to violence. Handley treats six authors: Owen Wister, Zane Grey, Willa Cather, F. Scott Fitzgerald, Joan Didion, and Wallace Stegner. Using the novels of Wister and Grey as the model of the Western, Handley claims that the other novels are more concerned with marriage and domesticity, in which they find the same struggles "concerning democracy and empire, promises kept and betrayed, greed and possession, optimism and pessimism, romance and violence that are played out in the West but with a sense of national stakes" (16).

Since violence in the traditional novel parallels violence in the Western, Turner's idea of frontier individualism is subject to reconsideration. Turner's individualism "created expectations that not only could not be met in the West but could not sustain social life in the West where kinship was key to communal survival (Handley 17). Violence is a common denominator in the two fictions, but it is casual violence in the Western and domestic violence in the traditional novel. The two come together as showing an American identity that is larger and that goes beyond Turner's individualism.

Handley brings a radically different focus to bear in examining the West in terms of the conventions of marriage. His discussions are often rich in their treatment of adjacent themes, such as the latent violence that seems pent up in the family and the consequences of deviation from traditional marriage, as with the Mormons and the Indians— themes more or less irrelevant to Turner's thesis when not conjoined by Handley. But in making marriage his thematic center, Handley introduces an element that did not concern Turner and takes us into a literary West of his own invention. Handley does what most revisionists do: he undoes Turner's theses in the name of his own. His interpretive strategy takes him away from Turner into his own narrative realms, from which he can then abstract imaginative but misleading conclusions. Handley has transformed Turner's thesis into something it was not, creating a fictional Turner and pointing to a realm of concern that never involved Turner.

These variations in emphasis give us a series of wilderness frontiers, from the more benign frontier of Turner to the more lawless frontier that Slotkin depicts. Each generation interprets the data anew, most often in accord with the political and economic changes at work in an evolving nation. Once the many versions of the frontier have been tabulated, the next step is to weigh their credibility and importance. In that context, Turner's thesis would seem to triumph as the vision most long-lasting and most sustained as an idea. Despite the variations, reciprocity (a mutual sense of process) was at work. The idea of the frontier and the idea of America were at one: the idea of the frontier became embodied in an idea of the West, which the historian could extrapolate to the idea of America. The idea of America could then be read back again as a mandate of the frontier; the circularity kept realms ideologically consistent with each other.

III

While historicism was the controlling mode of historical study involving the gilded age, there were within historicism three schools of concern, with differing priorities and hence with differing beliefs about what was the controlling issue, the center, of the era. The schools that examined the Populist-Progressive movements were the Wisconsin school, the Vanderbilt (Fugitive) school, and the Columbia school. All three concerned themselves with regional matters and took political positions that accommodated their ideology.

The Wisconsin school (Turner, Curti, Billington, Bogue, and Cronon) supported the attempt to move the prairie states into the ideological center and, although generally sympathetic to protectionist policies, was divided on the matter of isolationism. Merle Curti saw the Midwest as the heartland of America and its intellectual center, as opposed to Richard Hofstadter, who saw the intellectual force of America emanating from the East. The Vanderbilt school (Ransom, Penn Warren, and Tate) took the prewar South as the ideal society and supported an agrarian society and isolationism.

The Columbia school (Hofstadter, Bell, and Lipset) took the city as the ideological center, supported immigration, and was sympathetic to imperial pursuits. Arthur Schlesinger's *The Age of Jackson* (1945) insisted that Jackson restored the egalitarian desire in America and qualified the Turner approach to this era by stressing the urban rather than the rural source of reform (Brown 2006, 57). Richard Hofstadter felt that the Progressive movement was a weakened response to the abuses of the new industrialization of America. He believed the reform impulse had been picked up by the New Deal, which also failed in its attempt to mollify the effects of the depression, fascism, and racism or to supply a substitute for the ideal of the yeoman pioneer or the myth of the frontier (54). The intensity of the attack of the New York critics reveals the radical difference in political consciousness between Turner's wilderness frontier and New York urbanism. The New York intellectuals insisted that the vitality of their own region was living proof that

Turner had unjustifiably exaggerated the influence of the frontier in his reference to American history.

If the New York critics took their agenda from the urban workings of their region, the southern Agrarians took their agenda from the wilderness frontier as formulated by Turner and his disciples. And just as there is a subliminal connection between the agrarian and literary agendas, there is also a submerged connection, a symmetry of meaning, between frontier theses and the realms of intellectual history: the contrast between the theses of Turner wilderness and urban reality finds a parallel in the contrast between the Wisconsin-and-Fugitive historians, proponents of the Turner thesis, and the New York historians, products of the city.

Put differently, we have two realms of competing interpretation: on one hand, the agrarian thesis as proposed by Turner and the Wisconsin historians and their Fugitive counterparts and, on the other hand, the urban thesis as proposed by a host of New York intellectuals. There are thus parallel interpretations between frontier theses involving agrarian versus urban pursuits and historical interpretations based on the same systems of dichotomy; the end products of these interpretations give us radically different versions of America based on competing ideas of origins.

Richard Hofstadter supplied the momentum for the urban interpretation and can be linked with such New York liberals as Lionel Trilling, Alfred Kazin, Irving Howe, Saul Bellow, Leslie Fiedler, Daniel Bell, Philip Rahv, Nathan Glazer, Sidney Hook, Susan Sontag, Seymour Lipset, and Norman Podhoretz. This group shares many points in common: They all come from a Jewish background. They were aware of the long tradition of European anti-Semitism and took solace in having access to the more open political system in America. Politically, they maintained leftist sympathies, at least initially, before some of them (including Trilling, Bell, Hofstadter, Podhoretz, and Hook, to cite the most adamant) moved to the right.

This move in part stemmed from the disillusionment experienced by the radical Left in the 1930s and 1940s and is larger in context than the shift among New York liberals, as witnessed by the political transformation from liberal to conservative of such an influential spokesman as John Dos Passos. Part of the shift in political alignment was international in concern, traced to the lost innocence that followed Stalin's gulags. Part was domestic: as the federal government became stronger and more intrusive, it encountered the danger of manipulation by special interests, politicians influenced by lobbyists, and projects that benefited personal mandates and regional interests, often involving rampant waste. The influence of literary modernism can be added to such practices, especially its emphasis upon aesthetic matters and the priority of consciousness, which moved the discussion away from socioeconomic concerns and toward what Trilling called matters of the mind. And part of the shift came from the restoration of confidence in a financial system newly energized by wartime spending and engaged in resisting forms of totalitarianism in both Germany and Russia. As it became more prosperous, the Jewish population came to believe that Jewish well-being was better served by the Right than the Left. But carried over in this transition was a disdain for the agrarian hinterland with its evangelical beliefs and its disdain for the city and its urban values.

That liberal values continued to apply was a key point in Lionel Trilling's *The Middle of the Journey,* in which New York liberals fail to come to terms with the morally dubious policies of Stalin and with Communism in the modernist era. The backstory here includes Whittaker Chambers's disillusionment with the Communist Party and his implicating Alger Hiss before the House Un-American Activities Committee. This moment of history is fictionalized in the story of John Laskell, who feels empathy for Gifford Maxim (the Chambers figure). The problem is discussed in the summer home (testimony to the middle-class comforts of many Communist Party sympathizers) of Arthur and Nancy Croom, fellow travelers (sympathetic to but not members of the party). The Crooms believe the end justifies the means; despite the wrongs perpetuated by Stalin, they believe good can come from those actions. It was this sense of expediency that drove Trilling and other New York liberals to the Right and to neoconservative politics.

IV

The rise of literary modernism made inroads into both the idea of romantic destiny and historicism. Ezra Pound, T. S. Eliot, and William Carlos Williams all had different theories of how history worked.

Central to Eliot's concept of history was his belief in "tradition," the assumption that history builds upon itself and that continuity is part of the historical process, an idea that Pound believed was the basis for the "repeat" in history. To this end, Eliot's world involved the crossroads: an intersection between order and disorder, the spiritual and the material, the City of God and the city of man, the savage Sweeney and the decadent Prufrock. There were levels where these opposites met: man and God, for example, in Christ; man and animal in Sweeney; desire and inhibition in Prufrock. Like Turner, Eliot tried to reconcile the union of savage and civilized, the primitive and the city. Like Turner's thesis, Eliot's views were part of the neoconservative thinking that imbued literary modernism. And like Turner, he saw the industrialized city as a container separating the inhabitant from a spiritual realm emanating from something as basic as the soil. Eliot was writing in a world more urban and industrialized. A faceless crowd that never quite became a community, Eliot's modern inhabitants were cut off from the redeeming vitality that Turner allowed his agrarian pioneers.

Closer to Turner was the poetic world of William Carlos Williams. Williams resisted Pound and Eliot's attempt to find a historical ideal in the European past; he took radical exception to Eliot's idea of tradition when he insisted on history as a series of "new beginnings," an idea that challenged the belief that the past builds upon itself. He believed that meaning was not built into time or nature: history was discontinuous, a process of evolution subject to revolution. Like Turner, he leaned toward the indigenous, looked to America for historical ideals, and found his own ideas codified by Emerson and Whitman. Meaning was not found in the mind or in objects but in the conjunction (the combined workings) of the two. The poet created rather than discovered meaning. Williams anticipated what would become structuralist assumptions as well as rewriting American history from a dialectical perspective of origins. In this context, the Indians, rebellious in the face of Puritan authority, came to stand for a new freedom. While Turner took little interest in the role of the Indians, Williams's liberating position was consistent with Turner's idea of an open frontier.

Hart Crane (1899–1932) also inherited Whitman's vision and sustained beliefs that justified his connection to the *Seven Arts* group. Crane tried to bring Whitman's pronouncements up to date, moving from "Crossing Brooklyn Ferry" (1856) to *The Bridge* (1930). Crane wanted to heal what he called "the iron-dealt cleavage," the great divide between an agrarian and an industrial culture. The Brooklyn Bridge is Crane's symbol for cosmic unity: the connection of the finite and the infinite, past and present, East and West, agrarian and industrial, the bridge reconciles the disharmony between man and machine, primitive and mass culture. As a suspension bridge, it holds itself up by displacing stress, as the arch does, by the dispersion of its own weight, internal forces absorbing external pressure. He believed that, likewise, there could be an organic unity between an industrial culture and nature, and he tried to create a poetic vision that would reveal such harmony. Crane made use of the major modernist themes: *The Bridge* moves from the city to the frontier, to the West, and then back to the city in what has become an archetypal American journey. He was relying on material—the myth of the land, the power of Dionysus, the theme of the West, the hope for a New Atlantis—that took its meaning more from a tradition of mythic belief than from the convictions of his poetic argument. Crane tried to steer a course between T. S. Eliot's sense of cultural exhaustion and William Carlos Williams's belief in new beginnings, but he could not find the historical elements that would lift Eliot's vision or justify Williams's. As he worked on the poem, he began reading Spengler, and doubt clouded hope. Like Whitman's before him and Williams's after, his sense of hope foundered when it had no way to reconcile mythic belief with historical reality.

A third modernist who caught the attention of the *Seven Arts* group was Sherwood Anderson. Like Hart Crane, he grew up in a small Ohio town (Clyde) that was in the process of moving from an agrarian to an industrial base. Anderson believed such cultural mixture led to a lack of identity and psychological displacement, and in his major works he portrayed the effects of such displacement as the source of the grotesque.

The modernist mind was often torn between opposed beliefs, with the desire to reconcile them. While the *Seven Arts* authors focused on the critical impasse between an industrial and an agrarian culture, Lionel Trilling could not reconcile the modern disparity between an idealized and a profane reality. In *The Liberal Imagination,* Trilling speaks of two forms of modern reality—that of the Real and that of the Mind. He discusses the mind as a superior form of reality, linking it with the fiction of Henry James, as opposed to the "inferior" reality of Dreiser, who is the product of realism. In questioning the role of environment as a psychological factor, Trilling's exercise went a long way in delimiting both the rugged individualism of Turner's frontier reality and the environmental determinism of literary naturalism. Trilling created an intellectual vacuum outside of literary modernism, into which were pulled the dictates of the wilderness frontier and the controlling assumptions of literary naturalism. In disparaging the realms of frontier wilderness and the dictates of literary naturalism, he gave us a new, albeit a literary, America. We were now in a world of aesthetic consciousness, ambivalent by nature, self-contained in its organic workings.

Turner's frontier mandate, essentially a material construct, gave way to the idea of consciousness as the basis of this intellectual movement, to what can be called "the inward turn" of the modernist agenda. The result led to more nuanced thinking, to different shadings of intellectual reality, and removed from the center Turner's rugged individualist, who was the product of New World democracy and romantic destiny. An American prototype moved over, making room for John Archer and J. Alfred Prufrock. Trilling, and the modernist movement he helped sustain, created a far more cerebral embodiment of the American type. Indeed, the American democrat now shared a sense of authenticity with an extended, albeit European, consciousness.

V

As even the terminology suggests, the move toward modernism anticipated a postmodernism that is an intellectual break with modernism, gives us a form of reality separate from modernism, and is a further impingement on the Turner thesis of the wilderness. The idea of the West is transformed by the idea of history that we bring to it. We have previously discussed the transformations implicit in an Enlightenment and romantic reading of history. A similar transformation occurs when the idea of the West is subjected to a postmodern reading of history. The postmodern assumption is that we do not know history: what we know are the paradigms (constructs) we bring to our historical explanations. Once history becomes a system of signs, we need a transcendental signifier (be it God, nature, the mind, or a system of history itself) to hold the signs in place. Without a transcendental signifier, we have clues without conclusion, information without definition, content without context. Meaning is no longer a process of discovery but resides in the structures the mind furnishes.

Modernism begins where Nietzsche left off—with human consciousness confronting an unmade universe. Postmodernism takes us one step beyond modernist perspectivism and assumes that consciousness has been collapsed into the culture as part of a system held in place by institutions (that is, by forms of power). Such a procedure negates the influence of the subject (the idea of self) and substitutes the influence of the culture itself (e.g., the workings of capitalism) functioning as a state of mind, which in its pervading reach now "thinks us," individual motives subsumed to the collective ideology of a power base. The postmodern view negates the belief that meaning is built into history. Nature is no longer a mirror, its workings to be read symbolically. We create rather than discover meaning, and the epistemological process is hermeneutical (interpretive). There is an echo principle at work: we are the products of the meaning we bring to an issue.

The postmodern text is really the product of structuralism, which takes its being from the belief that reality functions semiotically, like a self-contained language system in which all meaning is present at once. In practice, it involves reading cultural signs in a transhistorical context, an assumption that was challenged by poststructuralism, with deconstructed meaning now emerging from disembodied signs, clues without conclusions. The difference between modern and postmodern thought turns on the difference between structural and organic principles. The organic assumes that a text is self-fulfilling, that each text completes itself like a plant working toward bloom in nature. The structural is based on the working of critical paradigms supplied by the critic. The organic takes its being from the idea that forms are autotelic.

Structural thought is the product of paradigms; organic thought is the product of an informing principle—dynamic, living, developmental, and self-fulfilling. The world of organic ideas, like plants and animals, takes on the property of living things. This idea supplies common ground, binding common elements—such as the southern Agrarians' belief in the vitality (fecundity) of the soil and the New Critics' belief in the vitality (autonomy) of the literary text. But when looked at as interpretive methods, and as applied to an idea like the wilderness frontier, the two systems produce totally divergent realities.

A text that illustrates the structural workings of postmodern history is Thomas Pynchon's *The Crying of Lot 49*. Pynchon's novel is also an apt conclusion to the idea of the West and to this book. It is Oedipa Maas's task to determine the legacy of Pierce Inverarity, a capitalist (think of Howard Hughes) on whose fortune much of America rests. Oedipa comes to believe that this legacy rests on the workings of an underground communication system that she must reveal to public scrutiny. Entering this maze, she comes upon series of clues, but each clue proves tentative and leads only to another clue. Forms of power hold the clues together, but once Pierce is dead, that power is diminished and no longer tangible. Oedipa comes to realize that there is no transcendent ideal holding the system together—that the idea of the West had its moment and then gave way to other forms that promised redemptive power, including the promises of Inverarity's capitalism with its submerged legions of investors and advisers. This was the source of power that held together Pierce Inverarity's legacy. Behind the front that Inverarity offered to the world was a counterfeit reality—a system built upon its own waste that depleted rather than energized, was entropic rather than organic, working in mysterious ways. The illusion of destiny was overtaken by a system now manipulated by special interest and greed. The power of illusion had produced an idealized America, but it met its limits in the postmodern realm of intellectual doubt.

Coda

I

This has been the story of two American realms, the wilderness frontier and its urban counterforce, and the historical assumptions and ideological transformations to which they gave rise. The wilderness frontier helped transform a European peasant into an American democrat: individualistic by instinct, optimistic in perspective, pragmatic in practice, inventive in disposition, and restless by nature. Such a character, of course, was a historical abstraction, a composite of mostly idealized virtues, a definition richly suggestive in human terms to extended application, supposedly the product of frontier life and Protestant religion, combining commitment to the land and to a harvest that justified God's grace. As in any complex social definition, the depiction of this frontier type involved a whole that was greater than the sum of its parts—a reality more complex than its abstract or summary. Each definition went beyond itself, often to a realm of fantasy, with each fantasy heightening the reality. The illusion was in great part the product of literary representation by the Western as it came to be transformed by literary naturalism; naturalism was later transformed by neorealism and noir fiction and film—narrative modes in which the characters have more self-understanding and the plot lines less naturalistic commentary.

II

Another way of summarizing this process is to see it as a study in historical interpretation. We have examined the changes that Turner believed stemmed from origins in the frontier wilderness: such changes came with the rise of a commercial-industrial-urban nation and were accompanied by the shifting of literary modes. Over time these changes anticipated the move toward an imperial nation with an extended frontier that included nation-building.

American history presumptively was built upon a sequence of ideals that put the best cast possible on the future and kept a sense of promise alive. That hope was initially connected with the will of God, with a sense of romantic destiny (heroic in its expectations), with political and social meaning inseparable from history, embedded in time's unfolding. This religious order eventually gave way to the secular order of the Enlightenment and the belief that the power of reason could help define a new political order and realize a destiny unique to the idea of America. A primary Enlightenment idea was the democratic belief in the rights of the individual and, by extension, the rights of the people implemented by the need to restrict the rule of royalty and feudal law by limiting the authority of government. Each generation sustained or transformed past ideals. The federalist colonies built upon the forenamed Enlightenment ideals before they were transformed by the idea of a frontier beyond the Appalachians, which in turn gave way to the idea of one form of imperialism (domestic expansion), to be eventually replaced by another form of imperialism (foreign expansion).

While we have concentrated on two, we have had in effect four frontiers. We have discussed at length the wilderness frontier as defined by Frederick Jackson Turner and the urban frontier as defined by the rise of an industrial America. As a consequence of the Spanish-American War, America laid claim to a third frontier that included Puerto Rico, Guam, and the Philippines, along with territorial rights to Cuba. And after World War II, America felt the need to protect the extended implementation of capitalism, which led to military intrusions in Korea and Vietnam and to nation-building in the Middle East, primarily but not exclusively in Iraq and Afghanistan, which areas constitute in effect a fourth frontier.

The imperial reach has brought consequences. As Spengler (among others) has told us, the demands of history bring decline to the mandates of empire, no matter how defined. The sense of promise that sustained Washington and Jefferson, Emerson and Whitman, and many others gave way to the sense of decline we find in their later writing as well as in the works of Twain, Adams, Cather, Fitzgerald, West, and

Steinbeck. The idea of the West was only one of numerous ideals that sustained the promise of America as a New World order. These ideals were subject to the reality of decline that comes with exploitation, with the greed and overreaching that is built into human aspiration. A new literature, as D. H. Lawrence saw, turned against the basic assumptions of Puritan values at the same time as that literature became darker in meaning.

III

This book has built upon several assumptions. The major assumption involved the process that led to the transformation of landed myth into its industrial equivalent. The theme of romantic destiny brings with it much baggage: not only is it the basis for the claim that the frontier inculcated a rugged individualism; it also explains the American insistence that the individual is superior to forms of the establishment such as the police (a narrative cliché of a tough-guy novel like Chandler's *The Big Sleep*) and the equally dubious claims that the government is inept and that military action demands rogue assistance (a plot element of TV drama and films like *Rambo*). While long a staple of American culture, these assumptions were renewed in the 1980s and became part of the Ronald Reagan legacy that built upon the myth of the West with its distrust of political authority (except for its own) and its belief in limited government and the priority of the individual.

The historical assumptions behind the myth of the West are based on the old historicism with its economic determinism and the corollary belief that historical events unfold in predictable ways (e.g., that empire-building leads to national decline). The literary context here involves the Western as the literary genre that best depicted the heroic aspects of the wilderness frontier and literary naturalism as the one that best depicted urban reality and the more diminished aspects of the wilderness frontier.

We have seen the effect of the melding of the primitive and the civilized, the pros and cons of keeping to the territory ahead. We have seen how each frontier can be transformed by the way it is defined or by changes in the mode of history that we bring as context. Central to all of these issues is the awareness that these major assumptions emerged from the primary conflict between agrarian and industrial culture.

Each culture possessed a system of demands, often leading to conflict between realms of law and realms of lawlessness.

Another assumption that runs through this book is that each generation builds on the failures (usually the decline) that it predicates of the previous generation as well as the promises of the new generation that it takes as its own. When generational change fails to occur, we have the basis for legend (a historical moment) or myth (a universalized moment). Both legend and myth take on symbolic value and are central to the cultural functioning of the society that produces them. In the John Ford western *The Man Who Shot Liberty Valance* (1962), Jimmy Stewart, who plays the central character, an effete easterner, is credited with the shooting and killing of Liberty Valance, when in reality Valance, a sadistic outlaw played by Lee Marvin, was shot and killed by the character played by John Wayne. Many years later, when Stewart tries to correct the record by confessing the truth to a local newsman, he is told, "When the legend becomes fact, print the legend." Once fact has become legend, it takes on a life of its own and constitutes the flash points of history: the landing of the Pilgrims, the call to the Minutemen, Custer's stand, the fight at the Alamo, Pearl Harbor (the event may involve a defeat that is later redeemed).

The myth of the frontier may have validated the Korean war, the Vietnam War (Norman Mailer suggests as much in *Why Are We in Vietnam?*), and perhaps other recent incursions such as into El Salvador and Granada, as well as the invasions of Iraq and Afghanistan and the bombing of Libya: the enemy becomes the equivalent of the Indians whom the cavalry must eventually vanquish. The frontier forts that supplied military purpose to the wilderness frontier find their equivalent in the seven hundred military bases that the United States now operates throughout the world. The idea of the frontier produced an ongoing commitment to a political agenda involving national purpose. The past may be emptied, but the transformed vision is renewed when needed to restore a new call of the military mind. As we have defined the frontier, we have defined America.

IV

The myth of the West lives on, transformed into shibboleths like the American Dream and the inevitability of Progress ("better days lie ahead"). The reality dies; the illusion lives on, and the illusion powers progress: the ship of state seems to sail on yesterday's wind. We look to the past for the future. And so we have it, as Scott Fitzgerald eloquently has told us; when we are not transforming the past, we pursue a past ideal now dead, a mirage beyond retrieval. Fitzgerald depicted in *The Great Gatsby* the misleading belief that we can relive an idealized past, which in the working of historical process has been transformed by time.

Each generation confronts a crisis of change. We use political myths to justify a national agenda. When the myths are no longer useful for political purposes, we idealize them, even as we discard them. We use up our pasts and the ideals that we bring to them. We have thus come full circle and end this study on the keynote with which we began. Frederick Jackson Turner supplied us with a set of cultural ideals: a mythical idea of the American West, grounded in the historical ideal of a wilderness frontier, both supporting the corollary ideal of romantic destiny—ideals that we struggle to keep alive as we perpetuate their historical equivalent, when in reality we are borne back to a past emptied long ago of the political ideals we still vainly seek.

CHRONOLOGY

1607   Jamestown becomes the first English colony in America.

1620   Pilgrims land at Truro on Cape Cod, then cross the harbor to settle what will become Plymouth Colony.

1630   Massachusetts Bay Colony is founded.

1693   Cotton Mather's "The Wonders of the Invisible World."

1776   The colonies ratify the Declaration of Independence on July 4.

1803   Jefferson oversees the Louisiana Purchase.

1805   Explorers Lewis and Clark travel from St. Louis to the Pacific Ocean.

1837   John Deere invents the steel plow.

1843   Mass migration to Oregon begins.

1851   The population of the United States reaches more than 20 million free men and 2 million slaves.

1853   The railway between New York and Chicago is completed.

1862   John D. Rockefeller founds the Standard Oil Company to refine oil.

1869   A golden spike driven into a railroad tie at Promontory, Utah, on May 10 marks the completion of the transcontinental railroad.

1871   Walt Whitman's "Democratic Vistas."

1873   Andrew Carnegie's Bethlehem Steel Company begins production in Homestead, outside of Pittsburgh.

The Crédit Mobilier scandal occurs.

Mark Twain and Charles Dudley Warner's *The Gilded Age*.

1876 Alexander Graham Bell patents the telephone on February 14.

The Sioux Indians kill Custer and his 265 men at Little Big Horn in Montana on June 25.

1877 Thomas Edison invents the phonograph.

1879 Edison invents the light bulb on October 21.

Henry George's *Progress and Poverty*.

1883 Twain's *Life on the Mississippi*.

1884 Twain's *Adventures of Huckleberry Finn*.

1885 The Santa Fe Railroad reaches Los Angeles.

1886 The American Federation of Labor is founded.

1890 The Sherman Anti-Trust Act is passed.

The work week in the United States is sixty hours.

The population west of the Mississippi reaches 16,766,000.

1892 The Populist Party is formed.

1893 Frederick Jackson Turner's "The Significance of the Frontier in American History."

1896 In *Plessy v. Ferguson,* concerning black-white racial relations, the Supreme Court approves the separate-but-equal provision.

William Jennings Bryan delivers his "cross of gold" speech at the Democratic Convention.

1898 The Spanish-American War is fought, April 25–August 12, resulting in the defeat of Spain at Manila Bay and in Cuba and Puerto Rico. The United States cedes the Philippines and Puerto Rico, marking the transformation of the United States to an imperial nation.

1901 William McKinley is assassinated; he is succeeded by Theodore Roosevelt, president 1901–1909.

J. P. Morgan establishes the United States Steel Corporation.

Frank Norris's *The Octopus*.

1902 Owen Wister's *The Virginian*.

1904 Lincoln Steffens's *The Shame of the Cities*.

Ida Tarbell's *The History of the Standard Oil Company*.

1907 *The Education of Henry Adams* is published.
Henry James's *The American Scene*.
William James's *Pragmatism*.
1908 Henry Ford begins mass production of his Model-T car.
1911 The Supreme Court orders the breakup of the Standard Oil Company and the American Tobacco Company because of monopolistic practices.
1913 Willa Cather's *O Pioneers!*
1918 Willa Cather's *My Antonia*.
1922 Willa Cather's *A Lost Lady*.
1925 F. Scott Fitzgerald's *The Great Gatsby*.
1939 John Steinbeck's *The Grapes of Wrath*.
1955 Richard Hofstadter's *The Age of Reform*.

NOTES

2. The Mythic West

1. The most direct access to Turner's ideas can be found in his *The Frontier in American History* (1962). The best explanations of the Turner thesis—along with its defense—are Ray Allen Billington's *American Frontier Heritage* (1966, 1970), his *Westward Expansion* (1967), and his overview of the European response to the American frontier along with the primitive or civilization theme in *Land of Savagery/Land of Promise* (1981). Completing Billington's studies are Alan Bogue's *Frederick Jackson Turner: Strange Roads Going Down* (1988).

The idea of the West is well treated in Walter Allen's *The Urgent West* (1969). The idea of the wilderness is the subject of Roderick Nash's *Wilderness and the American Mind* (1967, 1982). Religious movements relevant to the theme of the frontier are treated in Perry Miller's *Nature's Nation* (1967). The mythic West is treated in Robert Athearn's *The Mythic West in Twentieth Century America* (1986).

The limitations of Turner's thesis and suggestions for revision occupy Patricia Nelson Limerick's *The Legacy of Conquest* (1987) and William Cronon's history of Chicago in *Nature's Metropolis* (1991), along with Robert Hine and John Faragher's *The American West* (2000), Richard White's *"It's Your Misfortune and None of My Own": A History of the American West* (1991), and Richard Etulain's *The American West: A Modern History, 1900 to the Present* (2007). Limerick, Cronon, and Hine and Faragher deviate from Turner by changing the terms that define the frontier, as do White and Etulain, who emphasize the racial and ethnic matters that seldom concerned Turner.

The Progressive movement is well treated by Richard Hofstadter in *The Age of Reform* (1955), and Hofstadter himself is the subject of David S. Brown's *Richard Hofstadter: An Intellectual Biography* (2006).

The theme of manifest (romantic) destiny is treated in Bernard DeVoto's *The Year of Decision, 1846* (1942) and *The Course of Empire* (1952), Frederick Merk's *Manifest Destiny and Mission in American History* (1963), William Goetzmann's *When the*

Eagle Screamed (1966), Kris Fresonke's *West of Emerson* (2003), and Evan Thomas's *War Lovers* (2010).

10. The Dark Side of the Way West

1. For a collection of essays on the Western, see William T. Pilkington, ed., *Critical Essays on the Western American Novel* (1980). For a collection of essays on *The Virginian*, see Melody Graulich and Stephen Tatum, eds., *Reading "The Virginian" in the New West* (2003). For the way literary naturalism transformed other narrative modes, see Richard Lehan's *Realism and Naturalism* (2005) and "Literary Naturalism and the Realms of the Text," in *Studies in American Naturalism* (Summer-Winter 2006): 15–29; for a discussion of naturalism as the product of mechanistic philosophy that transformed Emersonian transcendentalism, see Lehan, "The Response to Power in American Literary Naturalism: Visions and Revisions That Transformed a Narrative Mode," in *The Oxford Handbook of American Literary Naturalism*, ed. Keith Newlin (2011), 37–51.

WORKS CITED OR CONSULTED

Adams, Henry. *The Education of Henry Adams.* 1907. Reprint, Boston: Houghton Mifflin, 1946.
———. *The Formative Years: A History of the United States during the Administrations of Thomas Jefferson and James Madison.* 1889–91. Ed. Herbert Agar. London: Collins, 1948.
———. *Historical Essays.* New York: Scribner's, 1891.
———. *The Life of Albert Gallatin.* Philadelphia: J. B. Lippincott, 1879.
———. *Mont-Saint-Michel and Chartres.* 1904. Reprint, Garden City, NY: Doubleday, 1959.
Allen, Walter. *The Urgent West: The American Dream and Modern Man.* New York: E. P. Dutton, 1969.
Athearn, Robert G. *The Mythic West in Twentieth-Century America.* Lawrence: University Press of Kansas, 1986.
Beatty, Jack, ed. *Colossus: How the Corporation Changed America.* New York: Broadway Books, 2001.
Benson, Lee. *Turner and Beard: America Historical Writing Reconsidered.* Glencoe, IL: Free Press, 1960.
Billington, Ray Allen. *America's Frontier Heritage.* New York: Holt, 1966. Reprint, New York: Rinehart and Winston, 1970. Reprint, Albuquerque, New Mexico: University of New Mexico Press, 1984.
———. *Frederick Jackson Turner: Historian, Scholar, Teacher.* New York: Oxford University Press, 1973.
———, ed. *Frontier and Section: Selected Essays of Frederick Jackson Turner.* Englewood Cliffs, NJ: Prentice Hall, 1961.
———. *The Genesis of the Frontier Thesis: A Study in Historical Creativity.* San Marino, CA: Huntington Library, 1971.

———. *Land of Savagery/Land of Promise: The European Image of the American Frontier in the Nineteenth Century.* New York: Norton, 1981.

———. *Westward Expansion: A History of the American Frontier.* New York: Macmillan, 1967.

Blake, Casey Nelson. *Beloved Community: The Cultural Criticism of Randolph Bourne, Van Wyck Brooks, Waldo Frank, and Lewis Mumford.* New York: Norton, 1990.

Bogue, Allan G. *Frederick Jackson Turner: Strange Roads Going Down.* Norman: University of Oklahoma Press, 1988.

Bradley, James. *The Imperial Cruise: A Secret History of Empire and War.* New York: Little, 2010.

Brooks, Van Wyck. *America's Coming of Age.* New York: Huebish, 1915.

———. "On Creating a Usable Past." In Trachtenberg, *Critics of Culture,* 165–71.

Brown, David S. *Beyond the Frontier: The Midwestern Voice in American Historical Writing.* Chicago: University of Chicago Press, 2009.

———. *Richard Hofstadter: An Intellectual Biography.* Chicago: University of Chicago Press, 2006.

Cather, Willa. *A Lost Lady.* New York: Knopf, 1922.

———. *My Antonia.* 1918. Reprint, New York: Vintage, 1994.

———. *The Professor's House.* 1925. Reprint, New York: Vintage, 1953.

Cawelti, John G. "Prolegomena to the Western." In Pilkington, *Critical Essays,* 61–71.

Cooper, James Fenimore. *The Pioneers.* 1823. Reprint, New York: Library of America, 2012.

———. *The Prairie.* 1827. Reprint, New York: Rinehart, 1950.

Crawford, Jay Boyd. *Credit Mobilier of America: Its Origins and History, Its Work of Constructing the Union Pacific Railroad, and the Relation of Members of Congress Therewith.* 1880. Reprint, New York: Greenwood Press, 1969.

Cronon, William. *Nature's Metropolis: Chicago and the Great West.* New York: Norton, 1991.

———. "Revisiting the Vanishing Frontier: The Legacy of Frederick Jackson Turner." *Western History Quarterly* 18 (April 1987): 157–76.

Cronon, William, George Miles, and Jay Gitlen, eds. *Under Open Sky: Rethinking America's Western Past.* New York: Norton, 1993.

Deverell, William, ed. *A Companion to the American West.* Malden, MA: Blackwell, 2004.

Deverell, William, and Anne Hyde, eds. *The West in the History of the Nation: A Reader.* Vol. 2. Boston: Bedford/St. Martin's, 2000.

DeVoto, Bernard. *Across the Wide Missouri*. Boston: Houghton Mifflin, 1947.
———. *The Course of Empire*. Boston: Houghton Mifflin, 1952.
———. *The Year of Decision, 1846*. Boston: Houghton Mifflin, 1942.
Emerson, Ralph Waldo. *Selected Prose and Poetry*. Ed. Reginald Cook. New York: Holt, Rinehart, and Winston, 1961.
Etulain, Richard. *The American West: A Modern History, 1900 to the Present*. Lincoln: University of Nebraska Press, 2007.
———. "Origins of the Western." In Pilkington, *Critical Essays*, 56–60.
Faragher, John Mack, ed. *Rereading Frederick Jackson Turner: "The Significance of the Frontier in American History" and Other Essays*. New York: Holt, 1999.
Fiedler, Leslie. *An End to Innocence: Essays on Culture and Politics*. Boston: Beacon Press, 1955.
Fitzgerald, F. Scott. *The Great Gatsby*. 1925. Reprint, New York: Scribner's, 1957.
———. *The Last Tycoon*. New York: Scribner's, 1941.
———. "My Lost City." In *The Crack-Up*. New York: New Directions, 1945.
———. *Tender Is the Night*. New York: Scribner's, 1934.
Frank, Waldo. "The Land of the Pioneer." From *Our America*. New York: Boni and Liveright, 1919. Reprinted in Trachtenberg, *Critics of Culture*, 119–44.
———. *The Rediscovery of America: An Introduction to a Philosophy of American Life*. New York: Scribner's, 1929.
Fresonke, Kris. *West of Emerson: The Design of Manifest Destiny*. Berkeley: University of California Press, 2003.
Goetzmann, William H. *When the Eagle Screamed: The Romantic Horizon in American Diplomacy, 1800–1860*. New York: Wiley, 1966.
Graulich, Melody, and Stephen Tatum, eds. *Reading* The Virginian *in the New West*. Lincoln: University of Nebraska Press, 2003.
Greil, Marcus, and Werner Sollors, eds. *A New Literary History of America*. Cambridge, MA.: Harvard University Press, 2009.
Handley, William R. *Marriage, Violence, and the Nation in the American Literary West*. Cambridge: Cambridge University Press, 2002.
Hine, Robert. *The American West: An Interpretive History*. Boston: Little Brown, 1973.
Hine, Robert V., and John M. Faragher. *The American West: A New Interpretive History*. New Haven, CT: Yale University Press, 2000.
Hirsch, Foster. *Dark Side of the Screen: Film Noir*. New York: Da Capo, 2001.
Hofstadter, Richard. *The Age of Reform: From Bryan to F.D.R.* New York: Random House Vintage, 1955.

———. *Progressive Historians: Turner, Beard, Parrington.* New York: Knopf, 1968, 1979.

Hofstadter, Richard, and Seymour Martin Lipset, eds. *Turner and the Sociology of the Frontier.* New York: Basic Books, 1968.

Horsman, Reginald. *Race and Manifest Destiny: The Origins of American Racial Anglo-Saxonism.* Cambridge, MA: Harvard University Press, 1981.

Jacobs, Wilbur R. *Historical World of Frederick Jackson Turner.* New Haven, CT: Yale University Press, 1968.

———. *On Turner's Trail: 100 Years of Writing Western History.* Lawrence: University Press of Kansas, 1994.

Jacobs, Wilbur R., John W. Caughey, and Joe B. Franz, eds. *Turner, Bolton, and Webb: Three Historians of the American Frontier.* Seattle: University of Washington Press, 1965.

Jaeckle, Jeff. "American Literary and Film Noir." In *Oxford Handbook of American Literary Naturalism,* ed. Keith Newlin. New York: Oxford University Press, 2011. 483–84.

Jones, Gregg. *Roosevelt, War in the Philippines, and the Rise and Fall of America's Imperial Dream.* New York: New American Library, 2012.

Kaplan, Harold. *Henry Adams and the Naturalist Tradition in American Fiction.* Chicago: University of Chicago Press, 1981.

Kaplan, Lawrence. *Thomas Jefferson: Westward the Course of Empire.* Wilmington, DE: SR Books, 1999.

Klein, Kerwin Lee. *Frontiers of Historical Imagination.* Berkeley: University of California Press, 1997.

Kroes, Rob, ed. *The American West—As Seen by Europeans and Americans.* Amsterdam: Free Press, 1989.

Kuhn, Thomas S. *The Structure of Scientific Revolutions.* Chicago: University of Chicago Press, 1996.

Lamar, Howard R., ed. *The New Encyclopedia of the American West.* New Haven, CT: Yale University Press, 1998.

———, ed. *Reader's Encyclopedia of the American West.* New York: Crowell, 1977.

Lawlor, Mary. *Recalling the Wild: Naturalism and the Closing of the American West.* New Brunswick, NJ: Rutgers University Press, 2000.

Lee, Everett S. "The Turner Thesis Re-examined." In Hofstadter and Lipset, *Turner and the Sociology of the Frontier.*

Lehan, Richard. *The City in Literature: An Intellectual and Cultural History.* Berkeley: University of California Press, 1998.

———. "Fitzgerald's *The Great Gatsby* and the Myth of the Land." In

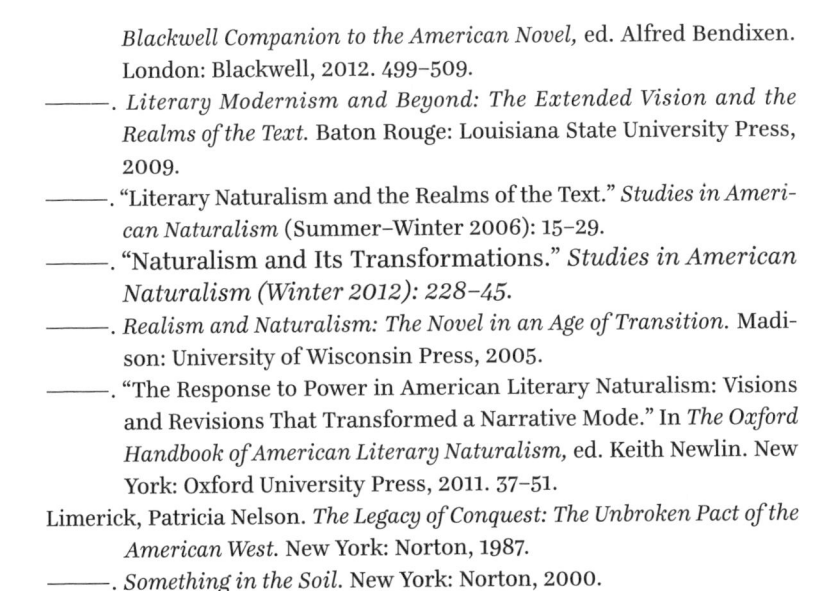

Blackwell Companion to the American Novel, ed. Alfred Bendixen. London: Blackwell, 2012. 499–509.

———. Literary Modernism and Beyond: The Extended Vision and the Realms of the Text. Baton Rouge: Louisiana State University Press, 2009.

———. "Literary Naturalism and the Realms of the Text." Studies in American Naturalism (Summer–Winter 2006): 15–29.

———. "Naturalism and Its Transformations." Studies in American Naturalism (Winter 2012): 228–45.

———. Realism and Naturalism: The Novel in an Age of Transition. Madison: University of Wisconsin Press, 2005.

———. "The Response to Power in American Literary Naturalism: Visions and Revisions That Transformed a Narrative Mode." In The Oxford Handbook of American Literary Naturalism, ed. Keith Newlin. New York: Oxford University Press, 2011. 37–51.

Limerick, Patricia Nelson. The Legacy of Conquest: The Unbroken Pact of the American West. New York: Norton, 1987.

———. Something in the Soil. New York: Norton, 2000.

Limerick, Patricia Nelson, Clyde A. Milner, and Charles E. Rankin, eds. Trails: Toward a New Western History. Lawrence: University Press of Kansas, 1991.

Malone, Michael P., and Richard W. Etulain. The American West: A Twentieth-Century History. Lincoln: University of Nebraska Press, 1989.

———, ed. Historians and the American West. Lincoln: University of Nebraska Press, 1983.

Marx, Leo. The Machine in the Garden: Technology and the Pastoral Ideal in America. New York: Oxford University Press, 1967.

May, Henry F. The End of American Innocence. New York: Knopf, 1959.

Merk, Frederick. History of the Westward Movement. New York: Knopf, 1978.

———. Manifest Destiny and Mission in American History: A Reinterpretation. New York: Knopf, 1963.

Mettler, Suzanne. New York Times, February 17, 2012, A23.

Miller, Perry. Nature's Nation. Cambridge, MA: Harvard University Press, 1956, 1967.

Milner, Clyde A. A New Significance: Re-envisioning the History of the American West. New York: Oxford University Press, 1996.

Milton, John R. "The Primitive World of Vardis Fisher: The Idaho Novels." In Pilkington, Critical Essays, 125–35.

Nash, Gerald D. The American West in the Twentieth Century: A Short

History of an Urban Oasis. Englewood Cliffs, NJ: Prentice Hall, 1973.

———. *The American West Transformed: The Impact of the Second World War.* Bloomington: Indiana University Press, 1985.

Nash, Roderick. *The Nervous Generation: American Thought, 1917–1930.* Chicago: Rand McNally, 1970, 1990.

———. *Wilderness and the American Mind.* New Haven, CT: Yale University Press, 1967, 1982.

Noble, David. "The American Wests." In Kroes, *The American West,* 19–36.

———. *Progressive Mind, 1890–1917.* Chicago: Rand McNally, 1970.

Norris, Frank. "The Frontier Gone at Last." In *The Responsibilities of the Novelist.* New York: Doubleday, Doran, 1903.

———. *McTeague.* 1899. Reprint, New York: Rinehart, 1955.

———. *The Octopus.* 1901. Ed. Kenneth S. Lynn. Boston: Houghton Mifflin, 1958.

———. *The Pit.* 1903. Reprint, New York: Grove Press, n.d.

Orr, Christopher. "Cain, Naturalism, and Noir." *Film Criticism* 25 (2000): 47–64.

Parkes, Henry Bamford. *The American Experience: An Interpretation of the History and Civilization of the American People.* New York: Random House Vintage, 1959.

Parrington, Vernon. *Main Currents in American Thought.* In *Documents of American Realism and Naturalism,* ed. Donald Pizer. Carbondale: Southern Illinois University Press, 1998.

Pater, Walter. Preface and conclusion to *The Renaissance.* In *Criticism: The Major Texts,* ed. W. J. Bate. New York: Harcourt, Brace, 1952.

Pierson, George Wilson. "The Frontier and American Institutions: A Criticism of the Turner Theory." *New England Quarterly* 15 (June 1942): 224–55.

Pilkington, William T., ed. *Critical Essays on the Western American Novel.* Boston: G. K. Hall, 1980.

Planck, Max. *Scientific Autobiography and Other Papers.* Trans. F. Gaynor. New York: Philosophical Library, 1949.

Pomeroy, Earl. "Toward a Reorientation of Western History: Continuity and Environment." *Mississippi Valley Historical Review* 41 (March 1955): 579–600.

Popper, Karl. *The Open Society and Its Enemies.* New York: Harper, 1963. Reprinted, Princeton, NJ: Princeton University Press, 1963. Reprinted, New York: Routledge, 1994, 2002.

———. *The Poverty of Historicism.* Boston: Beacon Press, 1957.

Postel, Charles. *The Populist Vision.* Oxford: Oxford University Press, 2007.
Santayana, George. "The Genteel Tradition in American Philosophy." In Trachtenberg, *Critics of Culture*, 14–32.
Schlesinger, Arthur M., Sr. *The Rise of the City, 1878–1898.* New York: Macmillan, 1933.
Simonson, Harold. *The Closed Frontier: Studies in American Literary Tragedy.* New York: Holt, Rinehart, and Winston, 1970.
Slotkin, Richard. *Fatal Environment: The Myth of the Frontier in the Age of Industrialization, 1800–1890.* Norman: University of Oklahoma Press, 1998.
———. *Gunfighter Nation: The Myth of the Frontier in Twentieth-Century America.* New York: Atheneum, 1992.
———. *Regeneration through Violence: The Mythology of the American Frontier, 1600–1860.* Middletown, CT: Wesleyan University Press, 1973.
Smith, Henry Nash. *Virgin Land: The American West as Symbol and Myth.* Cambridge, MA: Harvard University Press, 1950.
Stegner, Wallace. *Beyond the Hundredth Meridian: John Wesley Powell and the Second Opening of the West.* Boston: Houghton Mifflin, 1954.
———. *The Big Rock Candy Mountain.* New York: Sagamore Press, 1943.
Steinbeck, John. *The Red Pony.* 1938. Reprint, New York: Penguin Books, 1992.
Stewart, Donald. "A.B. Guthrie's Vanishing Paradise: An Essay on Historical Fiction." In Pilkington, *Critical Essays*, 136–49.
Susman, Warren. *Culture as History: The Transformation of American Society in the Twentieth Century.* New York: Pantheon Books, 1984.
Tarbell, Ida M. *The History of the Standard Oil Company.* 1904. Reprints, New York: P. Smith, 1950, 1963.
Taylor, George Rogers. *The Turner Thesis: Concerning the Role of the Frontier in American History.* Boston: D. C. Heath, 1949, 1956; Lexington, MA: D. C. Heath, 1972.
Thomas, Evan. *War Lovers: Roosevelt, Lodge, Hearst, and the Rush to Empire.* New York: Little, 2010.
Trachtenberg, Alan, ed. *Critics of Culture: Literature and Society in the Early Twentieth Century.* New York: Wiley, 1976.
———. *The Incorporation of America: Culture and Society in the Gilded Age.* New York: Hill and Wang, 2007.
———. *Shades of Hiawatha.* New York: Hill and Wang, 2004.
Turner, Frederick Jackson. *The Frontier in American History.* New York: Holt, Rinehart, and Winston, 1920, 1962.

———. "The Significance of the Frontier in American History." 1893. Reprinted in Turner, *Frontier in American History* (1962), 1–38.

Twain, Mark. *The Complete Novels of Mark Twain.* Ed. Charles Neider. 2 vols. Garden City, NY: Doubleday, 1964.

———. *A Connecticut Yankee in King Arthur's Court.* 1889. Reprint, New York: Morrow, 1988.

"Urban vs. Rural Values," *New York Times,* June 16, 2012, A21.

Wade, Richard C. *The Urban Frontier: The Rise of Western Cities, 1790–1830.* Cambridge, MA: Harvard University Press, 1959.

Ward, John William. *Andrew Jackson: Symbol for an Age:* New York: Oxford University Press, 1962.

Webb, Walter Prescott. *The Great Frontier.* Boston: Houghton Mifflin, 1952.

———. *The Great Plains.* Boston: Ginn, 1931.

West, Elliott. "Thinking West." In Deverell, *A Companion to the American West,* 25–50.

Westbrook, Max. "The Western Esthetic." In Pilkington, *Critical Essays,* 73–85.

White, Richard. *"It's Your Misfortune and None of My Own": A History of the American West.* Norman: University of Oklahoma Press, 1991.

———. *Railroaded: The Transcontinental and the Making of Modern America.* New York: Norton, 2011.

Whitman, Walt. *Complete Poetry and Selected Prose.* New York: Library of America, 1982.

———. *Leaves of Grass and Selected Prose.* Ed. John Kouwenhoven. New York: Modern Library, 1950.

———. *Song of Myself.* Ed. James E. Miller. New York: Dodd, Mead, 1964.

Wills, Garry. *Henry Adams and the Making of America.* Boston: Houghton Mifflin, 2005.

Witschi, Nicolas S., ed. *A Companion to the Literature and Culture of the American West.* Malden, MA.: Wiley-Blackwell, 2011.

Wylder, Delbert. "Emerson Hough and the Popular Novel." In Pilkington, *Critical Essays,* 111–17.

INDEX

Abbey, Edward, 146
Absalom, Absalom! (Faulkner), 107
Across the Wide Missouri (DeVoto), 162
Adams, Baxter, 161
Adams, Brooks, 63
Adams, Henry: beliefs of, 63–65, 90; *Democracy* and, 72–73; the Dynamo and, 33, 41, 62, 64, 72–73, 127, 151; illusion and, 14; on One in the Many, 41, 42, 121–22, 155; wilderness frontier and, 13, 54
Adams, Richard, 120
"Addresses to the German Nation" (Fichte), 47
The Adventures of Huckleberry Finn (Twain), 15, 24, 38, 96, 116–20, 153, 184
The Adventures of Tom Sawyer (Twain), 116
After Strange Gods (Eliot), 33
The Age of Jackson (Schlesinger), 170
The Age of Reform (Hofstadter), 54, 88, 185
agrarian movement, 47–49, 54–56, 80–81, 85–86, 91–93. *See also* southern Agrarians
agrarian revolution, 67–68
Aldrich, Thomas Bailey, 93
Algren, Nelson, 158
Allen, Walter, 35, 163
All the King's Men (Warren), 103

America: agrarian-industrial development in, 54–56, 85–86, 91–93; geography of, 51–52; as gunfighter nation, 168; historical transformations in, 52–53
American Adam, 39, 113–15, 162
The American Adam (Lewis), 162
The American Claimant (Twain), 94, 116
American cultural construct, 160. *See also* Crane, Hart; Emerson, Ralph Waldo; Whitman, Walt; Williams, William Carlos
American "exceptionalism," 14, 20, 22, 57
American Federation of Labor (AFL), 184
American Hieroglyphics (Irwin), 163
American Historical Association, xi
The American Jeremiad (Bercovitch), 162
American Quarterly, 82
American Review, 103
The American Scene (James), 33, 184
American Tobacco Company, 85, 185
The American West (Etulain), 55, 167–68
The American West Transformed (Nash), 55, 166–67
Ames, Oakes, 87
An American Tragedy (Dreiser), 150
Anderson, Sherwood, 174
anti-Semitism, 28, 75, 81, 88, 91–92, 99, 171
Apache tribe, 8

INDEX

Apollonian culture, 61–62. *See also* Spengler, Oswald
Arapaho tribe, 7–8
Aryan superiority, idea of, xvi, 48, 62, 98–100
Athearn, Robert G., 81, 144, 163–64, 167

Bancroft, George, 60, 92
Bar 20 (Mulford), 146
Barr, Robert, 94
Baum, Frank, 82–83
The Bear (Faulkner), 108–9
Beard, Charles, 21–22, 59, 160, 164
The Beautiful and Damned (Fitzgerald), 136
Bell, Alexander Graham, 184
Bell, Daniel, 170–71
Bellamy, Edward, 93, 119
Bellow, Saul, 171
Benton, Thomas Hart, 1–2
Bercovitch, Sacvan, 162
Bethlehem Steel Company, 183
Beyond the Hundredth Meridian (Stegner), 162, 163
The Big Rock Candy Mountain (Stegner), 162
The Big Sky (Guthrie), 148
The Big Sleep (Chandler), 157, 180
Billington, Ray Allen, 2–3, 8–9, 23, 50–51, 164, 187
Blaine, James G., 87
The Blithedale Romance (Hawthorne), 43
"The Blue Hotel" (Crane), 154
Bogue, Allan G., 163, 164, 170
Bohr, Niels, 45
Boone, Daniel, 1, 129, 132
Boss Tweed, 76
Bourne, Randolph, 64–65, 95, 162
The Brave Cowboy (Abbey), 146
Brooklyn Daily Times, 122
Brooks, Cleanth, 163
Brooks, Van Wyck, 64–65, 95–96, 128, 161–62
Brown, David S., 170
Brown, Dee, 8, 55
Bryan, William Jennings, 80–82, 184
Buffalo Bill. *See* Cody, William F.
Bunyan, John, 86
Burkhardt, Jacob, 57
Bury My Heart at Wounded Knee (Brown), 8, 55

Caesar's Column (Donnelly), 93
Cain, James M., 19, 156, 158
Calvinism, xiii, 35–36, 53, 110–11, 144. *See also* Puritanism
capitalism: Beard and, 22; Fitzgerald and, 126, 135–36; Germany and, 99–101; industrialization and, 92; Protestantism's effect on, 15–16; rise of, 27–28, 121–22; Twain and, 94, 117
Captains Courageous (Kipling), 148, 150–51
Carlyle, Thomas, 37, 63, 89, 122
Carnegie, Andrew, 70–71, 126, 183
Cash, W. J., 162
Cather, Willa: Handley on, 168; immigrant life and, 81; myth of the land and, xvi, 130; novels of, 123–25, 185; theme of pursuing a lost past and, 18; treatment of the West in literature, 41, 54, 118; view of wealth, 28
Catholicism, 75–77, 117, 119, 122
Cawelti, John G., 144
Century Magazine, 144
Chandler, Raymond, 30, 116, 149, 157–58, 180
Cheyenne tribe, 7–8
Chicago, Ill., 43–44, 55, 84, 89
Christian Examiner, 37
cities, rise of, 69–70, 84–85, 89
The City in Literature (Lehan), 163
"Civil Disobedience" (Thoreau), 43
The Civilization of the Renaissance in Italy (Burkhardt), 57
Clarissa (Richardson), 107
Clark, Walter Van Tilburg, 147
The Cliff Dwellers (Fuller), 94
Cody, William F., 50, 129, 132, 168
Coeur d'Alene (Foote), 93
Coleridge, Samuel Taylor, 37
Collins, Seward, 103
Columbia school, 170–71. *See also* Bell, Daniel; Hofstadter, Richard; Lipset, Seymour
The Confidence Man (Melville), 43, 114–15

INDEX

Congregationalism, xiii, 11, 35–37, 53
A Connecticut Yankee in King Arthur's Court (Twain), 43, 95, 117–19
Conrad, Joseph, 149, 155–56
Cooper, James Fenimore, xvi, 1, 18, 39–41, 54, 114, 116
Crane, Hart, 2, 42, 160, 161, 173–74
Crane, Stephen, 151, 154, 155–56
Crawford, Jay Boyd, 87
Crédit Mobilier, 86–88, 184
Critique of Pure Reason (Kant), 37
Cronon, William, 55, 84, 89, 163, 170
"Crossing Brooklyn Ferry" (Whitman), 173
"cross of gold" speech (Bryan), 80–81
The Crying of Lot 49 (Pynchon), 30, 177
"cultural multiplicity," 12
cultural transformations: and agrarian to industrial society, 21–23, 30–34, 54–56, 180–82; corporations and, 90–91; dichotomy between rural and urban reality, 19–20; effects of in America, 2–3, 15, 38–39; Emersonian ideals and, 95–96; Hart Crane on, 174; historicism and, 57–62; immigrants and, 75–77; Progressivism and, 84–85; religion and, 35–39; revolutions and, 67–68; southern decline and, 103–4; Turner on, 5–7, 52; "usable past" and, 161–62. *See also* literary naturalism; noir fiction; regionalism; romantic destiny; romantic nationalism
Curley, James, 76
Curti, Merle, 163, 164, 170

The Dain Curse (Hammett), 156
Darrow, Clarence, 80
Darwin, Charles, 46, 80, 143, 144, 149, 154. *See also* Spencer, Herbert
Davis, Rebecca Harding, 94
Dawes Act, 8
The Day of the Locust (West), 137–39
decline, process of, 31–32, 58, 61–63, 107–10, 179–80
The Decline of the West (Spengler), 58, 133
The Deerslayer (Cooper), 39
De Forest, J. W., 94
Deism, 36

Democracy (Adams), 72–73
"Democracy" (Whitman), 122
"Democratic Vistas" (Whitman), 43, 122–23, 183
A Desert Romance (illustration), 144
Deverell, William, 8, 15
DeVoto, Bernard, 162
Didion, Joan, 168
Dippe, Brian W., 51
Donne, John, 49
Donnelly, Ignatius, 93
Dos Passos, John, xiv, 5, 130, 156, 171
Douglas, Amanda, 93
Douglas, Kirk, 146
Dreiser, Theodore, 33, 44, 84, 87, 150, 174
Drexler, Anton, 48, 99, 100
Durkheim, Emile, 16
"A Dynamic Theory of History" (Adams), 64
the Dynamo, Adams's idea of, 33, 41, 62, 64, 72–73, 127, 151

East of Eden (Steinbeck), 141–42
Edison, Thomas, 184
The Education of Henry Adams (Adams), 73, 184
Edwards, Jonathan, 36, 76
Eliot, T. S., 10, 31–33, 49–50, 104, 172–73
Emerson, Ralph Waldo: idealization of the West, 13, 28–29, 32; philosophy of, 72, 95–96, 161; transcendentalism and, xii, xvi, 36–38, 143; vision of the city, 42; Whitman and, 41–42
An End to Innocence (Fiedler), 162
Enlightenment, influence of, xiii, 23, 42–43, 52–53, 67, 138, 179
equalitarianism, 9–10
Errand into the Wilderness (Miller), 36, 162
Esther (Adams), 73
Etulain, Richard, 55, 167–68
expansion, American, 15–17, 21, 31–34, 92–93. *See also* imperialism; manifest destiny

"fall line," 7
Farewell, My Lovely (Chandler), 157–58
Farmer's Alliance, 78

The Fatal Environment (Slotkin), 168
Fatherland Party, 48–49, 100. *See also* Volk, German theory of
Faulkner, William: idea of landed frontier, 104; myth of the land and, xiv, 130; world of, 107–10
Faustian culture, 61–62, 132–33, 136. *See also* Spengler, Oswald
Fetterman Massacre (1865), 7
Fichte, Johann Gottlieb, xiii, 47, 99, 100, 130. *See also* Volk, German theory of
Fiedler, Leslie, 144, 162, 171
film noir, 18, 30, 56, 156, 158, 178. *See also* noir fiction
Fisher, Vardis, 147
Fitzgerald, F. Scott: *The Great Gatsby* and, xvi, 125–37, 185; Handley on, 168; on lost past, 18, 33, 41, 121, 182; myth of the land and, xiv, 129–30
Foote, Mary Hallock, 93
Ford, Henry, 184
For Whom the Bell Tolls (Hemingway), 38
Fourteenth Amendment, 88, 123
Frank, Waldo, 95–96
Frederic, Harold, 94
free land, 2, 6–7, 12, 25, 59, 123, 166
frontier, agrarian, 13, 21, 65–66, 84–85, 95, 162
frontier, industrial, 13, 65–66, 84–85, 162
frontier, urban: about, 97; historical progress and, 29–30; literary naturalism and, xii, 80; roots of, 17; Trachtenberg on, 12–13; transition from wilderness frontier, xi–xii, 144, 158, 160
frontier, wilderness: as agrarian v. urban nation, 16–17; collaborative efforts and, 11; conservative agenda as origin of, 16–17; ending of, 5, 10, 27; industrialism and, 28, 178–79; migration into, 1–4; pragmatic disposition of, 6, 14, 26, 41, 178; pursuit of lost vision and, 97; reality of, 161; romantic destiny and, 97; transition to urban frontier, xi–xii, 144, 158, 160; Turner and, xi–xii, xv–xvii, 5–7, 9–13; westward movement into, 7–9
The Frontier in American History (Turner), 128, 187

frontier thesis (Turner): about, xi–xvii, 2, 45, 144, 184, 187; Brooks's reinforcement of, 128; Cawelti on, 144; challenges to, 15–17, 55–56, 166; changes to meaning, 55–56, 155; *The Day of the Locust* and, 137; *The Great Gatsby* and, 126, 129, 133–34; and illusion of unity, 64; legacy of, 161–62; Mormonism and, 102; Pomeroy and, 164–65; Smith on, 54; Volkism and, 49–50; weaknesses of, 9–13, 14–15. *See also* Turner, Frederick Jackson
frontier to urban transformation, xi–xii, 15–16, 27–29, 144, 158, 160
Frye, Northrop, 13
Fugitives. *See* southern Agrarians
Fuller, Henry Blake, 94

Gallatin, Albert, 73
Garfield, James, 87
Garland, Hamlin, 94, 144, 162
Gemeinschaft versus Gesellschaft, theory of, 16
George, Henry, 59–60, 184
German Worker's Party, 48
germ theory, 5, 25, 92
Giants in the Earth (Rolvaag), 152–53
The Gilded Age (Twain and Warner), 28, 33, 94, 116, 117, 184
Gilpin, William, 1–2
Ginsberg, Alan, 30
The Glass Key (Hammett), 156
Glazer, Nathan, 171
Godel, Kurt, 45
Go Down, Moses (Faulkner), 108–9
Goebbels, Joseph, 100
Goodin, S. H., 84
The Gospel of Freedom (Herrick), 94
Grant, Madison, 81–82
The Grapes of Wrath (Steinbeck), 19, 140–41, 185
Great Awakening, 76
The Great Frontier (Webb), 22, 165
The Great Gatsby (Fitzgerald), xvi, 33, 124, 125–34, 182, 185
Greenblatt, Stephen, 57
Grey, Zane, 144, 145–46, 168
Growth of the Soil (Hamsun), 152

INDEX

Gunfighter Nation (Slotkin), 168
guns as symbol of the West, 12, 26, 143.
　See also violence in the frontier West
Guthrie, A. B., 147–48

The Hamlet (Faulkner), 109
Hammett, Dashiell, 156–58
Hamsun, Knut, 152–53
Handley, William R., 168–70
Hart-Celler Act, 75
Harvard University, 65, 81, 161, 164
Hawthorne, Nathaniel, 43, 113–15
Hedge, Frederic, 37
Heisenberg, Werner, 45
Hemingway, Ernest, 38, 39, 156, 158–59
Herder, Johann Gottfried von, xiii, 47–48, 60, 100, 130
Her Mountain Lover (Garland), 144
Herrenvolk. See Aryan superiority, idea of
Herrick, Robert, 94
High Noon (film), 116
Hill, James J., 126, 127
historical determinism, 2, 19, 29
Historical Essays (Adams), 63
historical process, 8, 10, 20, 57, 59–60, 163, 173. *See also* Spengler, Oswald
historical transformations, 6–7, 52–53.
　See also cultural transformations
historicism, xiii–xiv, 29, 57–66, 161–62, 163. *See also* Columbia school; Populism; Vanderbilt school; Wisconsin school
historiography, 64, 160
History of the Romantic and Germanic People from 1494 to 1514 (Ranke), 57
The History of the Standard Oil Company (Tarbell), 93, 184
Hitler, Adolf, 48, 62, 99–100, 101, 103
Hobbes, Thomas, 4
Hofstadter, Richard: on consensus, 160–61; on dark side of the West, 54–55; on democracy, 71; population and, 74; Turner thesis and, 21, 163; view of America, 88–89; view of Progressive movement, 170–71
Homestead Act (1862–1890), 10, 12, 94
Honest John Vane (De Forest), 94
Hook, Sidney, 171

A Hoosier Holiday (Dreiser), 33
Hopalong Cassidy (Mulford), 131, 146
Hope Mills (Douglas), 93
Horsman, Reginald, 98–99
Hough, Emerson, 144, 147
Howe, Irving, 171
How the Other Half Lived (Riis), 93
The Human Geography of the South (Vance), 103
Hunger (Hamsun), 152
Hyde, Anne, 8, 15

idealism, 9–10
I'll Take My Stand (Twelve Southerners), 102, 130
illusion. *See* myth of the West
immigration: Columbia school and, 170; history of, in America, 74–77; Immigration Act (1924) and, 75, 82; industrial/urban life and, 13, 15, 27, 47, 61, 90–91; into frontier, 3, 27; racism and, 81–82, 88
Immigration Act of 1924, 9, 75, 82
imperialism, 17, 20–21, 28, 31–32, 111–12, 179
The Incorporation of America (Trachtenberg), 12, 65
Indians. *See* Native Americans
individualism: curbing of, 90; effects of, 12, 25–26, 39, 180; frontier thesis and, 2–3; and transcendentalism, 37–38; Turner and, 6, 9–10
industrial revolution, 67, 68–69
Ingraham, Prentiss, 50
The Innocents Abroad (Twain), 116
innovation, 9–10
intellectual concern, 18–19
International Mercantile Marine, 85
interpretive theory, 13
The Iron Heel (London), 93
Irving, George Washington, 60
Irwin, John, 163
It Can't Happen Here (Lewis), 101
"It's Your Misfortune and None of My Own" (White), 55, 167

Jackson, Andrew, 26, 39, 136
Jacobs, Wilbur R., 163

INDEX

Jaeckle, Jeff, 156
James, Henry, 6, 33, 118, 174, 184
James, William, 41, 89, 143, 155
Jamestown, 183
Jay, John, 103
Jefferson, Thomas, 2, 6, 9, 22, 26, 28, 103. *See also* Jeffersonian vision
Jeffersonian vision, xi–xvii, 17, 32–34, 46–47, 78, 102, 121, 135, 139
John Andross (Davis), 94
Johns Hopkins University, 5, 92, 161
The Jungle (Sinclair), 80, 93

Kant, Immanuel, 37, 47, 100, 161
Kaplan, Harold, 154
Kazin, Alfred, 171
Keenan, Henry Francis, 93
Kennedy, John F., 26
Kennedy, William, 158
Kerouac, Jack, 30, 121, 158
Kipling, Rudyard, 148, 150–51
Klein, Kerwin Lee, 59, 163
Knights of Labor, 78
Know-Nothing Party, 75
Kristin Lavransdatter (Undset), 152
Kroes, Rob, 64
Kuhn, Thomas, 45

La Bête Humaine (Zola), 149
L'Amour, Louis, 165–66
land speculation, 26, 29–30, 54–55, 92, 94
The Last of the Mohicans (Cooper), 40
The Last Tycoon (Fitzgerald), 135, 136–37
Lawlor, Mary, 154
The Lawton Girl (Frederic), 94
The Leatherstocking Tales (Cooper), 1, 39–41, 145
Leaves of Grass (Whitman), 42–43
The Legacy of Conquest (Limerick), 29, 55, 165
Lehan, Richard, 162–63
Lewis, R. W. B., 162
Lewis, Sinclair, 101
Lewis and Clark, 183
The Liberal Imagination (Trilling), 65, 174–75
Life on the Mississippi (Twain), 33, 184

Light in August (Faulkner), 108
Limerick, Patricia Nelson, 22, 29, 55, 65–66, 163–64, 165–67
Lincoln, Abraham, 22, 26, 27, 42, 96
Lipset, Seymour, 170, 171
Literary Modernism and Beyond (Lehan), 162
literary naturalism, xii, 13, 14, 18–20, 30, 43–44, 56, 80, 149–55, 178, 188
literary noir. *See* noir fiction
Littlefield, Henry M., 82–83
Locke, John, 39, 103
London, Jack, 93, 96, 149, 151, 154
Lonely Are the Brave (film), 146
The Lonely Crowd (Riesman), 19
Look Homeward, Angel (Wolfe), 105
Looking Backward (Bellamy), 93, 119
Loria, Achille, 59–60
A Lost Lady (Cather), 28, 124, 185
Louisiana Purchase (1803), 26, 39, 40, 73

The Machine in the Garden (Marx), 65, 161, 162
Magian culture, 61–62. *See also* Spengler, Oswald
Mailer, Norman, 181
Main-Travelled Roads (Garland), 162
Malone, Michael P., 31
The Maltese Falcon (Hammett), 156
manifest destiny, xiv, 5, 20–21, 31–33, 52, 98, 151, 168, 187
Manifest Destiny (Weinberg), 31
The Mansion (Faulkner), 109
The Man Who Shot Liberty Valance (film), 181
market speculation, 43–44
Marriage, Violence, and the Nation in the American Literary West (Handley), 168–70
Marx, Leo, 65, 120–21, 161, 162
Marxism, 67, 99
materialism, 9–10
Mather, Cotton, 52, 183
May, Karl, 23, 51
McKinley, William, 80, 184
McTeague (Norris), 150
Melville, Herman, 43, 114–15

INDEX

Merk, Frederick, 3
Mettler, Suzanne, 17
The Middle of the Journey (Trilling), 172
migration, 1–4, 7–8, 11–12
Miller, Henry, 33
Miller, Perry, 32, 36, 45–46, 162
Milton, John R., 147
The Mind of the South (Cash), 162
Moby-Dick (Melville), 114
modernism, 16, 47, 142, 148–49, 155, 159, 163, 172–75, 176. *See also* postmodernism
The Money Captain (Payne), 94
The Money Makers (Keenan), 93
Mont-Saint-Michel and Chartres (Adams), 73
The Moon Metal (Serviss), 93
Moran of the Lady Letty (Norris), 151
Morgan, J. P., 71, 96, 184
Mormonism, 101–2, 145–46
Morris, William, 47, 119
muckrakers, 86, 88, 93
Mulford, Clarence E., 131, 146
Mumford, Lewis, 95
Munson, Gorham, 95
My Ántonia (Cather), 123–24, 185
"My Lost City" (Fitzgerald), 33, 136
"The Mysterious Stranger" (Twain), 43, 117
mythic Adam. *See* American Adam
The Mythic West (Athearn), 163–64, 167
myth of the land, xii, 46–47, 71–72, 128–31, 134
myth of the West: and agrarian to industrial culture, 21–23; Cooper and, 40; endurance of, 181–82; historical reality of, 53–54, 54–56; idea of, 27–29; illusion of, 46; immigrants and, 81; impact of, 5, 7, 34, 46, 153, 180–81; literary masks of, 30–34; as lost past, 18; Mulford and, 146; revisionary thinking about, 29–30; romanticism and, 23–26; Slotkin and, 168; Turner's thesis and, 14–17

Nash, Gerald, 55, 163, 166–67
Nash, Roderick, 68

National Banking Act (1863), 122
National Socialism. *See* Third Reich
National Socialist German Workers Party. *See* Nazi Party
Native Americans: Cody and, 50; depiction of tribes, xii, 23–24; Etulain and White on, 167–68; Fiedler on, 144; Handley on, 169; perspective on the West, 55; response of, to white migration, 7–9; Turner's thesis on, 56, 111; Williams on, 173
naturalistic fiction. *See* literary naturalism
Nature's Metropolis (Cronon), 55
Nature's Nation (Miller), 45–46
Nazi Party, 48, 99, 100
neorealism, 18, 56, 152, 156, 159, 178
New Criticism, 49–50, 130
New Critics, 104, 163, 176. *See also* southern Agrarians
New Deal, 17, 77, 79, 91, 97, 170
The New England Mind (Miller), 162
New Republic, 103
News from Nowhere (Morris), 119
New York Times, 77, 145
Noble, David, 22, 27
noir fiction, 18–20, 30, 56, 156–59, 178. *See also* film noir
Nordic superiority, idea of, 48, 81–82, 100, 145, 147
Norris, Frank: beliefs of, 111; Lawlor on, 154; literary naturalism and, 19, 43–44, 149–50; myth of the land and, 130; *The Octopus* and, 38, 87–88, 90, 143, 151–53, 184; on wealth, 28; and the Western, 144

O Pioneers! (Cather), 185
Oates, Joyce Carol, 158
The Octopus (Norris), 28, 38, 43–44, 87–88, 90, 111, 143–44, 149, 151–52, 184
Odum, Howard W., 103
Of Mice and Men (Steinbeck), 139
Of Time and the River (Wolfe), 105, 106–7
Olmsted, Frederick Law, 24, 39
One in the Many, 41, 42, 155. *See also* Whitman, Walt

The Open Society and Its Enemies (Popper), 59
Open versus Closed space, 77–78
"Orbic Literature" (Whitman), 122
The Ordeal of Mark Twain (Brooks), 95, 128
Order of the Star-Spangled Banner, 75
Oregon Trail, 2, 3–4, 26
Orr, Christopher, 156
The Oxbow Incident (Clark), 147

"Parable on Populism." *See* "*The Wizard of Oz*: Parable on Populism" (Littlefield)
paradigms, 45, 58, 64, 163, 175–76
Parkes, Henry Bamford, 22, 27
Parkman, Francis, 40, 60–61, 92
Parrington, Vernon L., 64, 72, 160–61, 162
Passage to India, 1–2
The Passing of the Great Race (Grant), 81–82
The Pastures of Heaven (Steinbeck), 140
Pater, Walter, 43, 155–56
"Patria Mia" (Pound), 33
Paulding, James K., 50
Payne, Will, 94
Pendergast, James, 76
People's Party, 78
"Personalism" (Whitman), 122
perspectivism, 149, 176
Phelps, Elizabeth, 93
Phillips, David Graham, 93–94
Pierre (Melville), 43
Pierson, George Wilson, 7
Pilgrims, 53, 181, 183
The Pilgrim's Progress (Bunyan), 86
The Pioneers (Cooper), 40
The Pit (Norris), 43, 152
Planck, Max, 45, 69
Plessy v. Ferguson, 184
Plymouth, Mass., 7, 25, 138, 183
Podhoretz, Norman, 171
Pomeroy, Earl, 29, 164–67
Popper, Karl, 59
Populism, xiii, xv, 34, 71, 74–83
Populist Party, 184
Postel, Charles, 78
The Postman Always Rings Twice (Cain), 19, 156

postmodernism, 56, 149, 175–77
poststructuralism, 163, 176. *See also* structuralism
Pound, Ezra, xiv, 6, 33, 42, 63, 110, 130, 172–73
The Poverty of Historicism (Popper), 59
pragmatic disposition, 6, 14, 26, 41, 178
pragmatism, theory of, 143, 184. *See also* James, William
The Prairie (Cooper), 40
premodern American literature, 155–59
primitivism vs. civilization, 23–24, 38–39, 68–69
The Prince and the Pauper (Twain), 116–17
Princeton University, 92
The Professor's House (Cather), 124–25
Progress and Poverty (George), 60, 184
Progressivism, vx, xiii, 28, 33, 84–96, 170, 187
Pudd'nhead Wilson (Twain), 116
Puritanism: Emerson and, 161; Fitzgerald and, 136–37; Great Awakening and, 76; Miller and, 162; obsession with evil, 8, 144; Puritan revolution, 84–85; sense of destiny, 22–23, 57; *Seven Arts* authors on, 95–96; and the West, xiii, 53. *See also* Calvinism
The Puritan Origins of the American Self (Bercovitch), 162
Pynchon, Thomas, 30, 58, 148, 177

Rahv, Philip, 171
Ranke, Leopold von, 57
Ransom, John Crowe, 102, 170
Reagan, Ronald, 91, 180
Realism and Naturalism (Lehan), 163
Recalling the Wild (Lawlor), 154
Red Harvest (Hammett), 156
The Red Pony (Steinbeck), 139–40
Regeneration through Violence (Slotkin), 168
regionalism, 5, 9, 29, 52–53, 164, 170–71
Remember to Remember (Miller), 33
Remington, Frederick, 48, 144, 145
The Renaissance (Pater), 155
The Return of the Vanishing American (Fiedler), 144, 162
Riders of the Purple Sage (Grey), 145–46

INDEX

Riesman, David, 19
Riis, Jacob, 93
The Rise of the City (Schlesinger), 69
The Rising Tide of Color (Stoddard), 81–82
Rockefeller, John D., 71, 96, 126, 183
Rolvaag, Ole, 81, 152–53
romantic destiny, 22–24, 57–66, 126, 179
romantic nationalism, 47–49, 57, 98, 100–101. *See also* Volk, German theory of
Roosevelt, Franklin Delano, 76–77
Roosevelt, Theodore, 26, 27–28, 40, 86, 92–93, 111, 168, 184
Roughing It (Twain), 116

Santa Fe Railroad, 184
Santayana, George, 36, 85
savagery, 5, 9–10, 23, 52, 59, 144, 147
The Scarlet Letter (Hawthorne), 113–14
Schaefer, Jack, 146
Schlesinger, Arthur M., Jr., 170
Schlesinger, Arthur M., Sr., 69–70, 163
Scopes Trial of 1925, 80
Sea Wolf (London), 151
"Second Treatise of Civil Government" (Locke), 103
self-creation, 126–27
self-reliance, 14, 17, 36, 38, 41, 116, 146
"Self-Reliance" (Emerson), 42
Serviss, Garrett P., 93
settlement, 8, 10, 11–12, 59, 74, 165
Seven Arts, 96, 161, 173, 174–75. *See also* Bourne, Randolph; Brooks, Van Wyck; Frank, Waldo; Mumford, Lewis; Munson, Gorham
Shaftesbury, Earl of, 4–5
The Shame of the Cities (Steffens), 93, 184
Shane (Schaefer), 146
Sherman Anti-Trust Act, 184
"Shooting Niagara; and After" (Carlyle), 122
"The Significance of the Frontier in American History" (Turner), 24–25, 184
The Silent Partner (Phelps), 93
Simms, William Gilmore, 50
Sinclair, Upton, 44, 80, 93
Sioux tribe, 7–8, 184

Slotkin, Richard, 12, 163, 168–70
Smith, Al, 76–77
Smith, Francis Hopkinson, 93
Smith, Henry Nash, 2, 22, 28, 54, 65, 161–62
Smith, Joseph, 101–2
social mobility, 9–10
Something in the Soil (Limerick), 166
A Son of the Middle Border (Garland), 162
Sontag, Susan, 171
southern Agrarians, xiii, xiv, 49–50, 102–5, 170–71
Southern Regions of the United States (Odum), 103
Spanish-American War, 21, 179, 184
Spencer, Herbert, 38, 149–50, 154–55. *See also* Darwin, Charles
Spengler, Oswald: Crane's use of, 137; decline and, 31, 58, 179; Faulkner's use of, 110; Fitzgerald's use of, 133–35; theory of history, 61–63, 133–34. *See also* historical process
A Spoil of Office (Garland), 943
Standard Oil Company, 85–86, 93, 183, 184
Star Wars (film), 148
Steffens, Lincoln, 93, 184
Stegner, Wallace, 51, 144, 162, 163, 168
Steinbeck, John, 18, 41, 130, 139–42, 185
Stevens, Wallace, 54, 64
Stewart, Donald, 147–48
The Stillwater Tragedy (Aldrich), 93
Stoddard, Lothrop, 81–82
structuralism, 58, 64, 163. *See also* poststructuralism

Tammany Hall, 76–77
Tarbell, Ida M., 93, 184
Tate, Allen, 102–3, 170
Tender Is the Night (Fitzgerald), 135–36
The Testament of Man (Fisher), 147
That Fortune (Warner), 93
The Bridge (Crane), 174
Third Reich, 99–101
This Side of Paradise (Fitzgerald), 136
Thoreau, Henry David, 43, 116
"To Build a Fire" (London), 149
Together (Herrick), 94

To Have and Have Not (Hemingway), 158–59
Tolstoy, Leo, 63
Tom Grogan (Smith), 93
Tom Sawyer, Detective (Twain), 116
Tom Sawyer Abroad (Twain), 116
Tönnies, Ferdinand, 16
"Toward a Reorientation of Western History" (Pomeroy), 164
The Town (Faulkner), 109
Toynbee, Arnold, 59, 61
Trachtenberg, Alan, 12–13, 65
The Track of the Cat (Clark), 147
The Tragedy of American Diplomacy (Williams), 22
transcendentalism, xii, 36–38, 143. *See also* Emerson, Ralph Waldo
transcontinental railroad: and agrarian to industrial nation, 4, 183; as corporate entity, 90, 154; effects of, 4, 68, 70–71, 122–23; farmers and, 44; Faulkner and, 109; funding of, 11; scandal and, 86–88; use of, in fiction, 94, 109, 124, 150–51
transformations. *See* cultural transformations; frontier to urban transformation
The Treason of the Senate (Phillips), 93
Trilling, Lionel, 65, 171–72, 174–75
Truman, Harry, 26
Trumbo, Dalton, 146
Turner, Frederick Jackson: Athearn on, 167; Etulain on, 167–68; on the frontier evolution, 8–9; *The Frontier in American History*, xi, 128, 187; germ theory and, 5, 25, 92; Handley on, 168–69; individualism and, 25–26; Limerick on, 165–67; sectionalism and, 9–10; Slotkin on, 168; and sources of historical change, 111; vision of the frontier, 5, 12, 33–34, 182; Webb on, 165; White on, 167. *See also* frontier thesis (Turner)
Twain, Mark, xiii, xvi, 18, 28, 33, 38, 95, 116–21, 184
Tweed, William Marcy. *See* Boss Tweed
two-party system, origins of, vi–vii, 79
Typee (Melville), 114–15

Uncle Tom's Cabin (Stowe), 50
Undset, Sigrid, 152–53
Unitarianism, xiii, 36, 53
University of Wisconsin, 65, 92, 164
urban counterforce, myth of, 15–16
The Urban Frontier (Wade), 69
urban reach, 67–73
The Urgent West (Allen), 163
USA (Dos Passos), 156
U.S. Steel Corporation, 71, 85, 184

Vance, Rupert, 103
Vanderbilt school, 170–71. *See also* Warren, Robert Penn; Ransom, John Crowe; southern Agrarians; Tate, Allen
Vanderbilt University, 102, 170
The Vanishing American (Grey), 146
Veblen, Thorstein, 5
Vico, Giambattista, 59
The Victors (Barr), 94
violence in the frontier West, 12, 137–38, 168–70
The Virginian (Wister), 48, 116, 130–31, 145–46, 168, 184
Virgin Land (Smith), 22, 65, 161, 162
Volk, German theory of, xiii, xvi, 6, 47–50, 98–101, 128, 161

Wade, Richard, 69–70, 163
Waiting for the End (Fiedler), 162
Walker, Francis A., 8
Warner, Charles Dudley, 93, 94, 117, 184
Warren, Robert Penn, 102–3, 170
Washington, George, 5, 28, 44
The Waste Land (Eliot), 31, 135
Weaver, James B., 78
The Web and the Rock (Wolfe), 105
Webb, Walter Prescott, 22, 165
Weber, Max, 16, 110
Weinberg, Albert K., 31
Wells, H. G., 119
The Well Wrought Urn (Brooks), 163
West, Nathanael, 18, 41, 54, 118, 137–39, 165
West, the: dark side of, 54–55, 113–42; guns as symbol of, 12, 26, 143; idea of, 187; migration to, 1–4, 7–8, 11–12; as

state of mind, xii, 14–15, 19–20, 35–44, 52, 121, 146–47; violence in, 12, 137–38, 168–70
Western novel, xii, 18–19, 115–16, 145–46, 149–55, 188
Westward Ho! (Paulding), 50
"What Is Man?" (Twain), 43, 117
White, Richard, 55, 65, 163, 167–68
Whitman, Walt: American cultural construct and, 160; "Democratic Vistas" and, 122–23, 183; Dynamo and, 41–43; in pursuit of lost past, 18; myth of the land and, xiii, xvi, 130; One in the Many and, 41, 42, 121–22, 155; reflections of America in the poetry of, 121–23; vision of the city, 42; wealth and, 28
Why Are We in Vietnam? (Mailer), 181
The Wigwam and the Cabin (Simms), 50
Williams, William Appelman, 22
Williams, William Carlos, 42, 64, 161, 172–74
Wilson, Woodrow, 80, 92, 132

The Winning of the West (Roosevelt), 26, 168
Wisconsin school, 170–71. *See also* Billington, Ray Allen; Bogue, Allan G.; Cronon, William; Curti, Merle; Turner, Frederick Jackson
Wister, Owen, 30, 81, 130, 145, 146, 158, 168–69, 184
With the Procession (Fuller), 94
The Wizard of Oz (Baum), 81–82
"*The Wizard of Oz*: Parable on Populism" (Littlefield), 82
The Wolf (Norris), 43
Wolfe, Thomas, 104, 105–7, 121
"The Wonders of the Invisible World" (Mather), 52, 183
World's Columbia Exposition (1893), xi
Wylder, Delbert, 147

You Can't Go Home Again (Wolfe), 105–7

Zola, Émile, 43, 84, 140, 149